DIALOGICAL SOCIAL THEORY

In his final work, Donald N. Levine, one of the great late-twentieth-century sociological theorists, brings together diverse social thinkers. Simmel, Weber, Durkheim, Parsons, and Merton are set into a dialogue with philosophers such as Hobbes, Smith, Montesquieu, Comte, Kant, and Hegel and pragmatists such as Peirce, James, Dewey, and McKeon to describe and analyze dialogical social theory. This volume is one of Levine's most important contributions to social theory and a worthy summation of his life's work.

Levine demonstrates that approaching social theory with a cooperative, peaceful dialogue is a superior tactic in theorizing about society. He illustrates the advantages of the dialogical model with case studies drawn from the French philosophes, the Russian intelligentsia, Freudian psychology, Ushiba's aikido, and Levine's own ethnographic work in Ethiopia. Incorporating themes that run through his lifetime's work, such as conflict resolution, ambiguity, and varying forms of social knowledge, Levine suggests that while dialogue is an important basis for sociological theorizing, it still vies with more combative forms of discourse that lend themselves to controversy rather than cooperation, often giving theory a sense of standing still as the world moves forward.

The book was nearly finished when Levine died in April 2015, but it has been brought to thoughtful and thought-provoking completion by his friend and colleague Howard G. Schneiderman. This volume will be of great interest to students and teachers of social theory and philosophy.

Donald N. Levine (1931–2015) was Professor Emeritus of Sociology at the University of Chicago and founder of an NGO, Aiki Extensions. He received a lifetime achievement award from the American Sociological Association.

Howard G. Schneiderman is Professor of Sociology at Lafayette College in Easton, Pennsylvania. He has written about some of sociology's leading scholars, and has recently authored *Engagement and Disengagement: Class, Authority, Politics* 2017).

DIALOGICAL SOCIAL THEORY

Donald N. Levine
Howard G. Schneiderman, editor

NEW YORK AND LONDON

First published 2018
by Routledge
711 Third Avenue, New York, NY 10017

and by Routledge
2 Park Square, Milton Park, Abingdon, Oxon OX14 4RN

Routledge is an imprint of the Taylor & Francis Group, an informa business

© 2018 Donald N. Levine and Howard G. Schneiderman

The right of Donald N. Levine and Howard G. Schneiderman to be identified as authors of this work has been asserted by them in accordance with sections 77 and 78 of the Copyright, Designs and Patents Act 1988.

All rights reserved. No part of this book may be reprinted or reproduced or utilised in any form or by any electronic, mechanical, or other means, now known or hereafter invented, including photocopying and recording, or in any information storage or retrieval system, without permission in writing from the publishers.

Trademark notice: Product or corporate names may be trademarks or registered trademarks, and are used only for identification and explanation without intent to infringe.

British Library Cataloguing in Publication Data
A catalogue record for this book is available from the British Library

Library of Congress Cataloging in Publication Data
Names: Levine, Donald Nathan, 1931-2015, author. | Schneiderman, Howard G., editor.
Title: Dialogical social theory / Donald N. Levine and Howard G. Schneiderman.
Description: Abingdon, Oxon ; New York, NY : Routledge, 2018. | Includes bibliographical references and index.
Identifiers: LCCN 2017037909 | ISBN 9781412865500 (hardback) | ISBN 9781351294928 (ebook) | ISBN 9780815375470 (pbk.)
Subjects: LCSH: Sociology--Philosophy. | Social sciences--Philosophy.
Classification: LCC HM585 .L4849 2018 | DDC 301.01--dc23
LC record available at https://lccn.loc.gov/2017037909

ISBN: 978-1-4128-6550-0 (hbk)
ISBN: 978-0-8153-7547-0 (pbk)
ISBN: 978-1-351-29492-8 (ebk)

Typeset in Bembo
by Taylor & Francis Books

To Ruth, lifelong partner in dialogue

CONTENTS

List of illustrations	ix
Preface and Acknowledgments	x
Editor's Note	xii
Foreword by Peter Baehr	xvi

Dialogue, Disputation, Dismissiveness and the Motives for Controversy *Howard G. Schneiderman*	1

PART I
From Combat to Dialogue 9

1 Dialogical Social Theory	11
2 Dialogue and Human Combat	15
3 Transforming the Adversarial Mindset: Japanese Martial Arts and American Litigation	26
4 Civilizations, Clashing and Harmonious	42

PART II
Dialogue Involving Shared Objectives 55

5 Universalism in the French Philosophes and the Russian Intelligentsia	57

viii Contents

6	The Sociology of Morality in the Work of Parsons, Simmel, and Merton	84
7	Theory and Praxis in Parsons and McKeon	96
8	Freud and Ueshiba: Pioneers of Therapeutic Human Interaction	113
9	Dewey and Hutchins at Chicago	124

PART III
Dialogues Involving Pointed Conversations   **137**

10	Hobbes and Locke	139
11	Montesquieu and Durkheim	153
12	Kant and Hegel	171
13	Positions on Conflict in Euro-American and Asian Social Thought	181
14	Two Tales of One City	191
15	The Forms and Functions of Social Knowledge	195

Bibliography	*207*
Index	*219*

ILLUSTRATIONS

Figures

3.1	Evolution from Raw Combat to Consensual Conflict Resolution	32
3.2	Elements of Aikido that Reduce Conflict and Promote Mutual Respect	35
3.3	Elements of Mediation Promoting Agreement Based on Mutual Respect	37
8.1	Parallels between Psychoanalysis and Aikido	118
8.2	Double Interchange in the Economy	119
8.3	Double Interchange in the Aikido System	120
8.4	New *Uke* Paradigm	122
9.1	Dewey's Chart of the School System	129
10.1	Links in the British Tradition	146
11.1	Links in the French Tradition	160
11.2	Comte's Theory of Knowledge	162

Tables

4.1	Exclusionary and Inclusionary Concepts of Selected Civilizations	52
9.1	Dewey-Hutchins Concordance	133

PREFACE AND ACKNOWLEDGMENTS

Doubtless the greatest surprise of my life took place in June 2002 at a dinner at my home with Charles Camic and Hans Joas after which, at dessert time, one of them slipped me an outline of the contents of what purported to be a Festschrift, *The Dialogical Turn*. I pushed my chair back and looked up in amazement at Hans, Chas, and my wife, Ruth. My face expressed sheer disbelief. One by one they shook their heads up and down, indicating that, yes, it was true, a group of my most respected colleagues had indeed conspired to produce a Festschrift in honor of my seventieth birthday in June 2002. One by one, I read off the names of the contributors. I never expected such an honor. Even now, thirteen years later, I am humbled by this gift. Not only was it an honor, but the contents led eventually to the production of this book. Even now, thirteen years later, I recall vividly the poignancy of this honor.

No less incredulous, I read that the editors and contributors were not simply honoring me, but were making the claim that I had somehow been responsible for a shift in orientation among significant members of the social science community. They were in fact alleging that I not only had played an important role in the work of that community, but had done so in a way that I had not been mindful of, a way that was close to my heart but that I had failed to previously recognize. That jolt left me with a sense of responsibility that before another decade elapsed, I had better get busy and make good on their recognition. They were alleging that my work had inspired a shift in orientation toward what might be glossed as dialogicality. That point then and there amounted to the planting of a seed which led to the present volume.

As I began to work on options for producing such a volume, it occurred to me that it could well fit as a second of two volumes of selected papers, each of which would make good on a theme from the final period of my work in social theory. One of these would celebrate my commitment to the theme of my 1997 address to the Theory Section of the ASA. The other would celebrate my commitment to the idea of dialogical social theory. All that remained to produce these volumes was to find a suitable publisher.

As it turned out, academic presses were no longer publishing volumes of this sort due to commercial pressures. Nevertheless, I resolved at the 2013 meetings of the ASA to push the idea along, a project facilitated by my winning the ASA lifetime achievement award.

By the greatest good fortune, when I visited the book display of Transaction Publishers, Howard Schneiderman recognized me and showed sufficient interest to introduce me to the president, Mary Curtis, and set in motion the process that led to contracts for both books, *Social Theory as a Vocation* and *Dialogical Social Theory*. There remained only the need for a capable and committed staff to help with all the necessary work. The staff of *Social Theory as a Vocation* lay right at hand. To Robert Owens, Jack Friedman, Stephen Weller, I owe a large debt of gratitude. As my health took a turn for the worse, I turned to a brilliant graduate student on the University of Chicago's Committee on Social Thought, Jonathan Baskin, to my office assistant, Joe Cronin, and to my ever faithful son, Bill Levine.

Donald N. Levine

EDITOR'S NOTE

At the time of his death, Donald Levine was the doyen of social theory, and surely one of the last of that great generation of theorists which included Robert Merton, Talcott Parsons, Edward Shils, Robert Nisbet, Raymond Aron, Robert Bellah, and Lewis Coser, among others. Don was well known for his intellectual and personal generosity; he understood that the calling of social theory as a vocation had already been taken up by a new cohort of scholars whom he lauded in his work, such as Peter Baehr, Hans Joas, Randall Collins, Charles Camic, Craig Calhoun, Daniel Silver, and others who labor in the fields of social theory today.

Don is an important link in the chain of social theorists who extend from the founding generation of Weber, Durkheim, Simmel, and Cooley through a succession of important sociologists including Park, Parsons, Shils, and Merton to the present generation. He was instrumental in keeping alive the work of some of the founding generation; Simmel scholarship was enlivened and enriched by Levine's custodial work in translating and collecting Simmel's essays. He also wrote extensively about Simmel; aside from a very few others, Levine's role in keeping Simmel central to modern sociology is unparalleled. He also augmented and transcended his own career as a heuristic social theorist by serving as Editor of the University of Chicago Press' Heritage of Sociology series. This series has kept the most important theorists alive and well in the minds of generations of social scientists. He was also an important part of the University of Chicago's Committee on Social Thought, and he served the college as Dean for many years. In 2006 The University of Chicago Press published his brilliant book *Powers of the Mind: The Reinvention of Liberal Arts Learning in America*, a paean and analysis of this topic as it developed at Chicago and an important sociological analysis of higher education in America.

Don was not just a social theorist and author of influential books such as his 1985 *The Flight from Ambiguity: Essays in Social and Cultural Theory* and the 1995 *Visions of the Sociological Tradition*; as if these were not enough to establish his lasting reputation as a pillar of social science theory, he also was a consummate fieldworker. His ethnographic work in Ethiopia led to such books as his 1960 *Wax and Gold: Tradition and Innovation in Ethiopian Culture* and his 1974 *Greater Ethiopia: the Evolution of a Multiethnic Society*. Rounding out his richly diverse life, Don became a master of the martial art of aikido, which he describes as a way of thinking and a way of life in both of his last two books as well as in *Powers of the Mind*. There he discusses a legendary course he taught at Chicago called "Conflict Theory and Aikido."

As his career reached its end, Don bravely struggled to complete his work on *Dialogical Social Theory*, which he saw as summing up his career, right up to his death in early April 2015. He and I began discussing this book in August 2013, but somewhat more than a year and a half later, as winter yielded to spring in 2015, our emails and phone discussions became both more somber and more urgent as Don's fight with cancer took on the dramatic ups and downs of a devilish roller-coaster ride. By March 2015, Don sensed that he might not be able to see this book to completion, and he asked me to help him get it done. Now that my promise to him has been kept, I'd like to share a few thoughts about Don, this book, and the various travails associated with the project.

As Don notes in his preface, the story of how I became involved with this project begins in August 2013 when he and I ran into each other in New York City at the book exhibit of the annual American Sociological Association meeting. We had met many years before when Don was invited to give a lecture at Lafayette College, where I teach, and we had exchanged manuscripts we were writing at the time: he about Georg Simmel, I about charismatic movements. Thus, we had some background together to smooth the path of what came next, which was Don's interest in publishing his next two books with Transaction Publishers, for which I served as editorial consultant. His interest was whetted upon seeing some of the Transaction books on display at the book exhibit, many authored by or featuring social theorists such as Robert Merton, George Homans, Talcott Parsons, and Robert Nisbet, not to mention theorists with University of Chicago connections such as Edward Shils, David Riesman, Harold Lasswell, Erving Goffman, and Philip Rieff, and friends of his such as Peter Baehr and Mary Jo Deegan. I introduced him to Mary Curtis Horowitz, the President and publisher of Transaction, and he and I agreed to meet and talk about the book projects he was proposing.

When we sat down together later that day to discuss the books he had in mind, I found Don impressively enthusiastic, even gleeful; I remember being surprised by Don's taking off his sport coat, unbuttoning his button-down shirt, and sitting at a table in the hallway in a T-shirt in front of his laptop computer. He saw the surprised look on my face and said with his characteristic sense of humor, "It's time to get to work." For an hour and half we talked about the ideas he had for a book to be called *Social Theory as a Vocation* and for another tentatively to be called *Dialogical Sociological Theory*. Both these volumes would, in essence, be knit together from selected essays Don had written over his career. He understood that many publishers avoid such an approach today and was happy to find that I would encourage

Transaction to publish both books. The first of these, which I mentioned above, *Social Theory as a Vocation*, was published in time to be exhibited at the ASA meeting held in San Francisco during August 2014. It is a magnificent volume chronicling, rethinking, and adding weight to Don's career as one of American sociology's premier social theorists. The book ranges over the contributions of social theory to understanding and elucidating themes for which Don is justly famous: ambiguity, modernity, rationality, freedom, and conflict.

Don was so appreciative that Transaction had been able to publish *Social Theory as a Vocation* within a year of our talking about it in New York the summer before that I was surprised when he wrote to say that he would not be able to make it to the 2014 ASA meeting in San Francisco because of failing health. It was then that the urgency he communicated about the second volume, *Dialogical Sociological Theory*, made more sense to me. Don clearly hoped to get it done before his health failed him, but the dark side of hope is always despair. Sometime in January or early February Don's emails seemed to be increasingly fraught with anxiety about getting the second book completed, and he talked openly about his medical condition and the treatments he was undergoing.

As a friend and colleague, I volunteered to help him in any way I reasonably could to finish *Dialogical Social Theory*, and as Don got progressively weaker, he took me up on my offer and asked me to see the book through to completion. Don worked feverishly with some of his graduate students, and with his son Bill, to produce editable Word documents that would be the basis of a manuscript that could be used in the publication process. When Don died, he left me all the chapters for the book except one pivotal one on dialogue and dismissiveness, which he never had the chance to write. Unfortunately, Don died before he had an opportunity to actually read through these newly scanned and converted chapters, so he had no idea how much work needed to be done to make them publishable. When I read through the chapters, what had appeared to be a relatively straightforward editorial task began to seem overwhelming.

The process of scanning the original articles and turning them into Word documents created so many errors, deletions, transpositions, and other problems that I immediately realized that I was in over my head in what was essentially an unusable manuscript. As an academic teacher and writer, I didn't have the skills or the time to do the technical work necessary to prepare Don's manuscript for the publisher, so I asked Julia A. Dinella, one of my students at Lafayette College and one of the best undergraduate writers I have known, if she would help me out. Julia has been a godsend. Without her persistence and brilliant editorial skills, this book would not have been completed. On top of the work I put into editing *Dialogical Social Theory* before Julia began helping me, she and I worked together, going over every word, sentence, paragraph, and page to find and repair errors, even to the point of my having had to actually rewrite and add to parts of the text that were obliterated in the conversion process. Indeed, some of the text was turned into unreadable and unrecognizable scratch-doodle figures that required hunting down clean source copies. I relate these troubles here not as complaints, but to explain to those who cared about Don why this project has taken so long to bring to completion. It was a case of trying to have a working dialogue about this book with a much-loved, but deceased author. Now that the book is finished I believe that Don would be justly proud of it.

When *Social Theory as a Vocation* was published, Don saw it as the culmination of his life's work, an exclamation point, so to speak, closing out a laudable career as a social theorist. In this penultimate volume Don set out to categorize what he called "the genres of theory work in sociology." These include "custodial work," or the recovery of texts not readily at hand. Don's own custodial work on Georg Simmel is unambiguously important. Don also did yeoman's work to help make available important works by Max Weber, and he tied these together with the contributions of Robert Park, Robert Merton, and Emile Durkheim. The other meta-theoretical form of theory work is "heuristic"; that is, work that helps to aid in discovery and understanding of social phenomena. As Don knew, heuristic work always faces the major hurdle of ambiguity, and this is confronted by attention to careful definitions which hopefully clarify and obliterate ambiguity on the one hand and which open new areas of inquiry and new ways of thinking about old issues on the other. In the closing chapters of *Social Theory as a Vocation*, Don sets the stage for his last book—the one before you now—*Dialogical Social Theory*.

If *Social Theory as a Vocation* is mainly about the types of theory work, *Dialogical Social Theory* is about Donald Levine's particular contribution to how theory work may be done differently than it has been up to now; and that is dialogically. That Don spent the better part of his career doing theory as if it was a dialogue was first recognized by Charles Camic and Hans Joas in their 2003 Festschrift for him titled *The Dialogical Turn*. Don made me laugh when he alluded to having been doing dialogical social theory all his life without knowing it, and he was glad to realize that his brand of theory work could be called "dialogical."

The main thrust of *Dialogical Social Theory* is based on the idea that Don derived from Richard McKeon, one of his teachers at the University of Chicago. From McKeon, Don learned that theoretical understanding can be perverted by various forms of conflict among theorists, such as misunderstanding, mistrusting, ideological bending of the truth, debunking, and unmasking. The essays that Don has included in *Dialogical Social Theory* are used to illustrate the meaning and importance of dialogue and dialogical social theory. They emanate from his devotion to peace over war and conflict as well as his commitment to furthering our understanding of philosophers and social theorists despite jealousies, willful perversions of understanding, and the like.

Donald Levine was a gentle man, a good man, and a great social theorist. *Dialogical Social Theory* completes his life work and consolidates his central importance to contemporary social science.

Howard G. Schneiderman

FOREWORD

The big thinkers of the social sciences and humanities distinguish themselves along various axes. They may doggedly pursue a grand idea or they may chase down many smaller ones—the strategies of the proverbial hedgehog or fox. They may be lumpers or splitters. They may be ideologically passionate or scientifically disciplined. *Dialogical Social Theory*, the second volume of Donald Levine's selected papers to be published by Routledge, cuts across all of these familiar distinctions. It reveals a thinker who for over half a century has refined, taught, and transmitted a distinctive intellectual craft, who prefers synthesis to division, and who eschews ideology for intellectual honesty. Professor Levine's latest book confirms his standing as America's preeminent social theorist.

What are the defining features of his achievement? The first is a philosophical sensibility. It bears recalling that with the exception of Max Weber, whose methodological studies show a profound knowledge of philosophical argument, all the seminal thinkers of continental sociology began their careers with a philosophical training. Neo-Kantianism, phenomenology, and existentialism exerted a profound influence on Durkheim and Mauss, Simmel and Mannheim, and Aron and Bourdieu, whether by attraction or repulsion. If they became sociologists and social theorists, it was not in ignorance of philosophy; it was in frustration at its limitations. All the same, their thought is imprinted by a rigor, by prolonged reflection on epistemological and ontological questions, that only philosophical study affords. Donald Levine's oeuvre incorporates this legacy. One sees it not only in his discussion of Hegel, Herder, Kant, Husserl, Buber, Dewey, and MacIntyre (among others), but also in the large topics he addresses, such as freedom and rationality. A philosophical turn of mind is also evident in the care he takes to draw distinctions among apparently similar phenomena. Almost every chapter of *Dialogical Social Theory* divides one topic into several species and subspecies so as to clarify analytically what we are all too likely, otherwise, to conflate and muddle. Today's sociology students—torn between the subject's extremes of hyper-professionalism and hyper-politicization—typically know nothing about philosophy aside from what they may have learned in a general education course. *Dialogical Social Theory* offers a welcome corrective to this institutionalized innocence.

A second hallmark of Donald Levine's social theory is its comparative emphasis. It is one thing to talk grandly about "modernity" or "civilization." It is quite another to anchor these ideas in the close-grained study of nations and cultural traditions other than one's own. No American social theorist or sociologist has contributed more than Donald Levine to our understanding of Ethiopia. And none is more capable of surprising us with unlikely social juxtapositions such as, in the present volume, the parallels between Japanese aikido and American legal practice, or French and Russian intellectuals. But it is not just nations and historical experiences that Levine compares. Great thinkers, too, fall under his lens as in the conversations he hosts here between, inter alia, Hobbes and Locke, Weber and Freud, Parsons and Simmel, and Dewey and Hutchins. These comparisons between and among authors are sensitive to historical location without being historicist; Levine does not believe that the ideas of great thinkers are exhausted by the questions of their time; that would not make them great. Rather, we return to these writers because of their expansive contribution to issues both vital and enduring; for instance, rival or complementary conceptions of the individual, of human cultivation, of conflict, of interaction, and of a whole stream of arguments that relate human beings to the moral texture of life.

Social theory can be, and often is, a vertiginous subject. We can commend it for being broad. We can also tax it for being amorphous. It is a rare scholar who is able to describe lucidly and in detail the nature of this intellectual hybrid—the third salient attribute of Donald Levine's craft. At the University of Chicago, he is recalled as a seminal figure in the reorganization and broadening of the undergraduate curriculum. The passion with which Professor Levine defends liberal education is obvious to all readers of his many books. So, too, is his commitment to the teaching of social theory as an integral part of this education, a topic discussed at length in the companion volume to this one, *Social Theory as a Vocation*. There the reader will find syllabi and a practicum to guide students of any age who really want to know what social theory is and how best to exercise it.

At the beginning of this Foreword, I summoned different paths that major thinkers take to define their own intellectual signatures. Another fork is less commented on. It is the contrast between social thinkers who seek to unmask their subjects—individuals, practices, and institutions—and those who desire to forge connections among them. Donald Levine is the foremost representative of the latter camp. The unmasking stance is a commonplace in sociology and social theory; it recapitulates the polarization of politics and public discourse that is so widely lamented today. One finds unmasking in the reduction of all social relations to power, in the pervasive suspiciousness that requires us to "interrogate" or invert arguments in preference to understanding them, in the conviction that radical scholars are duty bound to educate a populace mired in false consciousness, and in the belief that the proper stance of the intellectual is to be the antagonist of his own society. Describing the unmasking mode in his 1970 Inaugural Lecture to the Collège de France, Raymond Aron put it this way:

> To our customs and beliefs, the very ones we hold sacred, sociology ruthlessly attaches the adjective "arbitrary." For our lived experiences, in their unique richness and indescribable depth, it substitutes indicators. It is concerned only with acts that repeat themselves, with manifest or latent classes; each act becomes one among many, anonymous and uninteresting if it remains alone in its peculiarities, marginal or atypical if it insists on combining features that are normally separate. In the wake of Nietzsche, sociology forces social actors to the light of day and uncovers their hypocrisy. As a millenarian vision, Marxism goes back to those mythologies by which men have wanted to assure themselves of winning in a just war. Insofar as it unmasks the false consciousness of all and the good conscience of the powerful, Marxism, like psychoanalysis, belongs more than ever to our time. In a way, all sociologists are akin to Marxists because of their inclination to settle everyone's accounts but their own.
> ([1970] 1978, 76)

Donald Levine's social theory offers something more edifying and more humane than the unmasking reflex that Aron describes. Rather than orchestrate enmity between various thinkers and traditions, Levine offers himself as a conduit between them. Rather than strip writers of their own sense, he seeks to elicit their relevance to a larger conversation about the grandeur and paradoxes of social life. Rather than adopt an adversarial posture to society, he urges us to avoid denunciation and, instead, communicate with those whose principal challenge is to deepen and broaden us. This generosity of vision is evident everywhere in Professor Levine's work and in the language he chooses to express it: understanding, mediation, negotiation, integration, disambiguation, and, of course, dialogue.

Why do we write? If we are honest, most of us doubt that our work will make much difference to even the small part of the world we inhabit. It probably will make no difference at all. We write to clarify problems that intrigue or bother us. We write because writing is what we do. But then there is another class of writers whose work survives to be read, re-read, and perennially discussed. Their work is the best of its type. Donald Levine stands tall among this class. Neither a dim light nor a flare of brief illumination, his books and essays are the brightest of beacons for all who value the life of the mind and who, with the aid of a wise teacher, wish to understand deeply our social and moral existence. "What good does it do a man," says Montaigne, "to lay in a supply of paints if he does not know what he is to paint?" *Dialogical Social Theory* and its companion volume, *Social Theory as a Vocation*, are the testaments of a master painter. Read them for their keenness of vision and sureness of touch. Read them as a canvas on which we, fellow students, are invited to draw in our turn.

Peter Baehr

DIALOGUE, DISPUTATION, DISMISSIVENESS AND THE MOTIVES FOR CONTROVERSY

Howard G. Schneiderman

The most well-known dialogues are almost always attributed to Plato; thus it is appropriate that the very term dialogue can best be understood as the epitome of Platonic discourse in which *dialegesthai*, a term of art, became *dialektike*, a term representing the art of philosophical dialogue (Arendt 1978, 110–18; Timmerman and Schiappa 2010, 17–18). It is just this form of dialogue as collaborative "group thinking" that Richard McKeon had in mind when he juxtaposed dialogue as a more irenic and cooperative way to resolve intellectual disputes than contentious debates and controversies in which opponents often dismiss each other's position out of hand out of confusion, doctrinaire adherence to ideologies, or drives for power (McKeon [1956] 1990).

McKeon was one of Donald Levine's mentors at the University of Chicago and had a defining influence over him as he developed his ideas about dialogical social theory. Especially important to Levine was McKeon's foundational 1956 essay, "Dialogue and Controversy in Philosophy" (ibid.), but McKeon's thinking about the place of dialogue in resolving intellectual conflicts without resorting to irreconcilable controversies began earlier in his 1952 essay "Love and Philosophical Analysis" (McKeon [1952] 1954). In this essay, McKeon said that philosophy "has been a long dialogue in which old insights and old errors have been forgotten and revived, reinterpreted and refuted, and in which new insights and new errors have been supported by old and new proofs," and the ability to engage in dialogue depends upon what Aristotle called friendship and manifests itself "when a problem requires for its solution many kinds of competence and many kinds of information: each member of the group then makes his contribution to the common task, and the solution is a composite result" (34–5).

Unlike disputatious forms of controversy which aim to produce winners and losers, dialogue depends upon what Aristotle described as friendship, the common purpose of which is "the advancement of knowledge by common thinking in the service of the love of wisdom" (35). Another Aristotelian thinker, Hannah Arendt, picked up this same point and extended it to thinking as a dialogue with one's self, and as she said, "dialogue of thought can be carried out only among friends, and its basic criterion … says: do not contradict yourself" (Arendt 1978, 189). From Aristotle to McKeon to Arendt, we see Don Levine's main point about dialogue as a cooperative form of discourse that stands in opposition to agonistic forms of group thinking such as controversies and debates.

Since all the above is essential to what Levine wanted to discuss in this chapter, but never had the chance to write beyond a mere outline, I will share some of his notes here. Don meant for this set of paragraphs to be the opening for the chapter:

> Although tendencies toward combativeness and exclusivity are inherent in human experience, humans have, we've seen, developed an increasingly rich repertoire of attitudes and techniques that counteract them. This chapter asks how and why that repertoire of dialogical forms has so often been cast aside among social scientists in favor of a panoply of discursive forms that embody acrimony, caricature, un-masking, labeling, and methodological dogmatism.
>
> In his State of the Union on January 21, 2015, President Barack Obama pointed out that better politics isn't one where Democrats abandon their agenda or Republicans simply embrace mine; a better politics is one where we appeal to each other's basic decency instead of our basest fears. A better politics is one where we debate without demonizing each other, where we talk issues and values and principles and facts, rather than "gotcha" moments or trivial gaffes or fake controversies that have nothing to do with people's daily lives.
>
> Given that that sort of discourse has long been the staple of democratic discourse, one would expect that a different sort of norm would obtain among social scientists, who are beholden to upholding academic norms of integrity, mutual respect, and fidelity to the quest for truth. Can anyone deny that what McKeon wrote of philosophical dialogue a half century ago is all the more dominant among social scientists today? As one of my colleagues once quipped, nowadays, the only thing the two social scientists can agree on is that the work of a third is no good.[1]

At the time of writing the presidential election of 2016 is almost upon us, and the contest between the Republican candidate, Donald Trump, and the Democrat candidate, Hillary Clinton, is certainly the most contested, acrimonious campaign in memory. I bring this up here since these candidates have proven that politics is about debates, disputes, base fears, and demonization of one's opponents. In other words, politics is not about dialogue in any sense of the word. The latter can only operate where the will to reach cooperative solutions to problems is much greater than the will to defeat an opponent. Debating is the perfect form of discourse for politics, while dialogue is the perfect form of discourse for intellectual life. Don and I discussed Max Weber's *Wissenschaft als Beruf*, which lays out all the important reasons to keep politics out of the classroom, and I'm sure that he would agree with me that dialogue is what should separate the professoriate from the politicians. While Don admired Barak Obama's notion of a better politics based on debate without demonization, I have to think that he would have agreed that political debates are essentially the antitheses of philosophical dialogues.

So, what are the appropriate forms of engagement and disengagement in the world of scholarly intellect, and how are these different from the forms of engagement in the demagogic world of politics?

My old teacher and friend Philip Rieff once wrote that "scholarship is polite argument." Rieff's quip comes close to what we call dialogue, which is obviously one of the main concerns of this chapter. And as I have suggested above, and as Don suggests throughout this book, while dialogue is an important basis for sociological theorizing, it still vies with other more combative forms of discourse that lend themselves to controversy rather than cooperation.

Among these more contentious forms of controversy, we find the following in the writing of pragmatist philosophers such as McKeon and others: blunt refutation, pejorative labeling, rejection of method, errant restatement of other's ideas, and dogmatic adherence to ideological positions at odds with another's thinking. Beyond these philosophical triggers for controversy, sociological thinkers from Karl Mannheim to Kenneth Burke to Don himself have shown how caricature, disavowal, selective and partial reading of theory, and discounting of theories and formulae with which we disagree, may distort the meaning of a particular work by a particular author. More recently Peter Baehr has shown how debunking and unmasking can also have similar distorting effects on sociological theory.

Thus, while dialogue is a cooperative effort among theorists, controversy more often resembles what I call "word-to-word" combat, where winning and losing become more important than deriving workable and generalizable theoretical frameworks that are akin to what Burke called bridging devices.[2]

As noted above, throughout this book about dialogical social theory, Levine leans heavily on the work of McKeon, who delineated three forms of argument and analysis, (1) Dialogue, (2) Disputation, (3) Dismissal, but the chief lesson to be derived from McKeon is that dialogue is opposed by controversy. For McKeon, as well as Levine, dialogue takes place when "two or more speakers or two or more positions are brought into a relationship in which it becomes apparent that each position is incomplete and inconclusive, unless it is assimilated to a higher truth" ([1956] 1990, 106).

In other words, dialogue is about the assimilation of ideas rather than the refutation of them. Addressing this, McKeon wrote that "dialogue concerning basic philosophic issues takes many forms—such as (1) the synthesis of contraries, (2) the assimilation of divergent views, and (3) the development of differences and the examination of unresolved oppositions" (107).

So, if cooperative dialogue is a method for enhancing mutual respect and integrity among social theorists who are trying to find and describe various truths about how societies operate, dialogue is thwarted when it gets degraded into disputation and controversy and when the work of a theorist is dismissed out of hand, as when ideological dogmatisms come to the fore.

In his original plan for this chapter, Don intended to discuss motivations for turning from dialogue to controversy, but he merely listed two of these, "pathology" and "incentives," and provided no further comment. Thus, I shall now take up the question of motivations for favoring controversy over dialogue.

Social science has done much to describe, explain, and predict motivations for action, and some of this might be useful to us in thinking about the motives which individuals have for turning dialogue into controversy. In a 1940 essay, "Situated Action and Vocabularies of Motive," C. Wright Mills ([1940] 1963) famously brought together the ideas of Max Weber and Kenneth Burke to give us a sociological understanding of the decomposition of dialogue into various forms of controversy. Mills presents us with a virtual dialogue between himself and Weber and Burke about a sociology of motives and motivations.

In *Economy and Society*, Weber defined a motive as "a complex of subjective meaning which seems to the actor himself or to the observer to be an adequate ground for the conduct in question" (1968, 11). Weber and, consequently, Mills, who was influenced by him, saw motives as normative rather than as strictly personal psychological artifacts of individual personalities. This idea was reinforced by Burke (1965) in his indispensable sociological analyses of motives in his book *Permanence and Change*.

For Burke, all concepts are reductive in the sense that they circumscribe what he called the "vast complexity of life" by reducing it to "principles, laws, sequences, classifications, and correlations, in brief, abstractions or generalizations of one sort or another" (1945, 96). The reductive nature of theory and concepts makes dialogue possible by leveling the playing field of social theory, allowing us to discuss the same things with each other, albeit in a variety of terms. This same reductive nature, however, allows for the distinct possibility of sometimes allowing controversy to prevail over dialogue.

To understand how reductive theory sometimes evolves from dialogue into controversy, we pay attention to the idea of a normative grammar of motives, in which competition is paired against cooperation; "I" is pitted against "thou"; debunking squares off against idealization; and a *tragic sense*, where everything is taken too seriously, is opposed by a *comedic sense*, in which nothing is taken seriously enough. All these motivations to turn away from dialogue and towards controversy are, in one way or another, about staking out one's identity.

The quest for a professional identity as a motive to become known as one type of theorist or another sometimes crosses the line and brings antagonism to the fore. McKeon anticipated this when he suggested that "Dialogue explores the plurality of positions, and it is transformed into controversy by dogmatisms which must therefore be refuted" ([1956] 1990, 104).

In extreme cases, controversy tends to degenerate into anomic forms, and it becomes, as McKeon suggested, "a symptom of confusion, mental disorder, and drives to power" (117). In a psychoanalytic sense, McKeon seems to see controversy as a regressive and immature form of "spoiled child syndrome" as opposed to the more mature and productive forms of dialogue with their requisite self-restraint and a willingness to consider arguments and evidence taken as a whole rather than in bits and pieces that fit one's ideological disposition. As he said, "This complex process of synthesizing is interrupted—and dialogue becomes controversy" (107).

To see the ways that controversy has created an atmosphere of dismissiveness among social theorists who might have benefitted from dialogue with creative thinkers, Don planned on examining the work of some theorists who have been disregarded, dismissed, ignored, debunked, or unmasked as a result of controversy. Among these theorists who were targets of abusive reading, Don proposed to name and describe the treatment of the following notable social scientists whose work has at various times been "misread, mistreated, and kept from being acknowledged and incorporated into mainstream social thought": Thorstein Veblen, Ernst Troeltsch, Emile Durkheim, Georg Simmel, Talcott Parsons, Raymond Aron, and William Graham Sumner.

To fulfill Don's plan to discuss each of these theorists as a target of controversy, rather than as a central focus of dialogical social theory, is beyond the scope of my intentions in this essay, which are to make clear what Don meant to accomplish in his pivotal but now unfinished chapter. Because Don and I discussed a few cases of abusive reading, disputation, and dismissiveness (including two that I have written about)—namely, those of Georg Simmel, Ernst Troeltsch, and William Graham Sumner and his most famous work, *Folkways*—I will close this chapter by briefly turning my attention to them as examples of what Don had in mind here.

Anti-Semitism in the German universities may have been the engine of Georg Simmel's dismissal in his own time, but Simmel's idiosyncratic writing style, which precluded the normative use of footnotes, caused peers to label him pejoratively, even though his writing is now considered creative and original to the point of being avant-garde. Simmel also seems to have evoked personal attacks, such as Albert Salomon's description of him as "physically unattractive" and fascinating and repellent alike when he spoke. Stereotypical descriptions such as these add fuel to the fires of prejudice and caricature that continue to make Simmel a controversial figure. Because Don was the leading Simmel scholar of his generation, we had hoped that he could have written about him for this chapter, but I should note that Don actually does discuss, throughout this book, Simmel's problems of acceptance by social theorists in his own day and beyond.

Partial reading, another cause of controversy mentioned by both McKeon and Levine, haunted the career of Ernst Troeltsch, who was also dismissed through caricatures of his work. Troeltsch's main ideas about church and sect, among others, are found in the massive and erudite *The Social Teaching of the Christian Churches*, a two-volume masterpiece of well over a thousand pages in which the sociological concepts are sandwiched in between learned discussions of theology, history, and philosophy. Troeltsch's work is more likely to be read today by students of religious studies than by sociologists. The sociological concepts in *The Social*

Teaching, and in *Protestantism and Progress*, have been preserved mostly as caricatures since the church-sect dichotomy has been cut loose from its mooring in the detailed historical and theological arguments in Troeltsch's books. Instead of a dialogue with Troeltsch, we find that sociologists have by and large dismissed him as more of a theologian than one of them (Schneiderman 2013).

Because William Graham Sumner plays a part in some of the chapters in this book, and given that I have written about how Sumner was displaced from a well-deserved central place in the history of sociology, I shall end this chapter with a brief description of his dismissal by contemporary sociologists.

Sumner's book *Folkways* is both monumentally long and monumentally important. Its 700 or so encyclopedic pages can be daunting. In *Folkways* Sumner ([1907] 2002) introduced some of the major concepts that continue to characterize modern sociology. Consider for a moment who coined and introduced the following terms: "folkways," "mores," "ethos," "ethnography," "in-groups," "out-groups," "we-groups," "ethnocentrism," "antagonistic cooperation," "strain of consistency," "conventionalism," "syncretism," "diffusion," and two types of social change: "enacted" and "crescive," which played an important part in the later work of sociologists such as Daniel Bell. However disparate these concepts may seem to be, they are all intimately linked by the fact that they constitute or are affected by "world views," another of Sumner's ideas. Sumner helped found what we call cultural sociology emphasizing the role of facts, values, and ideas in shaping our social behavior, while deemphasizing the role of social structure. Up to the late 1950s and early 1960s, American sociology relied at least as much, if not more, on Sumner's ideas about culture and values than on Weberian or Marxian concepts of power and structure. Even though Sumner helped to establish cultural relativism as the prevailing framework of sociology—"the mores can make anything right," he wrote—he is caricatured and dismissed today as a "conservative" sociologist.

Sumner wrote that crescive changes in the mores must precede changes in legislated rules or laws. Sumner's view of crescive changes (which Daniel Bell said are those that are derived from tradition, but surge, swell, and go on autonomously but willy-nilly) led to his being labeled and disavowed as an arch-conservative. This pejorative labeling eventually masked Sumner's influence and importance to the discipline. Indeed, in his day, Sumner was among the first sociologists to see the complexities of social and cultural change, and he tried to create a descriptive taxonomy and an analytic framework to understand it. But it is with his theory of change that Sumner eventually ran into the ideological wall of American sociology in the 1960s and beyond.

To say that mores have a persistent quality is one thing, but to say, as Sumner did, that "legislation cannot make mores" ([1907] 2002, 77) attacks one of the most stalwart liberal shibboleths. This quotation about the impotence of legislation to effect social change without previous changes in the mores turns out to have had pivotal implications for Sumner's reputation. It is often cited by sociologists as proof of Sumner's conservatism and even of what they see as his mean-spirited reluctance to advocate change. Because of this, Sumner has become the marginal man or, in a term he himself coined and made famous, the "forgotten man" of sociological theory. He was unmasked, on the one hand, by sociological liberals for his theory of social persistence and what they took to be his resistances to change through enacted legislation, and he was disparaged and labeled pejoratively, on the other hand, by some sociological conservatives for his liberal theories of ethnocentrism and ethical relativism. In Sumner's case dialogue has clearly been overwhelmed by controversy caused by abusive reading of the man and his work (Schneiderman 2015).

In honor of Don and his assimilation of McKeon's work on dialogue as a superior form of discussion among social theorists, I should like to close with one last quotation from McKeon:

> The basic problems of dialogue are, first, to find ways to make certain that there is agreement concerning what is in question and, second, to understand what is conceived to constitute a satisfactory answer to the question. ... Mutual understanding in the sense of agreement concerning what the question is and what is required in a satisfactory solution is necessary if philosophers are to resume their dialogue.
>
> *([1956] 1990, 125)*

Notes

1 Don was in considerable pain and getting close to death when I came to Chicago in mid-March 2015 to discuss completing this book. On Sunday, March 15, he read these paragraphs to me and Mary Curtis, and they should be taken as some of his last thoughts about the unfinished chapter 4 which he planned to call "Dialogue, Disputation, and Dismissiveness." During the ensuing weeks it became clear to Don and to me that he would be incapable of finishing this linchpin chapter. Rather than leave it out—and render the book truly incomplete—Don asked me to do what needed to be done, and, pragmatically, that clearly meant writing the chapter for him or, better, in place of him. As it stands before you, this is my best interpretation of what Don is trying to say about dialogue and controversy.

2 Burke defined a bridging device as "a symbolic structure whereby one 'transcends' a conflict in one way or another" (1984, 224).

PART I
From Combat to Dialogue

1

DIALOGICAL SOCIAL THEORY

Prologue. The Idea of Dialogue

> The psychological phenomena of intercommunication between two minds have been unfortunately little studied.
>
> – C. S. *Peirce*

On September 27, 1953—eight years after six million of his fellow Jews had been slaughtered by organized squads of the German government—Martin Buber delivered an address titled "Das echte Gespräch und die Möglichkeiten des Friedens"—"Genuine Dialogue and the Possibilities of Peace" (Buber 1957).[1] How he mustered the fortitude, the imagination, and the transcendent compassion to deliver such a talk at that time, in that place, I shall never know. What I have come to believe, however, is that the idea Buber was advocating for, the idea he had planted firmly on the landscape of modern culture in the 1920s—the idea of genuine dialogue—may be the most important idea to have survived the killing fields of the past century.

The classic formulation of this idea, in *I and Thou*, followed a period in which young Buber, like many of his peers, embraced a Nietzschean ideal of self-transcendence through ecstatic personal experience. Part of the shift in his perspective came from his study under Georg Simmel. Simmel lectured on the significance of the *Zwischenmenschliche*, the interhuman, and proposed that the forms of social interaction should be examined by contemporary sociology. Buber recalled later that in his youth, he had found this idea broached in the early writings of Ludwig Feuerbach, who saw the human essence contained in the relation between I and Thou; and Buber acknowledged others, from Friedrich Jacobi to Herman Cohen, as contributing to his "History of the Dialogical Principle" (1965). In his own *I and Thou* (Buber [1923] 2004) and subsequent writings, Buber delved deeply into this theme, which in essence signified treating others not as objects but as subjects and understanding the human self as derived from interacting with others.

Buber's seminal ideas were developed in various ways by some of the most creative minds in philosophy and theology of the succeeding decades. His colleague Franz Rosenzweig focused on ways in which dialogue helped to fashion the self and how participation in dialogue served to produce redemptive communal consequences. The philosopher Emmanuel Levinas emphasized the potential challenges and benefits of engaging fully with a radically different "other" in communication; the eminent hermeneutic philosopher Hans-Georg Gadamer engaged critically with Buber's ideas; and the Russian literary theorist Mikhail Bakhtin—who called Buber "the greatest philosopher of the twentieth century"—pushed a notion of "dialogism," holding that everything anybody says exists in response to things that have been said before and in anticipation of things that will be said in response.

The transformation of Buber's perspective from being centered on the personal self to being centered on mutually respectful social interaction doubtless drew on other elements besides those previously mentioned. The most profound source of that change arguably was the impact of the so-called Great War. Like most of his intellectual peers, Buber supported the war when it broke out, but at some point, the war's horrors affected his thinking and turned him into a lifelong promoter of genuine conversation as a means of promoting peace.

Half a century earlier, on another Continent, the horrors of war altered the outlook of some influential American thinkers. Oliver Wendell Holmes, valorous veteran of key battles of the Civil War, came to distrust commitments to absolute principles that motivated so many of the antagonists. For him, the chief lesson of the war was that dogmatic certitude leads to violence. Holmes concluded that the only way to keep certitude from producing violence is through inclusive democratic discourse.

In the 1870s, Holmes took part in a discussion group with friends and colleagues from Harvard, including C. S. Peirce and William James, who shared his distrust in concepts regarded with absolute certainty. From their discussions emerged what became known as the pragmatist movement in philosophy, which was energized by their younger colleague John Dewey when the movement went public in the late 1890s. Dewey, in turn, was influenced in Chicago by Jane Addams, who, following the violence triggered by the Pullman strike of 1893, convinced him that antagonism was unnecessary even when parties thought that they had opposed interests. Dewey devoted much energy to bridging what he considered false dichotomies.

The pragmatist thinkers, including G. H. Mead and Charles Horton Cooley, developed a number of kindred ideas related to their focus on sociality: genesis of the self through intersubjective communication; parallels between scientific and democratic discourse and processes involved in forming a public civil society. As a coda to all that work, John Dewey would sing in 1925: "of all affairs, communication is the most wonderful" (166). Following World War II, Continental philosophers of the dialogical tradition developed theories of communication that resonated with the thoughts of American pragmatist philosophers. Karl-Otto Apel developed his Transcendental-Pragmatic perspective by incorporating ideas about language drawn from Peirce. Jürgen Habermas, after engaging with G. H. Mead, sought to delineate the elements of an "ideal speech situation," in which distortions could be eliminated and parties to a conversation could thereby arrive at consensus.

Despite the richness of these and other philosophical investigations, the idea of dialogue has not achieved a prominent place in modern culture. Apart from some notable work in the field of communication studies, it has largely failed to enter the discourse of the social sciences. In philosophical treatments, moreover, it remains at a highly abstract level. For all that, I believe, understanding the dimensions and significance of dialogue presents a challenge of exceptional importance for the functioning of contemporary life, not least because of huge obstacles in communication among specialists and among partisans in the global community.

The task of this book, then, is to import the dialogical theme into contemporary sociology. Its underlying assumption is that *destructively conflictual modes of discourse among social scientists need to be transformed into discursive modes that embody dialogue.* This is so for the sake of the advancement of valid knowledge. It is important no less as an educational vehicle, one that offers concrete models of dialogical conduct for the world. The sociologist, Buber counseled, "must ... *educate* sociologically" (1957, 179); that is, must educate people how to live together, not to be just like one another, and how to express and respect their differences.

To my mind, the beginning of wisdom on the subject of dialogue versus combativeness follows from making two sets of distinctions. For one thing, the process of "intercommunication of two minds," as Peirce put it, takes many forms. The subject demands that we distinguish different forms of dialogical interaction. For another, some kinds of dialogue can actually involve conflict. Accordingly, we need to distinguish between what sociologists like Louis Kriesberg ([1998] 2014) have described as constructive versus destructive conflicts. These distinctions help analyze a number of discursive forms where proponents of different positions engage in destructive conflict, constructive conflict, and consensual diversity. More concretely, it critically considers styles of dismissiveness, unmasking, caricature, and disavowal in discourse among social scientists.

To accomplish this, I consider historical conditions that promote the evolution of modern nonconfrontational modes of communication (Part I) and then offer a differentiated analysis of forms of dialogicality in social theory (Parts II and III).

Chapter 2 introduces this topic by contrasting dialogue with its opposite: the multitude of phenomena that embody human combativeness. It surveys the dominant theories about the sources of combativeness and attends to the explosions of violence throughout the past century. It then turns to review the many nonviolent breakthroughs of the twentieth century and analyzes a complex of historic developments that lay behind these breakthroughs. Chapter 3 offers two case studies of this secular change. It describes the perceived obsolescence of received combative modes: in American adversarial litigation and in Japanese martial arts. Chapter 4 confronts a well-known claim that the post-Cold War international community would necessarily be marked by a "clash of civilizations" (Huntington 1993) with arguments regarding ways in which all world civilizations contain inclusionary as well as exclusionary assumptions.

The remaining chapters present essays that embody modalities in which contrasting intellectual positions in the social sciences can be related in non-adversarial ways. Part II presents forms of dialogue in which the parties, although holding different positions, nevertheless share common objectives. Chapter 5, a very old paper from 1950, demonstrates how radically different assumptions about human nature and the social world held by the eighteenth-century French philosophes and the nineteenth-century Russian intelligentsia produced similar visions of the global community. Chapter 6 revisits the work of Simmel, Parsons, and Merton—with their markedly varying assumptions and agendas—to find material that can be brought to bear on a single subject, the sociology of morality. Chapter 7, perhaps the most intellectually challenging chapter of the book, compares the complicated conceptual frameworks of Parsons and McKeon with an eye to finding ways in which the strong programs of each can compensate for the weak points of the other. These three chapters all illustrate the theme of dialogue as complementary contributions to a common problem.

The succeeding chapters demonstrate ways in which the ideas of authors who know little or nothing about one another can be brought together to form a novel dialogue. Chapter 8 brings together some key ideas of the Austrian psychoanalyst Sigmund Freud and the Japanese martial artist Morihei Ueshiba. Moving closer to the present, Chapter 9 considers statements about education by John Dewey and Robert Maynard Hutchins. It shows that the much-celebrated differences between them are overshadowed by what can be shown to be shared positions on a common topic.

Part III describes rhetorical forms that transfigure oppositional discourse into productive dialogue. It deals with two major ways in which parties displaying pointed confrontations with one another can contribute to ongoing dialogues that enrich the total discourse about a subject. Chapters 10, 11, and 12 do this for interlocutors from, respectively, the British, French, and German philosophic traditions. Chapter 13 schematizes three mutually exclusive interpretations of the somatic bases of social conflict, then moves toward a fourth interpretation that offers ways to connect them productively. Chapter 14 brings the discussion to a relatively recent political crisis which took place in Ethiopia following the violent reactions to the national election of 2005. My efforts there as a mediator between the government and the imprisoned opposition leaders forced me to find ways to bridge what seemed like implacably opposed positions.

In Chapter 15, finally, I reprint a 1985 essay, "The Forms and Functions of Social Knowledge," which offers an extensive paradigm of discursive commonplaces used by social scientists.

Note

1 The address was written for the German Book Trade in Frankfurt am Main.

2
DIALOGUE AND HUMAN COMBAT

Dialogue stands in opposition to human combat, a broad concept that covers everything from organized warfare to interpersonal violence, from jural litigation to antagonistic conversation. Of these, organized physical combat has attracted the most commentary. Even today, our cultural space seems dominated by reports of civil strife, policing actions, and terrorist warfare. Understandably, such phenomena prompt us recurrently to come up with explanations for human bellicosity in general.

Broadly speaking, I see the vast literature of explanations of human aggression framed by three perspectives: Nature; Society and Environment; and Micro-social Situations.

Nature: Aggression Instinctive

Perhaps the most enduring perspective locates a disposition to aggression in some form of natural endowment. The inherent sinfulness of human nature has been proclaimed in the West for millennia. Thomas Hobbes famously depicted the condition of unchecked human assertiveness as a war of all against all. Modern psychologists, however, have reworded the story. William James affirmed that "our ancestors have bred pugnacity into our bone and marrow, and thousands of years of peace won't breed it out of us" ([1910] 1974, 314). And to answer the stark question posed to him by Albert Einstein, "Why War?" Sigmund Freud replied in terms that have framed much modern thought on the question: "Human instincts are of two kinds: those that conserve and unify ... and the instincts to destroy and kill" ([1932] 1939, 90). Musing on the relations between the two instincts, Freud added:

> The ideal motive has often served as a camouflage for the dust of destruction; sometimes, as with the cruelties of the Inquisition, it seems that, while the

ideal motives occupied the foreground of consciousness, they drew their strength from the destructive instincts submerged in the unconscious.

(Ibid., 92)

Hans Morgenthau, in his landmark formulations of "political realism," argued that "forces inherent in human nature" lead inexorably to conflict among social groups (1960, 4).

Such assumptions were bolstered by the work of scientific naturalists, like ethologist Konrad Lorenz, whose research concerned "the fighting instinct in beast and man which is directed *against* members of the same species" (1966, ix). Lorenz demonstrated that aggressive drives form an essential part of the life-preserving organization of instincts. Among humans and many other species, conflict has provided clear adaptive advantages: balancing ecological distributions, selecting fit specimens through fights among rivals, mediating ranking orders for complex organizations, even instigating ceremonies that aid social bonding. Civilized man, he proposed, suffers from the fact that phylogenetically transmitted aggressive instincts that aided survival in prehistoric times now find no adequate discharge. Ethologist Nikolaas Tinbergen likewise posited a universal instinctual proclivity to intraspecific conflict, but remarked: "Among the thousands of species that fight … man is the only species that is a mass murderer" (1968, 180). Primatologists Richard Wrangham and Dale Peterson (1996) developed a point broached by Lorenz: they found the instinct for destructive aggression gender-specific. The proximity of humans to chimpanzees in genetic makeup signifies a chimp-like murderous drive in human "demonic males."

Society and Environment: Aggression Cultural

Not all evolutionary biologists accept the Wrangham-Peterson argument. In *Apes and Human Evolution*, Russell H. Tuttle asserted: "There is no paleoanthropological support for the notion that our stem ancestors regularly engaged in intragroup and intergroup killing, infanticide, cannibalism, or female bashing" (2014, 593). Tuttle thereby provides grounds for an opposite perspective, one that appears among social scientists who emphasize the malleability of human dispositions and hold that the scope of human aggression depends on cultural patterns. Anthropologist Ruth Benedict's *Patterns of Culture* stands as a classic exemplar of this position. Benedict contrasted the Native American Zuni, whom she described as orderly and peaceable, with the Dobu of New Guinea, among whom "treacherous conflict is the ethical ideal" (1934, 170). In this vein, Erich Fromm (1973) went on to examine anthropological accounts of 30 primitive societies with an eye to determining their levels of aggressiveness or peacefulness. He found several—like the Aztecs, the Dobu, and the Ganda—who evince a great deal of interpersonal aggression and violence both within the tribe and against others. The atmosphere of life within those societies he described as truly Hobbesian, a condition of constant fear and tension. On the other hand, Fromm found a number of primitive societies where precisely the opposite qualities manifest themselves. Among the Zuni Pueblo Indians, the Mountain Arapesh, and the Mbutu, for example, he found little hostility and violence, virtually no warfare, hardly any crime, little envy and exploitation, and a generally cooperative and friendly attitude. Appealing to the environmental factors subsumed under cultural variation, psychoanalytically oriented Fromm pointedly rejects the Freud-Lorenz notion of aggressive instincts as generating an inherent quantum of pent-up energies awaiting discharge.

Other social scientists locate environmental causes of aggressive behavior in various dimensions of social structure. William Graham Sumner, a founding father of sociology, famous for arguing that "the mores can make anything right and prevent condemnation of anything" ([1907] 2002, 521), formulated an enduring generalization: the general rule among social groups is to promote harmony within the group and combat against outside groups. A corollary of that assumption appears in his discussion of blood revenge within certain groups. The ingroup-outgroup notion was developed independently by political theorist Carl Schmitt ([1927] 2006), who regarded existential enmity between organized groups as the defining feature of all politics. For Schmitt, the identification of other groups as friends or enemies figures as the consideration that dominates all dimensions of human association.

In addition to Sumner's fruitful formulations regarding in-group–out-group combat (and his related concept, ethnocentrism), he also observed that commitments to warfare vary with the interests of elites—whether they find their interests better satisfied through war or through peace. In considering the importance of elites for the initiation of warfare, Sumner broaches a wider concept that engaged earlier theorists, like Alexis de Tocqueville, who associated bellicose motivations with aristocratic strata. This notion was developed more extensively by Riane Eisler (1987), who drew on a wide range of disciplines to make her case. She portrayed an aboriginal condition when humans subscribed to maternal sacred figures and were egalitarian and peace-like. Eisler's originary book, *The Chalice and the Blade*, traced the transformation into warlike societies as a "shift in emphasis from technologies that sustain and enhance life into ... technologies designed to destroy and dominate" (1987, xx). For Eisler, this transformation involves a change from a "partnership" model of social organization to a "dominator" model. Historically, she locates that transformation in a number of periods when invading pastoralists overcame relatively peaceable agriculturalist communities and introduced structures based on male dominance, hierarchy, and aggressiveness. Other analysts who ascribe bellicosity to social structural variables look not to aggressive elites but to strata oppressed by elites, a viewpoint shared by many in the Marxian tradition. Lewis Coser (1967), for example, pointed to subordinate groups who believe they have no outlet to redress their grievances other than violent protest. Ralf Dahrendorf (1959) generalized this pattern to include all those in subordinate positions who find authority oppressive and tend to revolt in some fashion or another.

Micro-social Situations: Aggression Interpersonal

At the micro-social level, social psychologists have identified situational configurations that generate aggressive orientations. An early proponent of this approach was John Dollard, who traced the eruption of hostile impulses to frustrations produced by social situations (Dollard et al. 1939). Thomas Scheff also traced interaction chains in which the emotion of shame performs an essential function, concluding that "protracted and intense hatred, resentment, and envy are all products of unacknowledged shame" (Scheff [1994] 2000). Thus armed conceptually, he provided a gripping interpretation of the origins of World War I. Several students have focused on aggression provoked by social patterns in families. Talcott Parsons ([1947] 1954) identified one particular dynamic by considering aggression to result from protest masculinity engendered by predominant parenting of males by their mothers. Murray Bowen (1978) and kindred family systems theorists/therapists connected conflicts in families and family-like relations to intense emotional involvement between two parties which lead to periodic outbursts to gain distance, outbursts that typically escalate conflict by recruiting other family members and then allies outside the family. In an overview of such dynamics, Richard Gelles and Murray Straus (1979) presented 15 distinct theories: a range of social factors that purport to account for the appearance of violence in families.

This overview of explanations of bellicosity serves two purposes. For one thing, I present it in order to keep us mindful of the range of persuasive ideas that have been put forward to account for the persistence of violence and other forms of combativeness, patterns that stand to obstruct the way of dialogue and in fact negate the possibility of future human societies without destructive conflict. Whichever factual account and theoretical perspective one prefers, one must acknowledge the existence of both old and novel forms of warfare and civil antagonisms as a constant reminder of obstacles to promoting more peaceful dialogue in the contemporary world.

More to the point, however, my framing of the literature on conflict and aggression can also serve to open up the larger goal of this book. It does so by raising the question of ways in which theoretical differences can either be exacerbated through controversy or related fruitfully through appropriate forms of dialogue. Thus, the opposition between genetic and sociocultural accounts of human phenomena embodies a long-established debate. And proponents of the sociocultural often subdivide into opposed perspectives on the basis of asserting the primacy of either cultural or social structural factors. It often happens that proponents of one perspective—and hasty readers of one compelling critique—are disposed to dismiss the other altogether. In dialogical communication, however, they may find attractive other options in spite of different theoretical positions. To cite a foundational notion of Buber's: Dialogue connects without enforcing uniformity, because "genuine conversation, and therefore actual fulfillment of relations between men, means acceptance of otherness" (Buber 1992, 65).

For example, although Tuttle pointedly argued that the Wrangham-Peterson thesis of male human bellicosity cannot conclusively be shown to derive from shared ancestry with chimpanzees, his work could be viewed as setting up a dialogue that still leaves the assumption of an instinctually based aggressive drive in human males intact. Similarly, although some critics of Eisler, like Lawrence Keeley (1996), took sharp issue with one aspect of her narrative (the assumption that primitive societies were essentially peaceable), her perspective still has value for competing viewpoints in pointing to the enormous increase of organized violence in societies ruled under male leaders with strongly hierarchical organization.

An actual example of respectful dialogue can be found in the September 2014 issue of *Sociological Theory*, which presents three responses to Jiannbin Lee Shiao's 2012 article, "The Genomic Challenge to the Social Construction of Race." The article argued that despite the strong social forces at play in the identification of races and ethnic groups, sufficient genomic evidence exists to support some notion of biological differences between human groups via ancestry. Critic Ann Morning (2014) argued that these differences can be accounted for by social constructivist theories of race, while others, like Fujimura et al. (2014), questioned the article's empirical evidence. In an exemplary demonstration of dialogical discourse, Shiao concurred with his critics that biological differences may at times not be causally significant while still standing firmly by the questioned empirical evidence. Shiao's response remains gracious to his critics, noting the merit of some of their objections while disagreeing with some of their conclusions. At one point, despite their many disagreements, Shiao praised Morning for "practicing what she preaches" in her "excellent book" (2014, 253).

Suppose we bring all three perspectives to bear on the question of how to account for the calamitous expansion of warfare in the world during the twentieth century. We can regard it as due to an explosion of instinct-driven impulsivity in a world of eroded values or maladaptive destructive technology; or as the consequence of ideologies of violence; or as the expansion of male-dominated, hierarchical, aggressive regimes. A firm commitment to any of the perspectives often results in dismissing all the others, while realizing that all can be considered as developing different variations on how the common theme of human combativeness opens new ways to productive dialogue. The cause of mutual understanding will, I believe, be served better by exploring options by which the different points of view can be connected productively, options that will organize the chapters in Parts II and III.

Option A: Complementary Contributions to a Common Problem
Option B: Forming a Novel Dialogue
Option C: Critical Extension and Progressive Transformation
Option D: Complementary Engagement through Reciprocal Priority

Whichever option is chosen, the result will predictably be more robust, since more facts and concepts will be introduced than would otherwise have been the case, and resulting ambiguities of terms can be used to discover and follow out diverse lines of discussion. With such an approach, we would gain more insight into the array of factors that dispose humans toward combat and into the apparent fact that, in spite of earlier expectations that the twentieth century would be a time of unprecedented peace, it turned out to be the opposite.

Rebels Against Aggression

Or was it? John Mueller, in a book to be considered shortly, claimed that appearances to the contrary, the institution of war, the prime example of combative violence, has actually been in decline. To whatever extent we follow his argument and the unusual variant he offers on the theme of human combativeness, at the very least we must acknowledge the fact that over the past century, assertive but nonviolent thinkers and political leaders have created new forms of nonviolent action that have attracted the allegiance of millions. William James (1910) broached this idea by proposing, on the eve of World War I, the need to find "the moral equivalent of war" through actions that later came to be illustrated by such New Deal programs as the Civilian Conservation Corps. Many of these inventions occurred in the wake of World War I. Martin Buber's classic *I and Thou* ([1923] 2004) promulgated a philosophy of open, mutually respectful communication. Created to replace atomistic, monological notions of the self with a dialogical conception, Buber (1957a) went on to explore its international political implications, as in the historic address mentioned in the Prologue, when he portrayed a world-historical battle between carriers of the *vox humana*, the human voice, against *homo contrahumanus*. War, Buber suggested, "has always had an adversary who hardly ever comes forward as such but does his work in the stillness" (236), and it is the depth of the contemporary crisis that prods us to hope.

Embodying this spirit of dialogue, Mohandas Gandhi applied his idea of Satyagraha, gestated in South Africa, to India in the 1920s. Gandhi embraced the Jain principle of *ahimsa*, nonviolence, in the conviction that using violence against another person amounts to depriving the world of that person's actual or potential contribution of the truth we all seek. His famous implementation of that principle in working to liberate India from colonial rule eventually drew hundreds of thousands. It proved so potent that it attracted the noted Muslim general Badshah Khan, who directed one hundred thousand Pashtun followers to lay down their arms and join the ranks of Gandhi's followers. Badshah Khan maintained that love can create more in a second than bombs can destroy in a century (Easwaran 1999).

Also in the 1920s, the famed Japanese martial artist Morihei Ueshiba revolutionized a millennial tradition of Japanese fighting arts into a medium for nonviolence. The goal of Ueshiba's new "martial art of peace" was to transform the whole world into one harmonious human family (see Chapter 2). It is notable that both Gandhi and Ueshiba were accorded titles that signify, respectively, "Great Soul" (Mahatma) and "Great Teacher" (O'Sensei) for their contributions to nonviolence.

Apart from these influential figures, we must also recognize the notable growth of social techniques that embody nonviolent principles. They include the nonviolent civil disobedience methods developed by Martin Luther King, Jr. and his followers in the 1960s, methods that have been adopted in dozens of political hot spots elsewhere in the world. King cited not only the model of Ghandi, but also the Christian tradition leading back to Christ and his suffering for mankind. More recently, the Nonviolent Peaceforce has trained volunteers to enter and diffuse situations where combat is imminent, which they have done successfully in places like the Philippines, Sri Lanka, and Guatemala. An organization devoted to applying the principles of aikido, Aiki Extensions, has organized seminars for citizens from countries with historic conflicts, such as Greece and Turkey, Serbia and Bosnia, and Israel and Arab states. And, among many other like-minded initiatives, special mention should be made of the Albert Einstein Institution, advancing freedom through nonviolent action, founded by Dr. Gene Sharp. Sharp's (1990) writings on "civilian-based defense" were used by the governments of Lithuania, Latvia, and Estonia as they separated from the Soviet Union in 1991. At that time, the Defense Minister in Lithuania, Audrius Butkevicius, declared, "I would rather have this book than the nuclear bomb" (Albert Einstein Institution 2014).

Within the domain of nonphysical, verbal interaction, the new nonviolent forms include practices that have transformed civil litigation from a tradition of adversarial legalism into processes of mediation (see Chapter 2). They also include the increasingly popular work of Marshall Rosenberg (2005a, 2005b), which has galvanized constituencies in some three dozen countries with ideas about how to constitute Nonviolent Communication (NVC). NVC offers a model for non-hurtful talk that offers rules for speakers to make observations in a nonjudgmental mode, attend to their feelings and those of others, express their needs clearly, and tender requests openly.

Secular Trends that Support the Reduction of Combativeness

In what kinds of theoretical and historical contexts can we make sense of these nonviolent stirrings and achievements? Several social scientists have analyzed long-term historical tendencies that replace institutionalized aggression with pacific modes of interaction. In Eislerian terms, this involves the development of forces that promote structures of partnership and collaborative problem-seeking, forces that she associates with feminine values. The following analyses focus on four different dimensions of action: (1) cultural values; (2) institutionalized norms; (3) collective interests; and (4) personal habits.

Cultural Values

The past two centuries have seen a cumulative increase in the number of people for whom the image of combat has become tarnished. That has been due in good part to the efforts of people organized in a number of peace movements. Nigel Young (1984) identifies ten such movements, from liberal internationalism and religious pacifism to socialist internationalism, feminist anti-militarism, and nuclear pacifism. These movements peaked on the eve of World War I, then resumed with growing strength in surges around 1921, 1932, 1958–60, 1968, and 1981. Relatedly, the status of conscientious objector has become increasingly respected over the past century. From Canada, Finland, and Israel to South Africa, South Korea, and the Marshall Islands, more and more countries have legitimated the option of conscientious objection. The horrific realities of World War I doubtless triggered widespread revulsion against war. John Mueller (2004) argued that this came about largely because the prewar peace movement presented successfully its once-novel argument for the abolition of war. For Mueller, the reduction of combativeness resulted from a cultural shift—a change in the way people conceive and evaluate war. The change has expanded. The Nobel Prizes, started in 1901, have become increasingly prestigious and from the outset have routinely included the Peace Prize—a prize devoted to someone who had done "the best work for the fraternity between nations, for the abolition or reduction of standing armies, and for the holding or promotions of peace congresses."

Two other cultural developments of the past two centuries in the West arguably contributed to a decline in combativeness. One appeared in the form of what Durkheim designated as the rise of a "religion of the individual": societal values shifted from those that sacralize collective symbols to those that sacralize the individual person. For Durkheim, this modern religion "springs not from egoism but from sympathy for all that is human, a broader pity for all sufferings" ([1898] 1973, 49). Relatedly, beginning with the American Declaration of Independence and the French Déclaration Universelle des Droits de L'Homme, the movement toward a Universal Declaration of Human Rights culminated with the United Nations proclamation in 1948. That Declaration slowly came to plant that ideal in the minds of citizens all over the world. In *The Sacredness of the Person: A New Genealogy of Human Rights*, Hans Joas (2013) has evocatively connected this pair of historic transformations.

The cultural shift toward peace took place not only in the realm of ideas, but also affected the lives of millions of people in many countries. Amnesty International, a global organization devoted to protecting human rights, began with the publication of an article in London in *The Observer* of May 1961. In an earlier period, it might have had limited effect. In the past six decades, however, it has gained three million members in over 150 countries, who campaign to end grave abuses of human rights anywhere in the world. An American NGO devoted to identifying and publicly shaming abusive governments, through media coverage and direct exchanges with policy-makers, Amnesty International fused in 1988 with Asia Watch, Africa Watch, and Middle East Watch to become Human Rights Watch, a potent force—with a budget of over $500 million. Around the time of its formation, the U.S. State Department, under President Carter, added a component to its embassies abroad to file an annual report on the state of human rights in their respective countries.

Both of these developments can be seen as part of a larger pattern that Stephen Pinker (2011) described as "the humanitarian revolution." Compressing a huge amount of data over a time span of the last three centuries, Pinker described the components of this revolution, which include the disappearance of human sacrifice, witchcraft, and blood libel; the reduction of violence against blasphemers, heretics, and apostates; the abandonment of cruel and unusual punishments; the decline in capital punishment; the end of slavery; and the rise of empathy and the regard for human life.

Institutionalized Norms

The German philosopher G. W. F. Hegel argued that the "slaughter-bench of history" would inexorably produce nation-states governed by the rule of law, which would provide a reliable means to curtail civil violence. This variable finds a strong advocate in Mueller (2004), who stressed the importance of competent domestic governments in promoting the decline of civil war and a shift in public attitudes toward war. Mueller saw persisting civil wars as high-intensity crime or criminal businesses rather than as low-intensity war. As a result, over the course of the last millennium, "warfare in Europe has gone from the commonplace and routine to the uncommon and avoided" (24).

A different aspect of the role of government in reducing the scope of aggressive actions was explored in Emile Durkheim's writings on criminal law. His most general formulation was that the number of acts covered by punitive reactions diminished over time as societies evolved from those governed by an extensive common culture to modern, differentiated societies, called "organic," where the scope of criminal law diminished while the scope of civil law vastly expanded. In his famed essay *Two Laws of Penal Evolution*, Durkheim ([1899] 1973) advanced this line of thought by analyzing two related variables: the extent to which the quantity of punishments inflicted diminished in the course of evolution, and a progressive moderation in the quality of punishments such that deprivations of liberty rather than physical injury tend to become more and more the normal means of penal control. In accounting for these changes, Durkheim identified a great change that occurred in the course of moral evolution: from a state in which crimes against the collectivity— represented by sovereigns, religious forms, and sacred symbols—become fewer and fewer to a state where crimes against individual persons become increasingly numerous. The vindictiveness and virulence of earlier punishments represents the emotional explosion incited by "an outrage directed against a being whose worth is incomparably greater than that of the aggressor" (179), whereas the more evolved penal institutions induce calmer, more reflective emotions provoked by offenses that take place among equals. In modern societies, we feel greater indulgence toward crimes against objects that represent the collectivity, such as *lèse-majesté*—those crimes, in other words, that are associated historically with violent retributions.

Collective Interests

Three nineteenth-century founding figures of sociology—Auguste Comte, Herbert Spencer, and William Graham Sumner—argued, in different ways, that Western industrial societies were evolving from being organized for warfare to being organized for peaceable commerce. For Comte, the historic "active" function of societies consisted of the production and utilization of military means, whereas the growth of modern science would create societies where the prevailing active function would be industrial production. Similarly, Spencer posited a long-term evolution from "militant" to "industrial" societies, wherein combative orientations would be replaced by cooperative habits useful in production and exchange and an army-like organization would shift to organizations that embodied "spontaneously evolved combinations of citizens governed representatively" (Spencer 1972, 162). Summarizing a number of points in this line of thought, Sumner wrote that great inventions and discoveries, new methods of agriculture and commerce, and the introduction of money and financial devices produced a situation in which

> industrial interests displace military and monarchical interests as the ones which the state chiefly aims to serve, not because of any tide of "progress," but because industrialism gives greater and more varied satisfactions to the rulers. ... Peace is necessary, for without peace none of them can enjoy power.
> ([1907] 2002, 49)

A contemporary proponent of this viewpoint is Michael Howard, who saw that industrialization "ultimately produces very unwarlike societies dedicated to material welfare rather than heroic achievements" (1991, 176).

Personal Habits

A number of analysts have commented on widespread changes in personal dispositions that have become manifest in the modern world. These changes in personal habits have in common a pattern of increasing control over impulses to aggression. Max Weber was perhaps the first of these, with his widely esteemed work that claimed that the institutions of modern rational capitalism required a radical change in self-discipline to accommodate the exigencies of industrial production. Philip Gorski (2003) has extended this idea to show that what he called the "disciplinary revolution" took place in domains outside the economy—most notably in bureaucratic offices. Perhaps the most noted of these is Norbert Elias, whose *The Civilizing Process* ([1939] 2000) traced how increasing social thresholds of shame and repugnance gradually transformed European standards for interpersonal violence and outward conflict into expectations of self-restraint. The development and diffusion of modern educational institutions can also be credited with a certain change in habits. From elementary school on, an increasingly large number of persons are brought up to control their temper, listen respectfully to others, and participate in cooperative learning situations.

Historically, shifts in values linked with the idea of war include a rise in the cult of the individual and the growing adherence to the idea of universal human rights, expanding authority of political institutions that control violence within politically organized societies, diminished violence in punishments for crimes, and the development of commercial interests tied to peaceful conditions. Additionally, the control of aggressive impulsivity as a result of changes linked with a civilizing process, a disciplinary revolution, a need for methodical work habits, and an expansion of education are some of the broader historical changes that might be related to the nonviolent breakthroughs listed above.

Nearly all of these changes have come about gradually. Often they are produced by people oriented by a factor that sociologists rarely attend to: an attitude of hope. At times, one can even trace directly certain breakthroughs from combative forms toward interactional forms that embody the spirit of dialogue. Such are the transformations in the domains of American civil litigation and Japanese martial arts I discuss in the following chapter.

3

TRANSFORMING THE ADVERSARIAL MINDSET

Japanese Martial Arts and American Litigation

In the course of human evolution, much thought and energy have gone into improving the techniques that parties with opposed interests have used to resolve conflicts. The most dramatic arena of such improvements concerns the instruments of combat: from stone to iron knives and spears, from plain to poison-tipped arrows, from slingshots to guns, from rifles to artillery, from man-powered bombers to automatized drones, from ballistic bombs to chemical and atomic bombs. The organization of combatants has also evolved: from bands of tribesmen to hordes, from ad hoc fighters to trained warrior strata, and from feudal legions to massive armies.

The prosecution of conflicts through verbal means has also evolved. Many preliterate societies have created customs that regulate disputes through procedures that entail various forms of litigation. In modern times, however, these procedures that regulate disputes among antagonists have become complex and highly institutionalized.

How and why might adversarial relationships be replaced by harmonious transactions that benefit both parties? Independently, portions of the traditions of both Japanese martial arts and of Anglo-American legal practice have developed methods to accomplish such a change. Both have replaced notions of defeat and victory with the idea of enhancing the well-being and autonomy of all stakeholders.

The Martial Arts in Japanese Culture

The evolution of the martial arts in Japan can be traced over two millennia. Those arts crystallized through the work of the samurai, a stratum of military specialists that came to the fore in the late Heian period (tenth to twelfth century CE). The samurai came to replace the stratum of professional warriors of preceding centuries—men from a different ethnic group it seems, who originally were hunters and manifested an extreme sort of raw violence. Other Japanese often viewed them as barbarians or wild beasts. However, seeds of the tutored samurai culture can be found in the eighth-century Japanese classic, the *Kojiki*. Before that, esoteric lore regarding sword work was cultivated at the imperial court.

Initially, the samurai (retainers) were positioned to serve the court nobility. In time, they acquired power in their own right, establishing domination over agricultural land and building their own hierarchical political organizations. This culminated in a semi-centralized military regime, the shogunate, in the late twelfth century. The samurai political organization rested on the formation of strong emotional bonds between military masters and vassals upheld by a strict code of honor (Ikegami 1995). By the sixteenth century, the samurai code was elaborated into a code known as *bushido* (the Way of the Warrior), consisting of seven *bushi* virtues: integrity, rectitude, courage, benevolence, honor, loyalty, and respect.[1]

Beyond qualities of comportment, samurai were expected to show proficiency in a number of non-martial spheres that were linked to the neo-Confucian notion of personal culture (*bun*). This connection was represented by an ideal that conjoined them by means of a compound phrase, *bu-bun*. One such art was the composition of highly stylized verse, most notably *haiku*. Another was calligraphy: the embodiment of *bu-bun* involved practice with pen and brush in a manner that evinced unselfconscious, fearless directness. Shogun Tokugawa Ieyasu proclaimed that the brush and the sword are one.

Nevertheless, the core *bushido* virtue consisted of fearless combativeness in battle and readiness to kill or be killed by a perceived enemy. In the words of samurai Kato Kiyomasa (1562–1611):

> [By] reading Chinese poetry ... one will surely become womanized if he gives his heart knowledge of such elegant and delicate refinements. Having been born into the house of a warrior, one's intentions should be to grasp the long and the short swords and to die.
>
> *(Cited in Wilson 1982, 131)*[2]

But grasping the swords was far from spontaneous; it required years of training in one of the specialized schools (*ryu*) that flourished toward the end of the medieval period. This involved mastery of one or more of the martial techniques for which complex curricula of instruction had become codified.[3] During the long period of peace under the Tokugawa shogunate, the martial skills could rarely be exercised on the battlefield. Even so, their cultivation remained no less sharp. The status of lords often depended on the number and quality of expert martial artists under their authority. The spirit of contests, even for matters of honor, dictated the ambition of seeking victory over an opponent, which often meant his death. As the arts of combat became "domesticated" during the long Pax Tokugawa, however, competition among different courts and *ryu* was no less fierce. During the Tokugawa period, it has been said, samurai ideals became close to a national ethic, for even the merchant class had become "*bushido*-ized" (Bellah 1957, 98).

With the overthrow of rule by the feudal lords (*shogun*), the system of Japanese martial arts faced major challenges. The advent of Western culture and the spirit of commerce dislodged the hegemony of samurai notions of victory and defeat in combat. Not many years after the Meiji Restoration of 1868, a prominent Japanese educator, Jigoro Kano, began to reconfigure the ethos of martial arts training. Kano Sensei started a dojo (training hall) in a Buddhist temple in Tokyo, the *kotokan*, which became the matrix for developing a discipline he called judo. In this effort, he sought to reconfigure the goal of training from defeating enemies into something purely educational: promoting the development of personal character and social engagement. He renamed the educational goal *shushin-ho*, "the cultivation of wisdom and virtue as well as the study and application of the principles of Judo in our daily lives" (Kano, in *AikiNews* 1990). As he later came to formulate it, "the ultimate objective of judo discipline is to be utilized as a means to self-perfection, and thenceforth to make a positive contribution to society" (Murata 2005, 147–8).

The view of budo training that Kano articulated became increasingly prominent in Japan in the twentieth century. This was especially true following World War II—the most disastrous outcome of the resurgence of the *bushido*-ized nation imaginable, a denouement that Kano opposed. By the 1980s, the Japanese Budo Association (Nippon Budokan) took the question of defining their goals so seriously that they spent years deliberating the matter, proclaiming in their 1987 Charter:

> Budo, the Japanese martial ways have their origins in the age-old martial spirit of Japan. Through centuries of historical and social change, these forms of traditional culture evolved from combat techniques (*jutsu*) into ways of self-development. ... Practitioners study the skills while striving to unify mind, technique and body; develop [their] character; enhance their sense of morality; and to cultivate a respectful and courteous demeanour. ... This elevation of the human spirit will contribute to social prosperity and harmony.

Even so, tensions remained between the age-old martial spirit of Japan and the pacific goals of moral development and social harmony. However as much as Kano Sensei espoused the ideals of ego-transcendence and societal betterment, judo retained something of the traditional martial goals of victory in combat. This spirit was rekindled by the incorporation of judo into Olympic competition. A Budokan was built to house the judo Olympics in 1964, and this continues to house national competitions among different martial arts, including karate, kendo, shorinji kempo, kyudo, and naginata as well as judo. In addition to the egoistic competitive spirit promoted by such matches, judo's goal of *victory* enabled the combatants to use whatever methods they like, such as "throwing, choking ... bending or twisting the opponent's arms or legs" (Kano 1932, 58). Recognizing this tension, the Japan Budo Association saw fit to express concerns over "a recent trend towards infatuation just with technical ability compounded by an excessive concern with winning" (Nippon Budokan 1987).

It was given to Morihei Ueshiba to complete the evolution of budo and resolve that tension. This involved configuring a curriculum of training that *embodies* in its foundational principles the elimination of competition and movements designed to avoid inflicting pain and promoting peace. Drawing both on superb training in traditional martial ways and on immersion in a universalistic new Japanese religion, Ueshiba's aikido journey took a new turn with an epiphanic experience in 1925, when he was 42. In the course of a particularly intense meditative/purification experience, he felt his body enveloped by a shimmering gold light, and he came to transformative insight about budo. At that moment, he said, he came to realize that

> the spirit of Budo is not defeating the opponent by our force, nor is it a tool to lead the world into destruction with arms. To follow true Budo is ... to keep the peace of the world, and correctly produce, protect, and cultivate all beings in nature.
>
> *(Cited in Saotome [1986] 1993, 10)*

Ueshiba continued forging new martial techniques throughout the 1930s. In vain he tried to forestall Japan's attacks against the United States. During the war, he withdrew in inner exile to Iwama, where in 1942 he renamed his practice aikido. In the postwar years, the catastrophes of Hiroshima and Nagasaki together with revelations from a Japanese soldier present at the liberation of Hitler's concentration camps spurred him into another turn. In 1948 he invited an old disciple, Hikitsutchi Sensei, to join him in promoting a "new kind of *budo*," one devoted explicitly to promoting world peace. Ueshiba Sensei continued to refine this practice for the rest of his life, which ended in 1969.

As Ueshiba came to formulate the end of his budo, the goal was not victory over the other, but *masagatsu agatsu* (the great victory is victory over oneself). The practice he created relied not on pain or physical force in any form, but a welcoming of the energy of an attack, neutralizing its aggressive direction, and caring for the attacker. The structure of combat had finally transformed into a harmonious exchange of gestures. This was an idea whose time had come. In the early 1950s aikido dojos were established first in France and the United States, then in the United Kingdom, Germany, and Australia; at present, more than a million practitioners pursue aikido training in all six Continents.

Litigation in Euro-American Culture

The transformation from combat to nonviolence in Japanese martial arts appears to have been prompted by educational, civic, and spiritual concerns. In contrast, the move from adversarial legalism to professional mediation in the legal profession was motivated largely by economic and political concerns.

As with the Japanese martial arts, arts of litigation in the West evolved over millennia, from resolving disputes through violence to civil litigation to socially mediated opposition to a process of seeking agreements that both parties freely assent to. The initial evolution was from spontaneous fighting between aggrieved parties to formal dueling with rules and witnesses. The United States inherited the roots of these changes from both Continental and English sources.

Among Germanic peoples, trial by combat—sometimes known as judicial dueling—appeared in the early Middle Ages. An eighth-century document prescribes a trial by combat for two families who disputed the boundary between their lands: the contestants were required to touch a piece of that land with their swords and swear that their claim is lawful; the loser would forfeit claims to the land and pay a fine also. Other issues settled through trial by combat concerned dynastic power. "Wager of battle" entered the common law of England following the Norman Conquest. In Renaissance Italy and France, codes for formal dueling emerged for conflicts in which honor rather than material interests were at stake. Similar codes emerged elsewhere in Europe, especially in Scandinavia (*Holmgang*) and Ireland (*code duello*). All these were forms in which Might makes Right, under conditions in which social and then judicial norms were in place to regulate the antagonistic encounter. In the United States, violent (though extralegal) forms of conflict resolution such as the duel persisted through the early decades of the republic, leading to such notable contests as the shooting of Alexander Hamilton at the hands of Aaron Burr.

In the course of the sixteenth and seventeenth centuries, trial by combat began to disappear, initially due to ecclesiastical opposition and then through legislative banning.[4] Instead, civil disputes came to be settled almost exclusively in courts through the arguments of lawyers and the testimony of witnesses. Modern European civil procedure begins with the Napoleonic era and the passage of the French Civil Code of 1806, which sought to standardize civil procedure. It promoted a court system that featured oral arguments between equal parties which were open to the public. This heightened the dramaturgical presentation of legal conflict in court trials. In the United States, the young country's litigiousness grew due to societal and economic conflicts of the Industrial Age and the resulting expansion of the network of courts. Those changes engendered a system that Georg Simmel analyzed more than a century ago, observing that the conduct of quarrels by professional counsels "serves the clean separation of the controversy from all personal associations that have nothing to do with it"; this makes it "the most merciless type of contestation because it lies wholly outside the subjective contrast between charity and cruelty" (Simmel [1908] 1971, 85). Robert Kagan aptly described this system as "'adversarial legalism'—a method of policymaking and dispute resolution with two salient characteristics: *formal legal contestation* [and] *litigant activism*" (2001, 9). The principle of adversarial legalism helped guide the construction of curricula in law schools. Beyond school, novice lawyers soon learn informal ways to uphold this principle; for example, by keeping the parties to a dispute talking only with their attorneys and not with each other.

Over time, critics began to target the socially dysfunctional aspects of this system. President Lincoln advised Americans to "discourage litigation" and instead encouraged them to consider "how the nominal winner is often the loser in fees, expenses and costs of time" (Steiner 1995, 2). Edward Bellamy called for the abolition of "law as a special science," seeing "no ... use for the hair-splitting experts who presided and argued in [the] courts" (cited in Hensler 2003, 169). Toward the end of the century, Austrian legalist Franz Klein broached ideas that would gain traction only half a century later, arguing that "parties to a lawsuit should co-operate in order to facilitate a judgment" instead of stretching facts and the law in a zero-sum showdown (cited in van Rhee 2005, 12). Opposition to litigious practices grew in the twentieth century as conflicts between families, contractual parties, and businesses grew more complicated, populations swelled, legal codes thickened, and court costs rose.

By the middle of the twentieth century, litigation had reached a saturation point in American life as civil case filings reached all-time highs and courts carried overloaded case schedules. One step toward relieving this situation was to give judges assistance from professional court administrators to set their calendars and manage the flow of cases (Hensler 2003, 174). Another was continued reliance on traditional arbitration, which had been a feature of the American legal system for generations. George Washington himself served as an arbiter prior to the Revolution, since it proved more efficient than the courts. In 1925, Congress ratified its role through the Federal Arbitration Act, drafted initially by the American Bar Association in response to ever-growing litigiousness. A robust arbitration system provided a seasoned alternative to traditional litigation. However, it was not malleable enough to account for the variety of nuanced disputes that later forms of conflict resolution had to address.

In the socially transformative 1960s, communities and disputants came to favor alternative forms of dispute resolution, including mediation. The community justice movement of the late 1960s and early 1970s increasingly supported mediation because participants felt that the litigation system in the United States disproportionately protected elite interests and neglected the need of the socioeconomically disadvantaged. Child custody disputants and divorcees came to see the bloated civil litigation system as too sclerotic and adversarial to produce nuanced outcomes tailored to the specifics of familial and individual disputes. Businesses found that mediation was better equipped to handle industry-specific disputes in a manner more in line with the ever-faster world of commerce. This evolved attitude towards forms of alternative dispute resolution (ADR) is one significant factor in the 84 percent drop in federal civil cases that went to trial between 1962 and 2002 (Stipanowich 2010, 4). ADR's newfound prominence in American legal life was ratified by the passage of the Alternative Dispute Resolution Act. As a result of the 1998 law, federal courts are required to offer "some form of ADR," and many state courts began to standardize such options voluntarily (Hensler 2003, 167). Other countries followed suit. In 2001, for example, the Government of Colombia mandated that all civil and commercial disputes undergo a conciliation process before being filed in court.

Evolutionary stage	JAPANESE MARTIAL ARTS	EURO-AMERICAN LITIGATION
1. Raw physical combat	Violent struggle	Violent struggle
2. Disciplined physical combat	Samurai martial engagement: *bujutsu*	Trial by combat
3. Regulated verbal combat	--------------	Civil litigation
4. Conflict subordinated to societal object	Martial forms subordinated to societal betterment: judo	Arbitration
5. Consensually achieved resolution	Conflict resolution through non-combative interaction: aikido	Mediation

FIGURE 3.1 Evolution from Raw Combat to Consensual Conflict Resolution

Indeed, this very cultural jump that produced a market for less adversarial forms of dispute resolution paralleled the shift that created an enthusiastic market for aikido teaching in the martial arts. After decades of reliance on adversarial conflict resolution in economic, political, and cultural concerns, Americans came to experience a hunger for alternatives that favor autonomy and consensus.

The Methodology of Aikido

To schematize the methodology of aikido as a resource to manage social conflict, I list below a set of factors known to promote the onset and escalation of conflict and explore how aikido deals with each of them. This is by no means an exhaustive list; complex tomes and thousands of papers have investigated the universe of internal and systemic variables related to conflict, escalation, and violence.[5] Those I have selected delineate factors which, in decades of teaching a course on Conflict Theory and Aikido, have seemed particularly plausible to me and relevant to engagement with aikido practice.[6]

Classic theories of conflict identify a number of factors internal to the parties inherent in social interaction: (1) bio-psycho-sociocultural dispositions toward aggression; (2) emotional reactivity; (3) hostile sentiments of the parties; (4) low self-esteem; and (5) memories of prior conflicts between the parties involved. Social science also has identified kindred factors located in the social and cultural environments, including (6) cultural beliefs about conflict and violence; (7) social controls that dampen conflict; and (8) availability of allies to help protagonists pursue the conflict.

Dispositions to aggressiveness in human personalities stem from a wide range of biochemical, psychological, social, and cultural factors (Levine 2006a, 2006b). The aikido theory assumes that humans will be subject to aggressive inputs from others as a matter of course. As a practice that seeks to promote harmony in action, accordingly, aikido seeks methods whereby attacks do not elicit counterattacks, but instead teaches ways to neutralize incoming aggression. Indeed, neutralizing aggressive attacks by others forms the core of aikido training. This involves both cognitive and kinesthetic responses. A major cognitive shift involves reframing the attacker as a training partner, not as an enemy; and reframing the attack itself not as a threat but simply as a charge, even a "gift," of energy. In words that noted Sensei Mitsugi Saotome has expressed in seminars, "when someone grabs your wrist, it does not mean the start of a fight; it is the beginning of a conversation." This reconfiguration can be extended to cognitive operations that critique distorted perceptions one has of others (Eidelson and Eidelson 2008).

Kinesthetically, neutralizing the aggression of an attacker involves a number of moves. It means moving in such a way that the attack is not permitted to impinge on the body or the feelings of the person attacked, which is known as "getting off the line." At the same time, it means allowing the energy of the attack to express itself fully—not "cutting the ki" of the attacker. Instead, it means conjoining with the attacker's energy and directing it in such a way that neither party is harmed. It does so, moreover, not in a spirit of directing attackers to change their ways, but by listening to them, concurring with them, and, indeed, even caring for them. If someone throws a punch at you, for example, you do not block it or counterpunch, but move deftly off the line of attack, connect harmoniously with the attack, and redirect the attacker's energy toward a nonviolent resolution.

In whatever manner the attacker is defined, there remains the psychological issue of how ready the person attacked is to experience a Fight-Flight response. In his classic work on conflict, economist Kenneth Boulding coined the expression "coefficient of reactivity" to represent the degree to which parties react to a negative gesture by the other, which Boulding described as the "touchiness" of the parties ([1962] 1988, 25–7). Aikido puts a premium on learning to "respond, not react" to attacks. Training for this includes learning how to remain calm by continued breathing, relaxed musculature, and staying "centered"—a state of being in which attention is directed to the lower abdomen.

Another factor that Boulding identified as inducing the escalation of conflict is the variable of what initial levels of hostility were evinced by one or both parties. Evidently, persons that are prone toward hostile feelings and gestures are likely to instigate attacks and to perform counterattacks. Aikido trains persons to control their hostile impulses in a number of ways. They habituate themselves to express gratitude frequently. They learn to be continuously mindful of their bodily states and to examine their own motives so as to subdue egoistic strivings that motivate aggressive gestures.

In a classic paper on community conflict, James S. Coleman (1957) began his inventory of causes of social conflict by considering whether the parties had a prior history of conflict. Memories of previous conflicts can be recalled quickly and thereby reactivate the neurons that carry traumatic memories. One way in which aikido minimizes this factor is by training people to be present in the moment, to work to avoid carrying the baggage of prior injuries or hurt feelings into current transactions.

Beyond these factors intrinsic to the parties in interaction, other elements in aikido practice work to substitute harmony for conflicts that are promoted by external conditions. As comparative cultural studies have demonstrated, cultures vary widely with respect to the positive or negative values they place on conflict and violence (Fromm 1973). The ideology of aikido implants strong dispositions to avert or counteract cultural dispositions to aggression. The very word aikido contains elements that signify harmony and love.[7] In the words of its Founder, "I'm not teaching you how to move your feet; I'm teaching you how to move your mind toward nonviolence."

The customary ways in which aikido is practiced include elements that theorists have shown to have a dampening effect on conflict. Coleman (1957) showed that social conflicts are likely to be contained when the antagonists shared allegiance to some sort of supervening authorities and/or symbolism that enabled them to transcend their local conflict and to third-party controls over their interaction. Aikido practice always begins and concludes with a ritual bow to the Founder of the practice and to the Japanese kanjis that signify harmonious interaction. On the mat, instructors intervene tirelessly to check students when their movements become the least bit aggressive. But some theorists point to the tendency of combatants to escalate conflict through the recruitment of allies among others in the system (Kerr 1988). Thus, dojo etiquette requires partners to solve their own problems and to seek assistance only when they cannot reach a solution in any other than a combative manner.

On all counts, then, aikido works to reduce, if not eliminate, factors understood to produce conflictual interactions, such that its practitioners do successfully replace notions of defeat and victory with the idea of enhancing the well-being and autonomy of both parties.

The Methodology of Mediation

While the aiki approach to managing conflict emerged from a continuous historical process of domesticating martial ways, from the most brutish combat to cultivated weaponry to a benign exchange of non-injurious gestures, the history of judicial litigation shows a substantial upturn before economic and political crises forced the turn to alternative forms of dispute resolution. Sociologist Georg Simmel was among the first to note that when interpersonal disputes get transferred to the jurisdiction of courts, they become uncompromising in content and vicious in execution. In a passage worth citing at length, he wrote:

FACTORS THAT PROMOTE CONFLICT AND ESCALATION	AIKIDO RESPONSES THAT COUNTERACT THOSE FACTORS
Aggression invites counterattack	Neutralizing the aggression: get off the line of attack; reframe the attack; permit energy of attacker to spend itself
Reactivity heightens Fight-Flight response	Relaxation and centering
Hostile sentiments feed the fight	Generalized gratitude; understanding and connecting with the other
Insecure egos cannot stand humiliation of defeat	Using setbacks or "failures" as occasions for growth
Memories of prior conflicts feed reactions	Focusing awareness on the present
Symbols glorifying war, macho aggressiveness	Symbols of peace and humanity
Ineffectual moral authorities	Instituting respected authorities
Recruiting allies heightens escalation	Search within to eliminate discord

FIGURE 3.2 Elements of Aikido that Reduce Conflict and Promote Mutual Respect

In judicial conflict … claims on both sides are pursued with pure objectivity and by employing all permissible means, without being deflected or in any way attenuated by personal or any other extraneous considerations. … Elsewhere, even in the fiercest battles, something subjective, some mere turn of fortune, or some interference from a third party is at least possible. In legal conflict, however, everything of that sort is excluded by the matter-of-factness with which the just fight and absolutely nothing else proceeds. … The prosecution of legal battles in more evolved societies serves the pure disentanglement of the controversy from all extraneous personal associations. When Otto the Great orders that a particular legal controversy be settled through trial by combat (*gottesgerichtlichen Zweikampf*) to be decided through professional swordsmen, only the bare form—the process of fighting and winning—is what remains out of the whole conflict of interests.

(Simmel [1908] 1992, 305–6; translation mine)

In this spirit, law school on the contemporary legal system trains lawyers to deal with conflict by out-strategizing and outmaneuvering their opponents through an arsenal of techniques that aim at convincing a jury or a judge to produce a decision favorable to their interests—without regard to the best interests of both parties, and surely without regard to the best interests of third parties and society more generally. In the words of Daniel Weinstein (2004), a former litigator and judge who became a professional mediator:

> The goal of convincing juridical authorities is achieved through employing a blitzkrieg of maneuvers that includes interrogatories, depositions, and advocacy aimed at influencing decision makers rather than the "opponent." The results are measured by how much you "win" ... like Rocky standing on the steps with his arms raised in victory. Unlearning this warrior-like behavior for any litigator who enters the world of mediation advocate is difficult and not at all natural. Winning by a verdict imposed on the other side is so much a part of our system that in order to inveigle lawyers to take mediation training, I once had to rename a course I taught on the subject from "Effective Mediation Advocacy" to "How to Win at Mediation," an oxymoron of sorts.

Accordingly, just as aikido practitioners have to unlearn so much that is associated with the samurai ambition to defeat an enemy, so do lawyers who wish seriously to pursue a career in mediation have to learn a whole new set of techniques, techniques which are rarely available in the curricula of law schools. As Weinstein phrased it:

> Effective mediation skills for the lawyer representing a client are very different from those of the litigators, whose skills do not translate from the courtroom to the mediation table. Stating your claims in terms that do not inflame the other side, and yet still integrate your clients' important interests, is a learned rather than a spontaneously manifested skill. Turning your opponents' fears, weaknesses, and anxieties into advantages, giving them a share of the outcome, and creating win/win solutions are new territory for the warrior litigator.

The skills and norms of mediation were codified initially by practitioners in the areas of family counseling and conflict resolution education. The mediation movement, however, was boosted substantially by the publication *Getting To Yes* in 1981, a book on the outcome of a Negotiation Project at Harvard University (Fisher et al. 1991, 2nd edition). The authors offered prescriptions for conduct that run precisely opposite to the paradigm of lawyerly practice that Simmel had articulated when writing about legal conflict. They advocate moving from a win-lose mentality in which personal feelings and biases are rigorously excluded to a process in which perceptions are clarified, emotions are recognized and legitimated, and listening to one another is prioritized. Additionally, what the participants really need and want is assessed honestly, finding solutions in which both parties gain is encouraged, and fair standards and fair procedures are agreed to.

During the 1980s, a growing number of lawyers and judges developed an increasingly sophisticated repertoire of ideas and techniques for resolving disputes through mediation. In *Mediation: A Comprehensive Guide to Resolving Conflicts Without*

Litigation, Folberg and Taylor provided a useful overview of the field. They supplied a succinct definition of the process of mediation:

> [A]n alternative to violence, self-help, or litigation that differs from the processes of counseling, negotiation, and arbitration. It can be defined as the process by which the participants, together with the assistance of a neutral person or persons, systematically isolate disputed issues in order to develop options, consider alternatives and reach a consensual settlement that will accommodate their needs. Mediation is a process that emphasizes the participants' own responsibility for making decisions that affect their lives. It is therefore a self-empowering process.
> *(1984, 7–8)*

The volume offers materials on the stages of the mediation process; relevant skills; diverse styles of mediating conflict; the educational, ethical, and practical dimensions of mediation as a profession; and an extensive bibliography.[8]

Although law schools were relatively slow to embrace this approach, since 2000 they have hastened to catch up. At present, many have introduced courses and even programs about mediation. Now almost every American law school offers a course in mediation; many in fact offer programs with a constellation of mediation courses, clinics, and certificates. In the process, numerous traditional law course texts have come to include some material on mediation in the domains of contracts, torts, and trial practice.

If one were to draw up a set of training points for mediators that bears some resemblance to the list presented for *aikidoka*, it might look something like Figure 3.3.

FACTORS THAT MAINTAIN A LITIGIOUS ETHOS	MEDIATOR RESPONSES THAT COUNTERACT THOSE FACTORS
Aggression as a stimulus	Lawyers and clients must not attack one another
Reactivity	Maintain a calm and friendly atmosphere
Hostile sentiments	Spot and build on points of agreement
Insecure egos	Praise willingness to be open and creative
Prior history of conflicts	Focus on present aspirations and future goals
Ideology favoring conflict	Appeal to general values of harmony
Nonexistent supra-local controls	Mediator stands to control escalation, and to adduce authority of shared values
Available allies	Identify allies as others who have successfully completed a mediation process

FIGURE 3.3 Elements of Mediation Promoting Agreement Based on Mutual Respect

Mutual Relevance

For a society and a time dominated by an ethos of competitive individualism—where the business world dominates public imagination and feeds upon the imagery and motivations of competitive sports and where the American dream is configured in terms of individuals' "getting ahead" and where heroes are celebrated by how they achieve victory and handle defeat—aikido and mediation represent cutting-edge, countercultural engagements in which the dominant motifs include a win-win outcome, subdue the ego, communicate openly, learn to trust, and build consensus. This is so, we have seen, even though both of them derive from traditions that have been informed by centuries of mortal combat but which have been transformed at their core.

Insofar as these practices have contemporary value, it may be useful to see in what ways they can be seen to reinforce one another and, even more, how each can enrich and contribute to the other. Both join a number of other contemporary modalities in which combative procedures are explicitly replaced by practices that eschew adversarial postures. These include Couples Therapy, Nonviolent Communication (Rosenberg 2005a), a wide range of Alternative Dispute Resolution strategies, as well as Principled Negotiation (Fisher et al. 1991).

Aikido's Gifts to Mediation

Aikido practice seems pertinent to all three of the domains in which mediators act:

1. the mediator's effect on the conduct of the disputing parties and their lawyers;
2. the mediator's effect on the interactional context of the mediation efforts; and
3. the personalities of the mediators themselves.

Aikido and the Litigators

The mediation process requires exactly the opposite of what conventionally trained lawyers and their clients are disposed to do. In the words of experienced mediator Antonio Piazza (2004),

> Litigators tend to think of themselves as warriors. Frequently they come into mediation and forcefully communicate to the other party that the other party is: (a) simply wrong, and (b) perhaps too stupid to know it, and (c) quite probably too venal to care, and (d) if they don't settle they will be beaten to a pulp in court.

Even though the actors in question understand that the goal of the process is a settlement agreement signed voluntarily by both sides, such counterproductive dispositions are a "natural" response based on aggressive instincts and a culture that values aggressive, macho attitudes.

An aikido approach here would be not to change the behavior of others, but to change oneself. This begins with the self of the mediator. That is, discarding the usual method of importing techniques into a situation designed to instruct or coach someone how to communicate less aggressively or less defensively, the mediator opens up him/herself to nondirective, non-manipulative communication. So Piazza said:

> For the mediator, the process is not one of standing outside a dispute and applying skillful techniques to it, but entering fully and wholeheartedly, and without importing yet another agenda (and its concomitant fears and desires) into an already changed situation. By way of example: Mediation theory may tell you that it is critical to allow a disputant with an emotional charge to vent their feelings, and experience being heard. But if "active listening" is practiced as a technique to remove an obstacle, the felt experience of the disputant is as likely to be "I am being manipulated" as "I am being heard." Paradoxically, aikido might well move you to fill the space between you and the disputant who is winding up for a tirade instantly, and so completely, that he never gets going at all. While that may sound brutal, the felt experience can be one of compassion. The difference is whether you are "doing to" or opening up to the person with whom you are interacting.

Aikido and the Interactional Context

People who train aikido walk into a dojo carrying whatever stresses, frustrations, peeves, and gripes the day has brought them. They are expected to leave these at the door, much as Ethiopians traditionally left their weapons at the door of the church or mosque before they entered. They bow into the dojo and begin and close their training with a communal ritual. Expectations for deportment while practicing in the dojo are then made clear.

It might be of value for mediators to direct some attention to the ritual setting of their deliberations. Another idea would be to distribute beforehand a list of points about etiquette in the mediation setting, such as many aikido organizations distribute information about dojo etiquette to newcomers. The emotional empowerment that aikido practitioners experience from expressions of gratitude can be brought into play intermittently. No less important would be words that remind the participants to reframe continuously the setting of their work: from a situation of combat to an opportunity to become more free and creative partners in a problem-solving conversation. One experienced meditator has suggested recently that the mediation process would be enhanced by attending more consciously to preliminary groundwork for mediation and concluding mediation with words of grace that acknowledge the work that has been accomplished consensually. Aikido promotes such moments somatically both through a moment of getting centered before each exercise and by bowing appreciatively to one another at the beginning and conclusion of every practice.

Aikido and the Personalities of the Mediators

Practiced *aikidoka* may understand the situation of mediators better than they do themselves, in the sense of being trained in mindfulness about inner somatic and emotional responses to a complex of aggressive actors swirling about them. On this point, experienced *aikidoka*-mediator Stephen Kotev (2001) maintained that there is a serious gap in the training of mediation practitioners:

> As mediators and conflict resolvers, our somatic education has been neglected. Mediators are starting to realize their body language is often communicating more than they know. A clenched jaw, an exasperated look can say more than you ever intended. Your stress may cause you to say or do something that you later will regret. Wouldn't it be nice to be able to notice where in your body you were feeling stressed and be able to release it? Wouldn't it be nice to be able to show our neutrality in our posture as well as in our words? Knowledge of your physical process will help you be a more effective conflict resolver.

The mediator's need to be neutral requires a level of emotional development that is not easy to come by. Aikido offers a variety of techniques and exercises that promote the state of being "centered," a state wherein the charged pushes and pulls of a subliminally litigious context can be finessed. Indeed, learning to be *centered under stress* forms a central part of aikido training. The state of being centered enhances abilities to perceive tense situations with more clarity and understanding and to become aware of openings and options in stuck situations. Beyond that, the mediator works best when manifesting a positive state of openness and love that litigants can be exposed to and mirror. One particularly relevant training is that of the *randori* practice, where one is being attacked simultaneously by a surround of aggressive bodies and moving in an aware and flowing manner to manage them effectively.

How Mediation Might Enrich Aikido Practice

This gets us into truly uncharted territory. The most I can do here is throw out a few suggestions. One is that the work of mediators provides greater awareness of the interpersonal dynamics involved in neutralizing aggression and harmonizing energies. This would be particularly true of those, like family or couples therapists, whose primary focus is on the emotional landscape of the parties they work with.

Another contribution could be to turn the attention of *aikidoka* to the whole area of three-party interactions. Virtually all of aikido training concerns what to do when one party is being attacked by another. Aikido as hitherto practiced has little to show about how to stop fights, how to turn combat among others into conversation, and how to attain peace other than working on each individual's potential response to negativity. In today's world, that cannot be sufficient.

All of the above is presented with a sense that we remain beginners in these new modes of communication. It remains to be seen—most certainly a worthy initiative to consider—what insights and fresh understandings of their own practices might emerge from occasions in which small numbers of mediators and *aikidoka* are brought together to share with one another reports of what they already do. I hope that these thoughts might stimulate others to carry the conversation forward.

Notes

1 The seven *bushi* virtues came to be symbolized by the seven pleats of the *hakama*, a skirt worn by *samurai* during the Tokugawa period (1603–1868).
2 Kato sama further prescribed: "One should rise at four in the morning, practice sword technique, eat one's meal, and train with the bow, the gun, and the horse. … When one unsheathes his sword, he has cutting a person down in mind" (Wilson 1982, 130).
3 Mastery of the dagger (*tanto*), glaive (*naginata*), bow and arrow (*kyujutsu*), empty hands combat (*jujutsu*), and, above all, the long sword (*katana*) and short sword (*wakizashi*).
4 Because Britain did not abolish wager by battle until Parliament's 1819 response to *Ashford v Thornton* (1818), and because no court in post-independence United States has addressed the issue, the question of whether trial by combat remains a valid American alternative to civil action remains open, at least in theory.
5 I find *Constructive Conflicts: From Escalation to Resolution* by Louis Kriesberg (2007) a particularly valuable overview of the field—not least for its useful distinction between destructive and constructive conflicts.
6 The syllabus of that course has been made public as an Appendix to my *Powers of the Mind: The Reinvention of Liberal Learning in America* (Levine 2005a).
7 "Aiki" translates as joining of energies, or harmony. "Ai" also has a homonym that signifies love.
8 The literature on mediation techniques has grown enormously in recent decades. Prominent treatments include such titles as *Mediation: The Roles of Advocate and Neutral* (Folberg and Golann 2011) and "The Secrets of Successful Mediators" (Goldberg 2005).

4

CIVILIZATIONS, CLASHING AND HARMONIOUS

In 1993, the late Samuel Huntington advanced a claim that the bipolarized world of the latter twentieth century would yield inexorably to clashes among civilizations. This alarm caught many social scientists by surprise. In the early 1990s, literate opinion still lingered under the glow of the Soviet collapse, which savored the sense that world consensus behind liberal democracy and capitalism stood to preclude future ideological clashes. The view that the array of culturally diverse historical societies would "converge" on a single common constellation of modern society—a principal tenet of the first two centuries of sociology—seemed reconfirmed.

Shmuel N. Eisenstadt figured prominently among those who had long challenged the convergence thesis. His noted conception of "multiple modernities" (Eisenstadt 2003) seemed to point to a world future in which gross cultural differences would perdure and, if anything, grow more intense. His perspective might thereby have been assumed a priori as fielding an argument consistent with the central claims of the Huntington thesis. However, this essay will demonstrate that in virtue of Eisenstadt's championing of two other ideas—the complexity of historic civilizations and the potentialities of dialogue—that assumption must be challenged.

Global developments since the early 1990s could be said to have corroborated Huntington's claim. As a rough indicator of that denouement, consider John Mearsheimer's recent summary: in the first years after the Cold War, many Americans evinced profound optimism about the future of international politics; but since 1989, the United States has been at war for a startling two out of every three years and with no end in sight, the public mood has shifted to an aching pessimism (Mearsheimer 2011). To be sure, it is a large leap from the frequency of post-Cold War international clashes to an assumption about the clash of civilizations. Warfare among contemporary societies stems from many sources: growing competition over increasingly scarce resources like land, energy, and water; struggles for political control and economic hegemony; and hostile reactions to economic insecurities and rapid social change. The management of such conflicts depends largely on the restraint of statesmen, negotiations among political stakeholders, and the attitudes of their followers.

Even so, the salience of those polemogenic factors does not rule out the thesis of a deeper-lying clash of civilizations. This sweeping claim deserves to be addressed in its own right.

In Support of the Huntington Thesis

The Huntington thesis holds that *diverse civilizations are marked by core symbolic complexes that ultimately stand in irreducible conflict*. This claim draws support from three truths.

First, ever since William Graham Sumner ([1907] 2002) provided the language to say so, social scientists have affirmed that all human groups manifest *ethnocentrism*. This designates a syndrome marked by an exaggerated view of a group's own virtues; a pejorative view of others; a relation of order, law, and industry among members of the in-group; and a relation of predation against out-groups. Related to these elements is a tendency to exaggerate the differences between in-groups and out-groups. The universality of this pattern can be linked in part to the ways in which it satisfies at once two of the most powerful human needs: the need for attachment and the need for differentiation.[1]

Second, as systematic studies on the matter have shown, the more complex and technologically advanced a society is, the stronger its level of ethnocentrism is likely to be (LeVine and Campbell 1972).

Third, ethnocentric beliefs become fortified when intertwined with imperatives that stem from strong cultural mandates. Certain of these mandates derive from the work of elites who have produced transcendent ideals for reconstructing worldly relations, ideals that were elaborated in what has been called the Axial civilizations (Eisenstadt 2003, I, chaps. 1, 7).

The great civilizations, consequently, have tended to defend and extend their respective domains through glorified ethnocentric processes involving conquest, conversion, and assimilation of those outside the pale. In Greco-Roman civilization, for example, Hellenes came to disparage outsiders who were ignorant of Greek language and civilization, thereby uncivil and rude. Calling them barbarians (*barbaroi*) encouraged the Greeks to conquer, enslave, and colonize others who were deemed culturally inferior. This conceit continued in Roman times, as Roman citizens justified their extensive conquests of alien peoples (*barbari*) by coercing them into adopting the Latin language and their religious beliefs. In the case of European civilization, this pattern found its denouement in the *missione civilatrice*, whereby Italian airplanes rained poisoned gas on shoeless Abyssinian peasants armed with spears and Nazi armies attempted to expand their notion of a superior German culture throughout Europe. The Greek/barbarian paradigm can also be found in all other major civilizations. Its omnipresence therefore underlies the plausibility of the clash of civilizations thesis.

The pejorative distinctions one associates with the great civilizations include, alongside the Hellenic distinction between Greek and barbarian, the dichotomies of Hindu/*mleccha*, Chosen People (*am segulah*)/gentiles (*goyyim*), Christian/pagan, *umma/fakir* (infidel), and *nihongo/gaijin*. Each of those dichotomies derives from certain core values in each civilization, values that implant criteria used to justify disparagement if not aggression against others. If, in fact, those values represent hegemonic notions that subordinate all beliefs and norms in their respective civilizations, then there would indeed be grounds for adducing theoretical support for the Huntington world view.

Challenges to the Huntington Thesis

Nevertheless, the Huntington thesis appears vulnerable when both of its key assumptions are subjected to question. The first assumption views civilizations as monolithic formations, organized around a coherent core of animating beliefs and values. The second assumption holds that the most likely interactional form in which serious differences tend to get aired is combat. These assumptions simply do not hold up under critical examination, but few thinkers have had the erudition and imagination to provide as much substance for those critiques as did Shmuel Eisenstadt.

The first critique was voiced by Edward Said (2001) when he discounted the Huntington view of civilizations as

> shut-down, sealed-off entities that have been purged of the myriad currents and counter-currents that animate human history, and that over centuries have made it possible for that history not only to contain wars of religion and imperial conquest but also to be one of exchange, cross-fertilization and sharing.

Few scholars have gone so far as Eisenstadt in elucidating the enormous complexity of all civilizations, not least in identifying strains within and between institutional structures and cultural complexes. In consequence of this, each civilization has evolved internally contradictory sub-traditions. Although each embraces a core value that separates some category of worthy humans from one that denigrates others, each also contains elements that promote a more inclusive orientation. All civilizations possess customs that promote hospitality toward strangers. They contain elements that can be used to encourage the toleration of diversity and they harbor teachings that cultivate understanding and compassion. This thereby offers seeds that can sprout into resources for interhuman dialogue—a form of open communication that could inspire ways of reducing clashes among contemporary civilizations. In fact, in an interview given shortly before his passing, Eisenstadt emphasized his belief that all civilizations contain universalistic elements (Weil 2010).

The second critique takes aim at implied assumptions about panhuman belligerence. It questions the notion that combat is the most likely interactional form in which differences are resolved. To be sure, much research—by biologists such as

Konrad Lorenz, Nikolaas Tinbergen, Richard Wrangham, and Dale Peterson—supports the assumption of an inherent human disposition toward aggression; and some ideologists regard the polemical principle as a defensible human ideal. A growing body of research in neurophysiology, however, supports the idea that humans are essentially motivated by needs for community and social harmony—claims that fit a long tradition of philosophical argument about the value of open communication and consensus. In its pure form, this yields to the Habermasian frame that stipulates ideal conditions of conversation under which concerned parties will expectably arrive eventually at similar positions.

In contrast to a notion of open communication as mutual aggression or harmonious consensus, dialogue signifies a type of discourse in which parties take turns listening respectfully and responding genuinely to one another's expressions. Empirically, the quest for dialogue draws support from the same human tendencies cited earlier—namely, the need both for attachment *and* for differentiation. It implies, in the words of the prophet of dialogue Martin Buber, "the acceptance of otherness" (1992, 65). The simultaneous wish for both attachment and differentiation forms a central theme in the social-psychological analyses of Buber's own teacher in Berlin, Georg Simmel.

Thanks to the anomalous circumstance that Shmuel Eisenstadt imbibed his sociology from books loaned by Buber, his professor at Hebrew University, he became acquainted with this notion of dialogue early on. Indeed, in later autobiographical reflections he acknowledged the deep impact of Buber's teachings, and he went on to edit a volume of Buber's writings for the series The Heritage of Sociology. What is more, in the course of writing *Visions of the Sociological Tradition*, I came to realize that Eisenstadt's narrative (in *The Form of Sociology: Paradigms and Crises*) was not, as I previously thought, strictly pluralistic, but rather took the form of a dialogical narrative: it saw diverse approaches to sociology as occasionally offering dialogical openings to one another, an interpretation that Eisenstadt himself corroborated in a personal communication (Levine 1995, 96).

From Clashing to Connecting Civilization: The Greco-Roman Case

If we were to conjoin Eisenstadt's affinity for the principle of dialogue with his passion for the comparative study of civilizations, we might be led to ask: how was it possible for historic civilizations, rooted as each was on a starkly exclusionary principle, to have evolved to a point where some of their elements could be used to support an ethic of dialogue? How, in other words, could each of the major world civilizations give rise to developments in which authentic traditional symbols were invoked in ways that heighten levels of openness and inclusiveness?

To adumbrate the transformational pattern that I have in mind, let me begin with a prototype of the process in Greco-Roman civilization. The concept of *physis* (nature) formed a central notion in the Greco-Roman world view. This concept defined nature, not in the post-Newtonian sense of an inherent force that directs the world, but as designating the essential quality of something in a universe of substances. Hellenic philosophers moved from questions about the nature of inorganic and organic bodies to a concept of nature that could be taken as a foundation for ethics. The texts of Plato and Aristotle provided a basis for superseding conventional notions of morality with a search for what is good by nature as distinguished from what is good merely by tradition or convention (Levine 1995).

At the same time, however, the notion of nature provided a basis for dividing people into superior and inferior categories on the basis of naturally given characteristics. This distinction was used to reinforce the Greek/barbarian dichotomy in that all barbarians were held to be slaves *physei* (by nature). In *The Politics* Aristotle quotes a line of the poets, "It is fitting for Greeks to rule barbarians," commenting that "the assumption [is] that barbarian and slave by nature are the same thing" (1984, Book 1, chaps. 2, 36).

In the minds of other Hellenic thinkers, however, the notion of nature was employed to overcome such political oppositions by envisioning a single polis of the entire world. For example, Diogenes the Cynic proclaimed the doctrine of a world state (*cosmopolis*) in which all humans would be citizens. This became a central doctrine of the Stoics, based on the assumption that all humans possess, by nature, an identical divine spark (*apospasma*). Accordingly, Stoicism undermined the former distinctions based on race, class, and gender. These ideas were amplified by Romans like Epictetus and Marcus Aurelius, who expanded the doctrine of humanitarian cosmopolitanism. Their doctrines drew on the core Greco-Roman idealization of nature, in ways that articulated the notion of a universal human nature, as a means for transcending the pejorative attitude toward outsiders that proponents of the civilized/barbarian dichotomy had fostered.

India and Japan

In the civilization of India, the idea of *purity* (Sanskrit: *sattva*) figured as one central symbolic theme. Connoting freedom from alloy, and so from defilement of the spirit by the impurities of matter, purity was tied to the belief that there is no possibility for humans to see and manifest divinity without being cleansed. In accord with this ontology, Hindus divided people into categories (*varna*) with respect to their levels of purity/impurity. Historically, the first group to be classified was the Brahmans. Although Brahmanic status rested on birth, to become a fully accredited Brahman, a man had to study the Vedic texts, learn certain ritual practices, and acquire a holy belt. He was obliged to provide literary instruction, priestly duties, and certain magical services, and to support himself from gifts, not by earning a salary. Brahmans were expected to manifest a number of virtuous qualities grounded on purity in several dimensions, including purity of body, purity of mind, and purity of heart, and the avoidance of contact with impure substances and persons.

Commitment to this ideal of purity had well-known consequences of an exclusionary and destructive character, both internally and externally. Within Indian society, one category designated a set of castes that came to be known as the

Untouchables. These individuals were considered irredeemably impure and therefore were excluded from such rights as to own land and to perform certain rituals. In addition, Hindu doctrine considered those outside their religious traditions to be impure as well. Groups who did not respect the Vedic rituals and the ban on killing certain animals were called *mleccha*, or outsider, a term that generally connoted impure. *Mleccha* and Untouchables were often thought of as being in a similar or identical category. Hostility toward Muslims was thus grounded, to some extent ideologically, on their being impure.

On the other hand, the enormous heterogeneity of Indian culture, together with absence of political pressures to impose religion and an egalitarian strain in Hindu culture, accounted for the proverbial syncretistic cast of Indian culture as well as the conspicuous absence of wars of religion (Eisenstadt 1996, 410). Evolving from such background a position of radical egalitarianism and inclusiveness, Mohandas Gandhi devoted himself to overcoming those established polarizing animosities. He strove to secure equal rights for the Untouchables, even renaming them as *harijan*, children of God. He also worked continuously for unity between Hindus and Muslims, aspiring to promote the notion of Indian nationals living together in a civic society. He strove valiantly to prevent the creation of a separate Islamic state following India's independence, but in vain. Identifying with the traditional Indian notions of *mleccha* and impurity, the Muslim League under Muhammed Ali Jinnah established a "Nation of the Pure," Pakistan.

Although Gandhi failed to prevent the Islamic split-off and the ensuing massacre of millions, he created a Way for Hindus to transcend tenacious animosities stemming from deeply held cultural convictions by drawing on other aspects of Indian tradition. He did so by turning to classical symbols such as *ahimsa* (nonviolence, drawn from the Jain tradition) and the quest (*graha*) for truth (*satya*). Gandhi found purity, above all, in what he called the search for truth. He categorically ruled out the use of violence on the grounds that it inhibited the search for truth, since no one could know more than a portion of what is true. In Gandhi's teachings, to use *satyagraha* to overcome injustice required considerable training and confidence. Training included understanding and controlling one's impure thoughts through regular meditation, because to transform the mind of an opponent, a *satyagrahi* needed this mental purity.

Around the time of Gandhi's transfiguration of Indian notions, a comparable breakthrough was taking place in Japan with efforts to reorient the heirs of the culture of Japanese warriors. For Japanese civilization, the core symbol to be considered here is *makoto*. Usually mistranslated as "sincerity," *makoto* signifies a disposition to discharge one's social obligations with utter fidelity, suppressing personal utilitarian goals. Considered the highest virtue of the Japanese hero, *makoto* connotes the value of calm action in whatever circumstances.[2] Although the focus of *makoto* has varied in different periods of history, a constant theme has been the disposition to act in a self-effacing manner on behalf of the well-being of others.

As Eisenstadt (1996) made clear, the ultimate ideal of Japanese civilization lies not in some transcendent value to which worldly actions are held accountable, but to the authority figures of this world, on whose behalf *makoto* actions are dedicated. Since the Middle Ages, the samurai were expected to display this conduct most consistently. The seven pleats of their traditional garb, the skirt-like pants known as *hakama*, allude to what are understood as the components of *makoto*: loyalty, honor, respect, affection, and sincerity (*shin*). The samurai ethos diffused through Japanese society; economic entrepreneurs even recast the notion of samurai *makoto* in ways that favored Japan's economic modernization (Bellah 1957). That ethos was further utilized following the Meiji Reformation by political modernizers, who directed it toward passionate allegiance to the emperor as symbol of the Japanese state.

That symbolism, notoriously, turned Japan in externally destructive directions: it fostered frequent violent combats among trained martial artists; and it eventuated in imperialistic ambitions that led Japan to embark on brutal conquests under Emperor Hirohito.

Yet those same samurai ideals that fostered violence served to transform Japan's traditional martial arts in an opposite direction. This began with the work of educator Jigoro Kano, who reconfigured the traditional teaching of *ju-jitsu* (lethal unarmed combat) into a practice of judo utilized only to develop character. It resulted in the teachings of Morihei Ueshiba, who reoriented martial arts training away from competitive struggle of any sort toward practices designed to produce an attitude of respect for all living beings and to serve as "a bridge to peace and harmony for all humankind" (Ueshiba 1984, 120). Ueshiba failed to persuade Japanese militarists to desist from launching war against the United States just as Gandhi failed to prevent the partition of India. Nevertheless, just as Gandhi's teachings in South Africa and India inspired subsequent political leaders like Martin Luther King, Jr., and Nelson Mandela to relate to their political opponents in a respectful, nonviolent manner, Ueshiba's teachings, through the practice he created, aikido, have inspired millions worldwide to embrace a Way that would enhance inter-civilizational dialogue.

The Abrahamic Civilizations

Christianity was founded on an ideal of universal love. Funneled through the Greek word *agape*, the teachings of Jesus propounded the virtue of unselfish and benevolent concern for the welfare of others. The universalistic cast of this teaching received classic formulations in the words of the proselytizing convert Paul, himself influenced by Stoic doctrines, who announced: "There is neither Jew nor Greek, bond or free, male or female; for ye are all one in Christ Jesus" (Galations 3:28). In society after society, these teachings have restrained violence and promoted generosity of spirit.

On the other hand, from Constantine on, Christians were responsible for slaying a huge number of people from other cultures, including millions of Native Americans, Africans, and Aboriginal Australians, not to mention, from among its own members, huge numbers of heretics and "witches." Western Christianity created a tenacious pattern of anti-Semitism that, as acknowledged in the statements of the late Pope John Paul II, played a nontrivial role in destroying the civilization of Continental European Jewry. Although Christian figures, from time to time, espoused a turn to the ethos of Jesus and early Christianity, almost none of them grappled conspicuously with the challenge of using the foundational statements of Christianity to oppose the waves of persecution launched against the Jewish people in their midst (Carroll 2001).

None of them, that is, until Pastor Dietrich Bonhoeffer. Inspired by the social activism of the Abyssinian Baptist church in Harlem, which he assisted during a postdoctoral year at the Union Theological Seminary in the early 1930s, Bonhoeffer returned to Nazi Germany to join Martin Niemoeller in his work with the Confessing Church (*Bekennende Kirche*), the center of Protestant resistance to the Nazis. He directed one of the underground seminaries of the Confessing Church in 1935. After the Nazis closed down the seminaries, he went on to engage in underground activity to help Jews escape and was associated with the conspiracy to assassinate Hitler. The theological and ethical statements that he worked out in the course of this resistance became a benchmark for a new brand of Christians. In justifying courageous pastoral intervention against Nazi oppression, he worked out a justification of political activism in an immoral world, based on a notion of "venture of responsibility": "It is better to do evil than to be evil," he decided. His theological creativity has been described as forging a kind of "religionless interpretation of biblical concepts in a world come of age" (Bonhoeffer 1963, 5). Bonhoeffer thereby paved the way for the more inclusive kind of rapprochement that many German Christians have displayed since the War, and he has been described as a key theologian for leading future generations of Christians.

For Islam, the core symbolic notion is, evidently, *Islam*; that is, submission. This signifies a posture of humble acceptance of and outward conformity with the law of God. The term is derived from Arabic *'aslama*, to surrender or resign oneself, which in turn is derived from Syriac *'a'slem*, to make peace. Islamic tradition focuses on a complex of laws found in the Koran and promulgated by Muslim clergy, laws which cover everything from family relations and civil accords to criminal codes.

Among the notions to which Muslims owe submission, nothing is more motivating than the injunction to pursue *jihad*. And nothing illustrates the capacity of civilization to promote different directions better than the different meanings this term has acquired in Islamic civilization. On the one hand, *jihad* refers to aggression against Unbelievers through the legal, compulsory, and collective effort to expand territories ruled by Muslims. Most scholars argue that despite ambiguities about the term in the Koran, this has been the principal line of interpretation of the doctrine in Islamic tradition. Thus, *jihad* was invoked to instigate the conquest, beyond the Arabian Peninsula, of the region from Afghanistan to Spain within a century of Mohammed's death and, later, to spur Muslim invasions of such territories as India, Anatolia, Balkans, Ethiopia, Sudan, and West Africa. More recently, however, it has been dramatically revived in modern Islamic fundamentalism by influential figures such as Sayyid Outb (1980), who has argued that the only way for Muslims to achieve religious purity is to establish an Islamic state through *jihad*.

On the other hand, *jihad* has been interpreted as a struggle for personal moral improvement in the sense of living more closely in accord with Islamic Law. Thus, in language that parallels Ueshiba's formulation that in his form of martial art, there are no enemies and that the greatest victory is the victory over oneself. The eleventh-century theologian Abu Hamid al-Ghazali maintained that the soul is an enemy which struggles with one and which must be fought, and that this *jihad* against the soul constitutes the "greater *jihad*" (1995, 56). In this sense of the term, it extends beyond overcoming baser instincts to a struggle for social justice. So understood, it could be viewed as an injunction to live peaceably with everyone and to cooperate with people of all faiths in a quest for social reform. This position on *jihad* has been embraced by virtually all Sufi theologians. This accords with the absence in Islam of any particularistic ethnic emphasis, apart from the status of Arabic as a sacred language (Eisenstadt 1992, 41). In fact, in many contemporary societies up until recently, including Ethiopia and India, public displays of solidarity between Muslims and other religious groups was the norm.

Although some progressive Muslims wish seriously to promote and extend the latter definition of *jihad*, no charismatic figure, such as a Gandhi or a Bonhoeffer, has arisen to challenge the contemporary drift toward an escalation of the other view.[3] In the past dozen years, Muslims appealing to the symbol of *jihad* have launched a worldwide campaign involving assassinations, vandalism, and terrorist acts—against Christians in Indonesia and Yemen, Jews in Israel, Hindus in Kashmir, and traditional religionists in Sudan; and against Buddhists through demolition of their world-prized mountain sculptures in Afghanistan. This trend has been exacerbated by another tenet of Islamic faith, the notion that the requirement to act in accordance with God's decrees as a condition of salvation—possible but difficult to fulfill—may be short-circuited when fulfilling the religious obligation of *jihad*, thereby enhancing one's chances of being sent to heaven at the Last Judgment or, if one dies a martyr, going directly to heaven.

For Jewish civilization, a core symbolic notion is *berith*, or covenant. This refers to biblical accounts of the covenants made between God and the Jewish people whereby God would provide certain benefits for the people of Israel in exchange for their loyalty to Him and obedience to His moral directives. Accordingly, a central distinguishing feature of Jewish civilization, in Eisenstadt's insightful account, consists of the semi-contractual relationship with the Higher Power, in contrast to the absolute status of the transcendental symbols in the other Axial Age civilizations.

Over time, as related in the Bible, the content of God's promissory note changed. With Abraham, it had to do with the Eretz, the Land, of Israel. With David, it had to do with legitimizing the political authority of a lineage. But the heart of the divine covenant for Jewish civilization lies in the central chapters of the Book of Exodus, where God promises to consider the Jews a Chosen People in exchange for their adherence to the numerous commandments enumerated therein.

The quality of being Chosen set up a constant invidious comparison with other peoples, referred to in what later became a pejorative Yiddish term, the *goyyim*.

This dichotomy never led to conquest or aggression, although when a sixth-century South Arabian king, DhuNuwaas, converted to Judaism, he began to persecute Christians (thereby provoking the Ethiopian Christian emperor at Aksum to send troops across the Red Sea to overthrow him). However, the conceit of chosenness produced at times an arrogant attitude toward outsiders that belittled their worth. (One account relates that Mohammed's turn against Jews was based on their rejection of his appeal for support at the beginning of his mission.)

On the other hand, the evident meaning of chosenness, as the covenant is spelled out in Exodus 19–24, signifies the adherence of Jews to a system of maxims that enjoin ethical behavior toward a wide range of people. Prominent among those maxims is the commandment to take care of strangers. Whatever narrow, cultic, or particularistic grounds for the covenant are entailed in the covenant with Abraham, or later with King David, these are far overshadowed in the history of Judaism by moral imperatives. And this history of Judaism is itself an essential part of the core symbolism. The central text of Jewish civilization takes the form of a historical narrative, not a straight listing of absolute commands or mythic portrayals. The course of its history moves steadily away from the primordial cultic observance and toward a universalistic ethical dimension. This shift is itself a subject of attention in the sacred text, as when God rebukes those who simply follow old ritual prescriptions for fasting, just bowing their heads, and spreading sackcloth and ashes under them: "Is not this the fast that I have chosen? To loose the bands of wickedness, to undo the heavy burdens, and to let the oppressed go free?" (Isaiah 58:6).

Even so, the particularistic aspects were never completely transcended; People and Land were perpetually celebrated. And when the time of the great return arrived, there were those who sacralized it in the terms of the earliest covenant. For them, the reappropriation of ancient soil amounted to a return of the earliest covenant. For some, that motivated a commitment to reclaim territory by building settlements on a vulnerable, contested area that became a constant provocation to the people with whom they were sharing this piece of the earth's surface. This appeal to the earliest covenant has been defended in some fundamentalist Christian groups more avidly than by most Jews.

A Challenge for the Future

The major source of civilizational clashes in the coming generation lies in the actions of the minority of Abrahamic religionists who are extreme fundamentalists. Most visible, of course, are those Muslims who insist on the aggressive side of *jihad*. There could be a kind of civilizational clash in the coming generation if those Muslims who insist on the aggressive side of *jihad* continue to grow in strength—if the politicized elements of Islamism continue to make headway in their recurrent assaults on the other world religious groups including Hindus and Buddhists as well as Christians and Jews.

Jews also play a part in perpetuating the clash of civilizational exclusivists. Those who do so include those settlers who occupy the West Bank not as a tactical move,

TABLE 4.1 Exclusionary and Inclusionary Concepts of Selected Civilizations

Civilization	Core idea	Benign consequences	Exclusionary framework	Expanded inclusionary concept	Creative agent
Greco-Roman	Nature	Rational ethics	Civilized/barbarian	Cosmopolitanism	Stoics
Indian	Purity	Brahmanic moral leadership	Pure/impure	Satyagraha	Gandhi
Japanese	*Makoto*	Social order Rapid modernization	*Nihon/gaijin*	Aikido	Ueshiba
Western Christian	*Agape*	Domestic pacification	Believer/pagan	Confessing Church	Niemoeller & Bonhoeffer
Islamic	Submission	Domestic pacification	*Ummo/infidel*	Peaceful jihad?	Badshah Khan
Jewish	Covenant	Promulgation of moral law	Chosen/gentile	Cohabitants on sacred land?	Buber

but out of deepest conviction. Just as militant jihadists draw on early Islamic beliefs and practices to inspire their terrorist attacks, so ardent Jewish West Bank settlers draw on archaic biblical symbols to justify this occupation.

Yet, to point out these particular worries is not to limit the danger of fundamentalisms to those with explicit or traditional religious commitments. Throughout the course of the twentieth century, secular fundamentalisms (e.g. extreme forms of communism and capitalism, various nationalisms, and even the more recent U.S. military focus on state building in the Middle East) have been equally as, if not more, violent and exclusionary than any particular religion's extremists groups. Thus, considering the continued decline of traditional religions in the United States and Europe, we should anticipate that emerging forms of extremism and fundamentalism might emerge from within secular ideologies as well.

One way these symbols can be recast is through the emergence of a charismatic leader or group who, steeped in traditional symbolism, will connect Islam with its deepest roots in ways that point to inclusionary imperatives. Within the Islamic tradition, the potential for turning *jihad* in a nonviolent, inclusionary direction was demonstrated by Khan Abdal Ghaffar Khan (1890–1988)—known as Badshah Khan—a Pathan (Pushtun) Muslim from Afghanistan. Khan defined Islam as a faith in the ability of every human being to respond to spiritual laws and the power of *muhabat* (love) to transform human affairs. So oriented, Khan raised a "nonviolent" army of some 100,000 Pathan warriors and worked closely with Gandhi to use nonviolent techniques to promote social justice and independence (Easwaran 1999). In this vein, strong statements against Islamic terrorism have been issued by contemporary Islamic spokesmen such as Abdal-Hakim Murad, who finds the taking of innocent civilian lives unimaginable in Sunni Islam, and Hamza Yusuf, a popular American Muslim speaker, who has declared that the "real *jihad*" for Muslims is to rid Islam of the terrorist element.

And as in Islam, potential for overriding such exclusionary claims lies near to hand in Judaism. The Talmudic tradition has recently been drawn on by Aaron Lichtenstein, in *The Seven Laws of Noah* (1981), to argue that observance of the Noahide laws sufficed to include non-Jews in the divinely approved community. Figures such as Joseph Abilea have eloquently endorsed a nonviolent, universalist position, as have participants in such groups as Oz ve Shalom, the Jewish Peace movement. A substantial portion of the world Jewish community considers the moral covenant of Exodus to supersede the territorial part of the covenant with Abraham.

To make these new openings does not require a purist *ex nihilo*. The charismatic innovators needed could come from perfectly conventional backgrounds, as did the exemplars who I described above. Gandhi began as an elitist who shared the white South Africans' disdain for blacks. Ueshiba served proudly in the Japanese army in 1904 and trained officers of the Japanese military academy until 1941. Niemoeller, a submarine commander in World War I, supported the National Socialists until they came to power in 1933. Bonhoeffer began as a conventional German who refused to perform the marriage ceremony of his brother to a Jewish woman in 1930. What all of them shared was a deep grounding in their respective traditions, which earned them credibility, and then a powerful impulse to break out of their elitist/ethnocentric molds in response to the ethical demands of the current world situation.

In a brief essay composed just after World War I, "What Is To Be Done?," Eisenstadt's mentor Martin Buber confronted the dilemma of our time in the voice of unknown comrades:

> Some say civilization must be preserved through "subduing." There is no civilization to preserve. And there is no longer a subduing! But what may ascend out of the flood will be decided by whether you throw yourselves into it as seeds of true community. No longer through exclusion but only inclusion can the kingdom be established.
>
> [...] Silently the world waits for the spirit.
>
> *(1957c, 111)*

Notes

1 These needs, as recent social neuroscience has demonstrated, are hardwired in the human species (Smith and Stevens 2002).
2 Success is not the criterion here. Ivan Morris (1975) suggests that the value of *makoto* action may be enhanced by failure. Other aspects of *makoto* are described in Gleason (1995).
3 This view was propounded with particular virulence by heirs to the thirteenth-century *jihad* revivalist Ibn Taymiyya and his eighteenth-century disciple, Mohammed Ibn Abdul Wahhab Najdi, from whom the fundamentalist Wahabi sect derives.

PART II
Dialogue Involving Shared Objectives

5

UNIVERSALISM IN THE FRENCH PHILOSOPHES AND THE RUSSIAN INTELLIGENTSIA

Men are born and remain free and equal in rights.
— *Declaration of the Rights of Man and the Citizen (1789)*

The barriers fall, the chains are smelted
By Divine fire,
And the eternal morning of new life
Rises in all, and all in one.
— *From a poem by Vladimir Soloviev*

I The Universalist Outlook

Defense of one's cave, battle for the clan, disgust for barbarians, slaves, and "furriners" is the bulk of history. Man's local needs are vivid, his local attachments strong. The assertion of these needs and attachments against those of outsiders has usually produced material gains and the pleasant security of group superiority. It has also created much color, nobility, and pathos.

Yet, now and then, a different theme is sounded. The brotherhood of all men is invoked as a live conception suggesting the direction of new action, the categories of new thought, and the development of new ideals in historic situations. We shall call this "universalism": the outlook with which one's primary attachments to his fatherland are transferred to the whole world, conceived either as a substantial entity (world republic, world church) or an abstract "humanity" (Bergson's "open society"), or just everybody anywhere.

The psychological disposition for membership in a world community, however conceived, is the recognition of some common denominator inherent in all people. This may mean universal descent from, or participation in, one God; it may be fellowship in a common historic or cosmic task; it may be possession of one common human nature. In one way or another, the worth of every individual figures in the universalist outlook, and part of the task of formulating the universalism of a given person or group is to study its conception of the individual.

That task also involves an understanding of the surrounding intellectual climate. A universalist outlook adds meaning when considered in terms of the localism(s) reacted against and the general world view behind it. It is unwise to study such a value term in isolation, as having a nature of its own, especially when the term does not serve explicitly a symbol for the person.

It is useful to distinguish between two forms of universalism, "abstract" and "concrete."[1] The former we call "cosmopolitanism," an attitude which sees the immediate union of the individual and mankind. It follows from a stress on the common nature and value of each individual. Conditions which favor its development include uprooting from native soil, intercourse with foreign people, and mobility— influence which dissolves the bonds between an individual and his native group. (Frequently the psychic power of the cosmopolitan's narrower solidarities persists, yielding ambivalence of some sort.) Art, science, and philosophy transcend boundary lines and develop this outlook.

Concrete universalism involves institutions as agents of union between the individual and humanity. In modern times this figures primarily as internationalism, which conceives of the world in terms of distinct national societies contributing their special ways to the world society. It does not seek to ignore national differences, as does cosmopolitanism but, rather, to utilize them constructively. It underlies the philosophy of world federalism, which seeks a supranational government for international affairs that allows active autonomy to national governments. A chief factor inducing internationalism in modern times is Durkheim's "moral density" on a worldwide scale, the result of increased communication and cultural independence.

The earliest recorded expression of the universalist ideal is that of Ikhnaton, emperor of the Egyptian Empire, ca. 1375 BC. Upsetting many traditions, including the sharp Egyptian chauvinism of two thousand years' standing, he proclaimed a universal monotheism and regarded himself as owing the same duties to all men, regardless of race or nationality. His hymn to Aton, the one (sun-)god, is to a benevolent father actively concerned with the maintenance of all his creatures, even the meanest.[2]

The Greeks inaugurated a significant tradition of universalism, which lasted through the Roman Empire and found its way through Stoicism into Roman law. Socrates is said to have proclaimed allegiance to the "cosmopolis," and Alexander the Great sought to fuse the civic ideals of the polis with the Eastern conception of world empire. His synthesis found ready adherents in those foreign entrants into the Greek world (Cynics and Stoics) who urged the open world state against the closed culture of the city-states. Diogenes the Cynic is held to have said "the only right state is that of the world" (Boehm 1931).

Cosmopolitanism was a central doctrine of the Stoics, developed from the idea that all men have an equally divine spark (*apospasma*). Stoicism devalued distinctions based on race, class, and sex. Plutarch says of Zeno that "he taught that there should not be different city-states ... that *all* men should be fellow-citizens" (Barker 1934). Greek cosmopolitanism was essentially the same throughout the Hellenistic-Roman period: a reaction against nationally conceived polytheism and local patriotism, uniting cultured minds, opposed by particularistic political and military forces.

Early Christianity proclaimed the worth of each person and his hope for salvation. St. Paul, himself influenced by Stoic doctrines, declared: "There is neither Jew nor Greek, bond nor free, male nor female; for ye are all one in Christ Jesus" (Galations 3:28). Judaism itself had long since outgrown its idea of a tribal god and was professing its present credo: the fatherhood of one God, the brotherhood of all men.

Elements of universalism are present during the Middle Ages, but in a less thorough spirit. Dante sought a world empire, to make the world one, politically as well as spiritually. The outlooks of many men in the universities, of traveling artists and merchants, and of some knightly orders in the Crusades were cosmopolitan. But not until the French Enlightenment do we hear universalist strains as loud and clear as those of the Stoics.

The aim of this inquiry is to formulate universalism in the broader context of Enlightenment thought and to compare it with an equally powerful development—the universalism of the Russian intelligentsia of the next century. We shall seek the direct influence of Enlightenment values on Russian thinking during the periods of their penetration into Russia, under Catherine II and Alexander I; then we shall study the universalist values of the Russian Intelligentsia during the rest of the nineteenth century.

It is beyond the scope of this essay to investigate adequately the thought of the Westernizing intelligentsia; we shall simply note the elements of universalism present at nodal points in the development of Russian socialist thought. Our primary concern in Russia, as in this essay, is with the religious universalists: Peter Chaadaev, the first original Russian social thinker, and that astonishing triad of his successors—Dostoevski, Soloviev, and Tolstoy.

II Universalism in the French Enlightenment

Despite considerable individual differences of approach and emphasis, the men of letters of the French Enlightenment, or philosophes, emerged from the dark woods of tradition with certain ideas and values as common property. They agreed that the new light of reason was to be a gift for all mankind, and they considered themselves citizens of the universe, emancipated. Their language was one with the enlightened of other countries. They hallowed reason, nature, and progress, whose corollaries—liberty, equality, fraternity—were to be on many lips by 1789. In this complex of values a vigorous universalism developed. We shall sketch its expression in the religious, cultural, and political attitudes of a few outstanding Enlightenment figures.

For the philosophes, the universal content of religion was to be found by each individual in apprehending the being of God and the universal moral order. Revealed dogma kept men in ignorance and slowed progress; some philosophes, like Diderot, carried their revolt to the point of atheism. Rousseau, at odds with his contemporaries on many counts, gave eloquent illustration of this new "natural religion" in the Abbé's confession of faith in *Emile*. Rousseau himself acknowledged only "the laws of nature, justice, and reason, and those of that religion, pure [and] holy ... which men have polluted" ([1782] 1861, book 8, 295); to him, the forms of religion were incidental and should be adopted according to the state where one lived.

Most of the philosophes were more aggressive than this in attacking the traditional forms of the church. In debunking religious institutions, they developed a religious outlook that made them at one with men everywhere. The Abbé de Saint-Pierre, a Jesuit turned theist, offered a new credo:

> I believe in God ... the common father of nature and of all men who are his children equally ... who has given them the same principles of morality, perceived by them when they reflect, & has made no other distinction among his children than that of crime and virtue.
>
> I believe that the just and benevolent Chinaman is more precious before him than an arrogant, carping Doctor from Europe.
>
> *(Cited in Voltaire 1935, I, 216)*

Voltaire explained that the theist belongs to none of the sects, which all contradict one another. The theist "speaks a language which all the peoples understand, while they do not understand one another. He has brothers from Peking to Cayenne, and he counts all the wise men as his brothers" (II, 264). One of the most outspoken crusaders for the new religion of humanity, Voltaire made clear the universalist nature of his creed: "I understand by natural religion the principles of morality common to the human race" (*Euvres*, XXII, cited in Becker 1932, 44).

In their cultural activities, the philosophes defined the cosmopolitan spirit in art and science which has survived, in varying degrees, to the present day. Thanks to their translations, foreign works (especially English writings) gained wide popularity by the 1740s. The word "cosmopolitan" came into vogue and figured in the titles of literary works.[3] The philosophes declared their allegiance to mankind; as Grimm put it, they hoped to be counted "among the small number of those who by their intelligence and their works have merited well of humanity" (*Correspondance littéraire*, IV, cited in Becker 1932, 34). Introducing his "Second Discourse," Rousseau wrote:

> As my subject interests mankind in general I shall endeavor to use a style adapted to all nations.
>
> [...] O man, of whatever country you are, and whatever your opinions may be, behold your history ... the life of your species.
>
> *([1752] 2005, 24–5)*

The universalism of the philosophes grew from the doctrine of the natural rights of man, a moral proposition meaningful and certain for them, independent of belief in God. Voltaire insisted on the inviolability of the person, freedom of conscience, equality; he urged respect for the universal essence of human nature despite ethnic differences. "Souviens-toi de la dignité de l'homme" is his charge to each individual (Voltaire 1935, II, 127).

Becker accounted for this penchant for abstracting the essence of man on the basis of inconsistencies in early Enlightenment thinking. The deification of the natural order led to the distasteful proposition that what is, is right, because it is so naturally. Hence the socially conscious philosophes were led to seek a permanent and universal nature of man against which to measure local customs and institutions, in spite of studies like Montesquieu's *Esprit des Lois*, which suggested moral relativity.

This problem was the natural outcome of undermining traditional religion and its absolute moral values. Their solution was pregnant with consequences. If all men are endowed by nature with rights of life, liberty, happiness, and equality, then superiority because of class, religion, race, or nation is false. Then there is no justification for torture or war. Then the world is one's fatherland.

These are crude abstractions of ideals held by most of the philosophes. Voltaire was at his witty best in revealing the absurdity of when Rousseau called war of any sort "an outrage to humanity." At the apex of the Enlightenment, Condorcet offered a sunny picture of future peace and progress as the philosophes' last will and testament to mankind. His hopes for the "tenth epoch," the future, testify to his vibrant universalism (Condorcet 1802). With the advancement of science and education, Europeans will learn to enlighten and aid, not exploit, Asians and Africans. Nations will seek security, not power; they will form confederations, will lose their commercial prejudices, and will invite foreigners to their countries to share their benefits. War, the most terrible of crimes, will disappear; men's object will be the "general welfare of the human species" (ibid.). All this and a universal language too.[4]

Besides refuting the claims to superiority by all belligerents, Voltaire submitted to his keen inspection the myth of fatherland. He noted that "to desire the greatness of one's country is to wish harm on one's neighbors. The one who would wish that his native country was never greater, smaller, richer, nor poorer, would be the citizen of the universe," (Voltaire 1935, II, 176) and concludes that "one's fatherland is everywhere where one is comfortable," a sentiment recalling that of the American philosophe Ben Franklin: "Where liberty is, there is my country."

Tom Paine's fighting retort, "Where liberty is not, there is my country," suggests the temper of revolutionary universalism. The "natural, inalienable, and sacred rights of man" drafted by the National Assembly in 1789 were shouted to the world. In his declaration of rights submitted to the Jacobins in April 1793, Robespierre proposed:

> The men of all countries are brothers, and the various peoples ought to aid each other ... like citizens of the same state.

> Whoever oppresses a single nation is declared the enemy of all.
>
> (Cited in Blanc 1847, IX, 29)

As De Tocqueville remarked, the French Revolution "sought not merely the particular rights of French citizens, but the general political rights and duties of all men ... [and it] appeared to be more concerned with the regeneration of the human race than with the reformation of France" (*L'ancien régime et la revolution*, cited in Becker 1932, 154).

This is only half the story: the Revolution had the dual nature of establishing France as a truly national state as well as proclaiming the universal rights of man. Throughout the eighteenth century, French national consciousness quickened. In opposing divine-right kingship, the Catholic Church, class, and provincial privileges, the philosophes were incidentally weakening the historic obstacles to the development of national spirit. The Revolution abolished distinctions based on class or locality, put the church on a national basis, and contrived symbols to incite patriotic loyalty to the new republic.

Rousseau's works were inspiration for the new nationalism. In *Considerations on the Government of Poland* (Rousseau [1772] 1947), he urged a healthy patriotism fostered by social institutions. Rousseau felt that "without that patriotic fervor which makes men surpass themselves, liberty is only an empty name, and laws merely an illusion" (cited in Becker 1932, 55). This sentiment sprang from his yearning for a society based on the natural virtues of simple people, with a minimum of the trappings of pan-European civilization. Such virtues could be maximized only when a nation, like an individual, gave full expression to its own natural personality—the same individualism behind his universalist outlook. These ideas set the pace at once for the romantic nationalism of the early nineteenth century and for the internationalism which sought peace in order to enjoy the several colorful contributions of each nationality. The outlook among the other philosophes, however, was more abstract and cosmopolitan.

Plans to unify the nations attracted a few philosophes. As early as 1713, the Abbé de Saint-Pierre, taking his cue from Grotius' codification of natural international law, composed his *Projet pour rendre la paix perpétuelle en Europe*. This won the enthusiasm of Rousseau, who wrote in his *Paix perpétuelle* in 1756, a freely rendered account of the Abbé's project coupled with some shrewd observations of his own.

Rousseau decried the fact that in joining a particular group of men, one declares himself enemy of the whole race. He saw that wars spring from the contradictions arising from the presence of civil states and the absence of interstate government. Like the good Abbé, he considered the only remedy to be a federation, uniting nations "by bonds similar to those which already unite their individual members ... under the authority of the law" (Rousseau 1917, 38). Such a federation is to have a legislative body and coercive powers and is to be composed of emissaries of the sovereigns of Europe.

Unlike the Abbé, who expected the European princes to federate out of the goodness of their Christian hearts, Rousseau appealed to the self-interest of the sovereigns with such enticing conditions as the use of the federal power to uphold their authority in case of rebellions by subjects. "If, in spite of all this," he declared, "the project remains unrealized, that is not because it is utopian; it is because men are crazy, and because to be sane in a world of mad-men is itself a kind of madness" (91). Rousseau knew his fellow men too well to expect princes to follow anything but their apparent, not their true, self-interest. At the close of *Paix perpétuelle*, he despaired of establishing such a federation except by force, which he felt might not be justifiable.

It remained for Immanuel Kant, with the thought of the Enlightenment and the examples of the American and French republics behind him, to propose a federation that would include the whole world and would be based on the consent of peoples, not absolute monarchs. In general, the philosophes were more concerned with establishing the abstract principle of the rights and kinship of all men than with working out concrete schemes for their organic union.

III Enlightenment Universalism on Russian Soil

The torrent with which Peter the Great sought to irrigate his arid Russian civilization was followed by a more or less steady stream of French influence in the succeeding century. The Russians soon reacted against the German bureaucrats whom Peter had imported, resenting the disdain of these "superiors," so that, when the ubiquitous French culture found its way into Russia, via French and Russian travelers and students in the 1730s and 1740s, it was well received. Its prevalence in Europe suited the Russian urge for maximum Europeanization, and the Russian nobility were attracted by the French urbanity and rich literature. The two peoples were mutually sympathetic. "The Germans resemble no one," noted a Russian traveling in France, "the French are less honorable, but they resemble us" (Haumant 1913, 520).

By the time of Catherine II (1762–96), Russian "society" was borrowing most of its ideas, aspirations, manners, and tastes from France. During her reign, interest shifted from aesthetic to social questions as Enlightenment social philosophy came to appear in Russian libraries. Montesquieu, Diderot, and especially Voltaire were widely read. Catherine herself was a devotee of Voltaire and corresponded with him and other philosophes for several years.

Yet the absorption of Enlightenment values by the nobility was by no means profound. Typical of their implementation of these values was the Free Society for Political Economy. Founded on a French model by Catherine, its members talked much about social and economic equality but never did anything. Despite her enthusiasm for liberty, the privileges of the landowners increased under Catherine, and the yoke of serfdom clamped down harder than ever. Catherine and the manifold Voltaireans accepted the new ideas so long as their status quo was not disturbed. *Nakaz* (Instruction), Catherine's book of proposals for reform, juxtaposed the principle of natural rights with that of absolute czarism; and she gave easy consent when her advisers toned down the more liberal measures. When it came to substantial social reform, these Voltaireans preferred to leave it "au temps et au progrès des lumières."

The military successes under Catherine began to stir up national pride. Hoping to be considered a genuine Russian, the German-born czarina flattered such pride. She included no Germans among her many court favorites and encouraged her court poets to write patriotic tragedies. She tried to Russify her non-Russian provinces, although her adherence to the Voltairean principle of tolerance made her proceed with care and moderation.

In this first period of Enlightenment influence in Russia, political values were treated much like French theater costumery. Hertzen has aptly termed the liberal agitation of the nobility "un jeu d'esprit." He observed that "among us, the Voltairean philosophy put nothing in place of the old beliefs, moral duties, traditions. ... The neophytes of civilization understood well only the Epicurean appeal" (Hertzen, *Le Développement des idées révolutionnaires*, cited in Haumant 1913).

They failed to take from Voltaire the conception of all men as brothers, as social equals, and a positive deism available to all men through the exercise of reason.[5] Delighted with French ways and anxious to "belong" to European high culture, they admitted those Enlightenment ideas which relaxed the restraining grasp of tradition without seriously affirming its radical values. In Russia those values became chiefly sympathy and philanthropy. Their cosmopolitanism stayed on a cultural level; they could not support the "natural rights of all men" which underlay the Enlightenment universalism.

There were a few of the intelligentsia, however, who were dissatisfied with the compromise of values as well as with the degenerate morals. Scerbatov, an enthusiast of Enlightenment rationalism, spoke for political liberty for the nobility and criticized their indulgence of "the Epicurean appeal." More radical was the satirist Novikov, whose espousal of liberty involved shocking attacks against serfdom and a demand for a "rule of law" over all.

Yet their orientation was primarily nationalistic. In decrying contemporary morals, Scerbatov contrasted them with the virtues of old Russia—prototypic of the next century's Slavophils. Novikov spent much of his energy in the Masonic movement, awakening public interest in the glories of Russia and her past.

The French Revolution dimmed Russian favor for the philosophes. Happily received at first, its democratic fervor and subsequent political excesses induced a general reaction among the nobility. It put a damper on Catherine's liberalism: she began to suppress political criticism and now dangerous works (*L'Encyclopédie*, Rousseau, even Voltaire). Novikov was imprisoned. The veneer of Enlightenment was wearing off.

But Catherine did not have all public opinion on her side as she had imagined (Haumant 1913, 178). The aspirations of many youths were stirred by the glorious revolution for liberty, despite its faults. Their sympathy for liberal ideas was kept inconspicuous until the advent of Alexander I (1801–25) released the government's close censorship. Alexander Radishchev dared to give literary expression to their ideals and suffered exile to Siberia. Radishchev had studied in Germany in the late

1760s, but quickly found his beacon in the writings of the philosophes. His was probably the most complete incorporation of Enlightenment values. Prototypic of the liberal intelligentsia of the next century, he exclaimed: "My soul was wounded by the suffering of humanity" (cited in Berdyaev [1937] 1960, 22). In his *Voyage from Petersburg to Moscow*, he was the first to seek the emancipation of the serfs as well as the end of absolutism.

In the early years of the nineteenth century, liberal thought was encouraged by Alexander I, whose reign began with high social aspirations. Radishchev was brought back from Siberia to the court. French émigrés (as teachers and abbés) were agents of renewed penetration of French culture into Russia. Some of their influence was reactionary and Catholic, but mostly it was in the anti-religious and liberal mode of the philosophes. The majority were Voltaireans, whose liberalism, if darkened by the storm of the revolution, was rekindled in the face of Russian conditions. With memories of the French terror fading, Russians increased in Gallomania.

These conditions planted the roots of a conflict which was to rock the Russian intelligentsia for over a century—Slavophil versus Westernizer, Stalinist versus Trotskyist. Enthusiastic over Russia's history and foreign exploits, disturbed by its *mœurs francisés* and lack of national pride, writers like Karamzin sought to stir up Russian patriotism. S. N. Glinka, in his review *Rousski Vestnik* (The Russian Messenger), formulated a complete philosophy of Russian nationalism—chauvinistic and xenophobic. Glinka lauded the Russian past,

> that happy epoch when, living in fear of God, our ancestors owed all their moral conceptions to the example of their fathers and the holy books, when they did not discuss the natural state of man or the indefinite progress of knowledge and human reason, but sought simply to fulfill their duties of man, citizen, and Christian.
>
> *(Koyré 1929, 20, author's translation)*[6]

This nationalistic trend became a reactionary battle against all Western civilization in behalf of a return to the traditional ways of the Orthodox faith. One's attitude toward the work of Peter the Great became an index to one's whole ideology. Karamzin's dislike for the Innovator was unambiguous; after Peter, he wrote, "we became citizens of the world, but ceased in some respects to be citizens of Russia" (Mazour 1937, 30).

Did universalism fare better in the camp of the liberals and Westernizers? Alexander I was a *fsyechelovek*—one who can share the point of view of all types or nations. He talked with Robert Owen about a new structure for society; he worshipped with Quakers. Yet his version of the Enlightenment values was more watered-down than Catherine's. His liberalism was never strong enough to oppose the wishes of his reactionary ministers, and it was lost completely in the mystical reaction of the Holy Alliance. The internationalism of that concert of powers was certainly not the universalism of the philosophes.

The cause of the liberal Westernizers was boosted by the War of 1812. The officers who fought in France inhaled republican ideas, and Russian soldiers were seduced by the greater freedom and respect for human dignity that they observed there. But the return to the harsh conditions of Russian life jolted them: was Russia to have freed Europe only to remain in slavery?

Moreover, in spite of an all-round patriotism during the war, French prisoners were treated well by Russian civilians, and after the war *nos amis les ennemis* were in great favor. Just after 1815, French culture, principally Voltaire and Rousseau, had reached a new high in popularity. Salon talk was on the abolition of serfdom and on constitutional government; the maxims of 1789 were rediscovered. It was this elite of officers and nobles, imbued with the philosophes' ideas and the French example, which formed secret societies (modeled after Masonic chapters) to push for liberal reforms. The first of these societies, the Union of Salvation, was set up by 1816, and it contained the core of men who were to lead the tragic uprisings of December 1825. The aim of the society was, according to Mazour, "social reform tinged with a strongly nationalistic sentiment and the establishment of a moderate constitutional government" (Mazour 1937, 68).

At first they hoped to proceed legally, but the government became more reactionary as they became more determined. After 1816 the government strictly suppressed the works of Voltaire, Rousseau, and Kant. By 1820 the members of the Decembrist movement were convinced that cooperation from the government was impossible, that revolution was necessary.

Despite the considerable inspiration for reform which the Decembrists took from the writings of the philosophes and from travels abroad, they were akin to the Gallophobes in their patriotic nationalism and in their hopeful wishes for Russia's future. The Decembrists never intended, as one of their survivors stated, "to transplant France into Russia" (Mazour 1937, 57). Some of them held that the Union of Salvation ought to work to rid the country of foreigners and alien influence (68). The Society of United Slavs, the least nationalistically oriented of the Decembrist societies, aimed for a free Slavic federation. Nevertheless, when it merged with the Decembrist Southern Society, the latter persuaded its members that Russia's problems came first.

Thus the first significant political action in Russia inspired by the ideas of freedom and equality for all men was carried on, for the most part, in a deeply patriotic and nationalistic context; revolution was necessary in order to fulfill Russia's mission.

IV Universalism, Russian Style

The saying goes that the Russian people responded to Peter's reforms by giving birth to Pushkin. In truth, they answered with the whole of nineteenth-century Russian creation: one of the richest literatures and one of the most admirable bodies of social and religious thought in world history.

The national-universal problem was one of the chief topics of the century's thinking, and Russian manifestations of universalism were as varied and all-absorbing as their reactions to the "social question." The Russian intelligentsia approached universalism with their characteristic intensity and dualism. For coupled with the many sincere demands for universal brotherhood in nineteenth-century Russian thought is frequently found the belief that Russia is destined to realize a unique mission in the world. At times this led to contradictions; but Berdyaev assured that "Russia and the Russian people can be characterized only by contradictions" (Berdyaev [1937] 1960, 14).

The belief in a Russian mission, however, was popular long before an uneasy intelligentsia had to rationalize Russia's existence on the map. The messianic tradition dates back to 1439, when the Orthodox church at Constantinople reunited with the Western church under papal supremacy, giving Czar Ivan III the opportunity to become the "only Christian ruler." Russia became the "God-bearing nation," Moscow the third and final Rome. This notion of a divine-historic mission was never effaced from the Russian soul.[7]

The universalist theme of Russian thought is of more recent origin. It came from the awakened intelligentsia of brotherly people protesting Russia's long isolation and estrangement from the rest of the world. The poignancy of their ideal of world brotherhood springs from their immersion in the vision of the Kingdom of God on earth.

Those for whom the national problem was of greatest practical consequence were the several converts to Catholicism during the early decades of the nineteenth century. Their practice of another faith often meant legal as well as cultural denationalization. A few of these spiritual exiles were content to forget about Russia in their new homes abroad, but most of them maintained a keen interest in Russian affairs and suffered deep nostalgia. One of these sufferers was Vladimir Petcherin, convert both to Catholicism and to utopian socialism, who wrote a poem beginning "How sweet it is to hate one's native land awaiting its destruction." His hatred of Russia's oppressive regime concealed a love for the motherland, whose salvation he saw in Catholic universality (cf. Iswolsky 1943, chap. x).

Michael Lunin expressed with Petcherin the social aspirations of most Russian Catholics. A disciple of Saint-Simon, and hence a bitter foe of autocracy and serfdom, he returned to Russia after his conversion to Catholicism and took part in Decembrist activity. With the universalist views fostered by his supranational religion, Lunin called himself a "citizen of the world."

The Catholic vogue was neither extensive nor long-lived; it was, as a contemporary wrote, "a drop of water in the ocean" (Haumant 1913, 240). We now turn to the main stream of Russian social thought.

The occasion for the formal outburst of the Slavophil-Westernizer feud coincided with the first articulate expression of Russian universalism. It was the untoward publication of Peter Chaadaev's "Lettres sur le philosophie d'histoire" in 1836. In these letters Chaadaev complained that Russia has no past, no future, no character of her own; that she has contributed nothing to the progress of reason and of humanity and that she has distorted whatever she has copied (Chaadaev 1913). He attributed this cultural poverty to her isolation from both Orient and Occident:

"the universal education of the human race has not reached us" (77, author's translation). Chaadaev's advice was that Russia rejoin the universal Christian movement, for Catholicism is the active, unifying, and social form of Christianity:

> The doctrine based on the supreme principle of *unity* and in the direct transmission of truth through its successive ministers corresponds most of all to the true spirit of religion, for it can be reduced to the fusion of all the moral forces in the world into one idea, one sentiment, and in the gradual establishment of a social system or Church which should establish the reign of truth among men.
> *(Ibid., 75)*

It was clearly its all-unifying aspect which attracted Chaadaev to Catholicism, not its rites or theology, for he never became a Catholic. He felt that one may forego traditional rites when one's beliefs come directly from the source of all faith. Catholicism and Orthodoxy were to him but forms of the Christian spirit, to which he preferred his own creed. "My religion," he wrote to Turgenev, "is not precisely that of the theologians ... but it is the religion at the bottom of men's minds ... and which ... will someday become the definite cult and entire life of humanity" (Koyré 1927, 600).

Steeped in German metaphysics and mysticism, Chaadaev believed that religion and its ideas determine the nature of existence and that history should be questioned to make people aware of its "idea," its mission. If peoples would learn their true national contributions from history, they would "combine to produce a universal and harmonious result, and one would perhaps see peoples extending their hands in the true sentiment of the general interest of humanity, which would be no more than the enlightened interest of each people" (Chaadaev 1913, 102).

Through his thoughts, actions, and opinions, Chaadaev had questioned history. In "Apologie d'un fou" he re-sketched Russia's barren past but predicted a brilliant future (ibid.). Urging the eclectic assimilation of Western culture as Russia's duty, he held that this would prepare it for fulfilling its mission. But Russia's time will come, he said: "We are called to solve the most problems of the social order, to complete most of the ideas which arose in the old societies, to answer the gravest questions troubling the human race" (230).

According to Chaadaev, this universal harmony would not result from the study of philosophy and the "progrès des lumières" as the sages assumed (and as Condorcet had so vividly prophesied half a century earlier). Intellectual activity involves feelings of individual existence and separate interest on the part of nations (who are moral beings) as well as people; this sentiment constitutes the *moi* of the collective human being. The path to world progress lies in learning one's nation's destiny from the past and implementing it more powerfully in the future.[8]

Chaadaev argued that he loved his fatherland more than any of the Slavophils; it was not patriotic to love one's country with closed eyes; "there is no point in stifling ourselves in our history, in dragging ourselves, like the people of the West, across the chaos of national prejudice, by the narrow paths of local ideas" (223).

The philosophical letters initiated the intense preoccupation with social questions and a bent for messianism and utopianism which were to mark the intelligentsia throughout the century. Like so many of his successors, Chaadaev wrote, in spiritual anxiety, "It is in the sweet belief of the future happiness of man that I take refuge when, obsessed with the annoying reality which surrounds me, I feel the need to breathe an air more pure, to behold a heaven more serene" (93). This was the refuge that all the intelligentsia, confronted with the bleak reality of Russia, were to seek in such varied and extreme forms.

The immediate result of the publication of Chaadaev's letters was a gust of protest from the increasingly prominent Slavophils. They resented his affirmation of the West and of Catholicism. Exploiting the idealistic notion (taken from Schelling) that religion determines the development of a people, as well as his point that Russia's growth had been isolated from Western civilization, they made Russia's separate culture based on Orthodoxy a supreme virtue.

The Slavophils' jeers were the applause of the Westernizers, who hailed Chaadaev as a leader in spite of his leaning toward Romanism. Hertzen called the letters "a shot fired in the darkness of night," and radicals saw them as a summons to liberation from Nicholas' tyranny (Iswolsky 1943, 124). Chaadaev was henceforth to wage a double conflict, against the extreme Westernizers as well as against the utopian chauvinists. No friend of radicalism, he opposed slavery and oppression because they would lead to revolution (Chaadaev 1913, 122).

With Chaadaev, Russian thought was mature and on its own. His mystical universalism, however, received the same slight acceptance that his Catholic sympathies did. The Slavophils, who shared his mystical premises, inverted his conclusions to produce an increasingly chauvinistic pride in Russia's isolated and exceptional history. Those who greeted his invitation to learning from the West usually disregarded his historical and religious concepts along with his metaphysics. These include the "German circle" of Westernizers, whose Hegelian rationalization of the status quo (and memories of the Decembrists' fate) kept them out of politics until their craving for social justice upset Hegel and cleared the way for the French socialists. Belinsky, leader of the circle, pioneered this reversal; from utter conservatism he shifted to

> a wild, fanatical love for the freedom and independence of personality ... possible only in a society founded upon right and chivalry ... I have now reached a new extreme—this idea of socialism. ... More and more I become a citizen of the world.
>
> *(Cited in Berdyaev 1948, 76)*

The Westernizers were bound to import more from the West than Chaadaev had bargained for; if they were to think of world harmony now, it had to be in positivist, socialist terms.

Elements of universalism were present in Russian socialist thought in its utopian, *narodnik*, and Marxian stages. The utopian socialists gained prominence in the

1840s, when the ideas of Saint-Simon and Fourier were hailed by romantic idealists as the cure for the social evils under Nicholas. Petrashevsky, a Russian landowner influenced by Fourier (who wrote a *Théorie de l'unité universelle*), declared in characteristic fashion that "Unable to find anything either in women or men worthy of my adherence, I have turned to devote myself to the service of humanity" (cited in Berdyaev [1937] 1960, 32). He held meetings for discussing socialism at his home in St. Petersburg until the police raided one. The most famous member of his circle was Dostoevski, whose memories of these utopian socialists were recorded in a couple characters of *The Possessed* ([1872] 1936): Virginsky, whose family professed the very latest progressive convictions, was dubbed a "universal humanity man"; and Liputin, who, when taunted by Stavrogin for borrowing his Fourierist ideas from the French, retorts, "That is taken from the universal language of humanity, not simply from the French. From the language of the universal social republic and harmony of mankind, let me tell you!" (51).

The universalism of the utopian socialists was based upon an optimistic view of a universal human nature. It conceived of brotherhood in terms of social utility and harmony; with the rational, voluntary organization of social institutions, irrational factors like economic inequality and national prejudice would disappear. It was an extension of Condorcet's vision into the next century.

Alexander Hertzen was one of the first of these utopian socialists. His disillusionment with Western socialism after the failures of 1848 gave his thinking a new twist. Russia was the last hope of Western civilization: it alone could solve the social question. Hertzen idolized the *narod* (common people; primarily the peasants) and the *mir* (village commune) and took pride in Russia's special historic development in avoiding capitalism. His synthesis of Slavophil and Westernizer ideals became the staple ideology of the *narodnik* (lovers of the *narod*) socialists, an agrarian socialism based on the *mir*. It is the least universalist of Russian socialisms.

In the 1850s and 1860s the temper of the socialists was changing. A change marked vividly, if perhaps unfairly, in the contrast between Stepan and Pyotr Verkhovensky in *The Possessed*. The new socialists were more "realistic," more interested in the *narod*, and more inclined to revolt. Some turned their hatred of the West and their love for the Russian *narod* into nationalistic feeling, while others moved in the direction of international revolution. Of the latter, Bakunin and Lavrov are two outstanding figures.

Michael Bakunin, known chiefly as an apostle of international anarchism (which, when spelled out, meant, for him, decentralized democracy), spent more than 20 years of his revolutionary activity in behalf of nationalistic causes.[9] He extolled the revolutionary virtues of the Russian peasants and continued the messianic tradition by prophesying in 1845: "Knowing [Russia], it is impossible not to be convinced that before it there stands a great mission to be fulfilled in the world" (cited in Hecht 1947, 75).

Only after the thwarted Polish uprising of 1863 did Bakunin turn to international causes with a vengeance. He formed an "international brotherhood" at Naples a few years later, which aimed for world revolution to end all forms of exploitation. Its "Revolutionary Catechism," which he wrote, rejected any policy based on patriotism and the rivalry of nations: "All political and authoritarian States existing at present ... will have to disappear in the universal Union of the free agricultural and industrial associations" (Nomad [1939] 1961, 185).

Bakunin had come to consider patriotism "the negation of human equality and solidarity" and saw its downfall through a common proletarian consciousness (cited in Hecht 1947, 75). Never a Marxist, he prophesied a proletarian federation of Europe and then of the whole world.

Peter Lavrov's alternative to Bakunin's insurrectionist program was largely the inspiration for the intelligentsia's "crusade to the people" in the middle 1870s, when thousands of *narodniki* went to live with the "common people" to raise their educational and economic level. Like all pre-Marxian Russian socialists, Lavrov's socialism was agrarian, aproletarian. Yet his social thinking was worldwide. He stressed the primacy of the proletariat in the revolutionary movements of western Europe and the United States and urged the socialists to make of the labor movement "one international struggle of the organized proletariat ... against its exploiters," recognizing "no ethnic and racial differences" (cited in Hecht 1947, 180). Lavrov wanted to achieve internationalism "in life and literature" through the peculiar contributions of each nationality.

Lavrov's phrases suggest the spirit of Marxism, and we are not far away. The failure of the *narodnik* socialists in the 1870s (to gain an understanding of the peasants) was a cue for more adequate theory and more effective techniques. With the systematic exposition of Marxism by Plekhanov in the 1880s, Marxian socialism attracted large numbers of the intelligentsia. The political struggle displaced the primacy of the social struggle, and universalism was now that of an organized class-conscious proletariat, destined to become the new mankind.

The most anti-universalist trend among the Russian intelligentsia was the Slavophil movement. It was started, however, by men well acquainted with and fond of European culture. Aksakov even spoke of a "universal human culture." The early Slavophils simply wanted Russia's contribution to world culture to be original, not a cheap copy of the West.

After the time of their chief spokesman, Alexis Khomiakov, the Slavophils pursued a narrow nationalism and endorsed many reactionary governmental policies. During the 1830s and 1840s, Khomiakov developed certain concepts which are relevant here because of their influence on Dostoevski and Soloviev.

Khomiakov revived and refined the conception of *sobornost*, or "congregationalism," a product of the Orthodox belief that the spirit in man is a gift to the congregation, not to individuals. The doctrine of *sobornost* holds that truth exists in the constantly developing consensus of the congregation. In Khomiakov's words,

> The highest knowledge of truth is beyond the reach of an isolated mind; it is open only to a society of minds bound together by love. Truth looks as though it were the achievement of a few, but in reality it is the creation and possession of all.
>
> *(Cited in Lampert 1947, 105)*

To Khomiakov, the idea and fact (!) of the Orthodox church were prototypes of *sobornost*. The Orthodox church, he wrote, has unity without the tyranny of Rome (since its unity is based on mutual love) and freedom without the rebelliousness of Protestantism (since its members are regulated by the humility of mutual love).[10] The social expression of *sobornost*, the *mir*, he praised as the perfect Christian society.[11]

Along with the church, *sobornost*, and *mir*, Khomiakov eulogized religious anarchism which he noticed among the people (and to which Tolstoy gave such a resounding "Yea" in his later years). This anarchism deplored the state's institutions and considered the prerogative violence as delegated to the czar, who assumed the sin for all. Orthodox believers need no masters; they have *sobornost*. In the spiritual order, autonomy is necessary and the free church ought to be superior to the state. Such ideas, needless to say, were held subversive by the state, and the early Slavophils were as suspect to the government as the Westernizers.

While these ideas of the Slavophils were being upheld defensively against the Westernizing onslaught, the evils of autocracy and serfdom were provoking young men like Fyodor Dostoevski into circles of quiet rebellion. Dostoevski, however, did not remain in the socialist camp for long. The exile on which he was sent for his revolutionary activity precipitated a deep spiritual conversion, which turned his social idealism to the way of Christian love. He found The Way in Siberia through the words of Christ, the precepts of Orthodoxy, and the boundless example of the "wonderful people!" The suffering, sinning, atoning, humanitarian Russian *narod* became his new ideology.

This ideology was made public through his magazine *Vremya* (Time), published in 1861. Its policy assumed that Slavophils and Westernizers were working for the same thing—the glorification of Russia—and urged both factions to seek, in the *narod*, the true national spirit and Russia's salvation. It emphasized Russia's difference from the West and extolled its mission and the unique character of its people. "We believe," wrote Dostoevski in *Vremya*, "that the Russian nation is an unusual manifestation in the history of all humanity. ... In [Russian character] ... is a highly synthesizing capacity, a capacity of universal reconcilability, of universal humanity" (cited in Simmons 1940, 98). This concept marks the main aspect of Dostoevski's universalism and explains his equally intense nationalism. By locating Russia's virtues and missions in the capacity of her people for universal brotherhood, Dostoevski is simultaneously national and universal. This polarity remained with him throughout the rest of his life.

As Dostoevski's contacts with western Europe and socialism increased, his views hardened. He came to detest the materialism and individualist selfishness in the bourgeois West and to exalt Russia's exceptional historic growth and her spiritual purity. Socialism was no answer to the evils of capitalism: it counts on the rational self-interest of human beings. In some notes on his trip to Europe, Dostoevski stressed the inability of men to submit to rational, mechanical rules of life for society. He criticized socialists because they want to legislate, by reason, those sacrifices of love which can come only from the heart, from faith, from love of Christ. The consequences of ignoring this are dangerous, and in *Crime and Punishment* and *The Idiot* he showed the specter of the contemporary radical generation and its lack of faith.

Speaking through Prince Myshkin in *The Idiot*, Dostoevski declared that there are two ways to unite society into a harmonious whole: via authority or via service. The former, using reason and force, is the way of Catholicism and socialism, a pair of evil forces Dostoevski often juxtaposed. The latter is the way of the Orthodox faith (of *sobornost*) and achieves universal harmony through submission and mutual love. "Submission," Dostoevski wrote in his notes to *The Idiot*, "is the most fearful force that can exist in the world," and it must be opposed to the way of violence (cited in Simmons 1940, 218). The Prince's religious faith calls for enraptured unification with the highest synthesis of life, attained when he has completely repressed his self. (It is similar to that ecstatic moment before his epileptic fits—a record of Dostoevski's own ecstasies.) This dynamic mystical union in love was the sure faith which dispelled Dostoevski's sporadic religious doubts. It was the feeling which evoked those visions of world harmony that haunted his later years.

Such a vision occurs in Stavrogin's confession in *The Possessed* and is repeated in *A Raw Youth* with the dream of Versilov. A paradise is pictured, inhabited by men whose boundless love and happiness flow from "the living life," the life of universal wholeness through feeling, as opposed to the reflective life. We meet this vision again in the story "The Dream of a Strange Man." There again is love and bliss, the people living "in daily live communion with the whole of the universe," in mutual universal love. The Strange Man introduces reflection and civilization into this utopia, which turns to science and the cult of rational self-interest. Its concord is ruptured; the society ends in almost nihilistic misery.

The lesson is plain. The Strange Man vows on waking to combat the view that "cognition of life is superior to life"; and we again perceive Dostoevski's disgust for rationalism and his passion for all-embracing love based on faith.

In terms of the contemporary world situation, this yearning for future world harmony presented the other aspect of Dostoevski's universalism. But only through adherence to the Christian idea could a warring civilization be saved.

The theme was developed journalistically in the installments of *The Diary of a Writer*. Catholicism had perverted the Christian idea by adopting the force of the Roman Empire to achieve spiritual unity. Through the violence of both bourgeois and socialists, the West was doomed to self-annihilation. The fate of Europe belonged to the Russians, who would bring world harmony through the principle of universal service through meekness: the Russians alone can be brothers to all people.

This last idea was the core of his famous speech at the dedication of the Pushkin statue in Moscow in 1880. There he praised Pushkin as a great national poet because he embodied a major faculty of the Russian nationality—*fsyechelovechnost*—its universal susceptibility, and its "all-embracing humanity":

> To become a genuine Russian means ... to show the solution of European anguish in our all-humanitarian and all-unifying Russian soul, to embrace in it

with brotherly love all our brethren, and finally, perhaps, to utter the ultimate word of great universal harmony of the brotherly accord of all nations abiding by the law of Christ's gospel.

(Dostoevski 1949, 980)

Recognition of this spirit by the intelligentsia will resolve the Slavophil-Westernizer quarrel, the latter learning that Russia's mission cannot be fulfilled by apish imitation of Europe's social order, the former learning that the Russian character yearns to be brotherly with Europe and share its cultural heritage. Dostoevski made another appeal for their reconciliation, exhorting both camps to cooperate in the mission, to clarify to the people, as he had written earlier,

our urge to render universal service to humanity, sometimes even to the detriment of our own momentous and immediate interests. This is our reconciliation with the civilizational cognition and *excuse* of their ideals even though these be in discord with ours; this is our acquired faculty of discovering and revealing in each one of the European civilizations ... the truth contained in it, even though there be much with which it be impossible to agree.

(Ibid., 361)

This is Dostoevski's universalism at its noblest. Yet it could be readily matched by passages whose attacks on Jews, Poles, and Frenchmen reveal an elemental chauvinism. Dostoevski's Slavophilism, however, he would argue, is not that of the narrow nationalists. He was primarily concerned with Russia's mission to the world and, in that framework, would justify his dualism.

In that framework he did justify what seems utterly inconsistent with his repudiation of violence—war. Dostoevski believed that Russia, the only bearer of true Christianity, sought to serve all by uttering to the world "her new, sane, and as yet unheard of word ... for the good and genuine unification of mankind as a whole in a new, brotherly, universal union" (780). But the servant to all is highest in the Kingdom of Heaven, and this spiritual priority gives Russia the right to fight wars to spread this new word and further human unity. Hence Dostoevski, who rejected wars for political or economic gain, continually insisted that "Constantinople must be ours" and cheered Russia's war against the Turks in 1877: "With war and victory the new word will be uttered and a new life will begin" (662). The war was a means to liberate the Slavs and to found a Russia-headed union of the Slavs as a step toward the unity of mankind. If this recalls imperialism, it is an inverted imperialism; for he insists that Russia's desire for universal service is not a demand for universal worship. The reward is not political, but spiritual.

Dostoevski's apocalyptic prophecy of a world united under Orthodox Christianity was by no means a picture of regulated calm among now fighting men. His one new world is the scene of dynamic love, entailing expiation through suffering and the active responsibility of all for all. His individual code and social panacea are one: individual religious self-betterment is the means to social reform. Disgusted with economic injustice, his remedy for economic inequality was seen "only in the spiritual dignity of man. If we were brothers, there would be fraternity; but without that, men will never agree about the division of wealth" (cited in Maynard 1946, 211). Ivan Karamazov's legend of the grand inquisitor is Dostoevski at his most socially challenging: man should reject legislated material and happiness and strive with the gift of freedom to attain new spiritual heights. It is axiomatic that he cannot reach them alone, that "a Russian sufferer in order to find peace needs precisely universal happiness—nothing less" (Dostoevski 1949, 968).

Dostoevski's novels were praised by Tolstoy for communicating "religious feelings toward the union and brotherhood of man" (cited in Simmons 1940, xi). This area of accord leads us to seek the profoundly different world view behind Tolstoy's universalism and the singularly tortuous path he trod to find the meaning of man's paltry existence.

Before he reached the spiritual crisis which brought him near to suicide and gave him the germs of a lasting faith, Tolstoy had written his most famous novels, *War and Peace* and *Anna Karenina*. Yet in his national epic we already find concepts which belong to his later religious universalism. It shows two influences which persist throughout his life: the love of the *narod* and a strain of Buddhism derived through Schopenhauer. These merge in the peasant Karataev, who is an expression of Tolstoy's pantheism, his drive to fuse individuality in the collective life of the laboring people. Tolstoy is saying through him, according to Maynard, "It is the ego and its affections which make sorrow: therefore, be thou merged in the common life of the people, and obey the promptings of the universal life" (Maynard 1946, 229). "Platon Karataev," another interpreter wrote, "was already a citizen of Tolstoy's brotherhood of man" (Sandomirsky 1949, 208).

Tolstoy's growing antipathy to war was expressed in the last part of *Anna Karenina*, where Levin condemns the chauvinistic sentiment that leads to war. However, the wave of patriotic enthusiasm accompanying the Russo-Turkish War muffled his qualms. Just a few years later, his thinking evolved the unconditional rejection of violence in any form.

After a lifelong spiritual struggle capped by his intense turmoil in 1879, Tolstoy found in the *narod* a meaning in life which death could not destroy: belief in God and desire for godly living. His subsequent writings, unlike Dostoevski's profession, which came as sporadic outbursts of artistic inspiration, developed a comprehensive, rational religious philosophy. Tolstoy could not accept anything which did not stand to reason, but, once accepted, he would adhere to it with maximal devotion. His new faith was built on Christ's injunctions on self-control and absolute love. The corollaries to these were conscientiously deduced and tirelessly expounded: self-perfection through the negation of personality, absolute nonviolence, rejection of church and state.

Tolstoy reasoned thus: Since life involves pain, decay, and death, one's animal welfare cannot be sustained; what alone is true and undying is love for God and his children; hence the reasonable man ought to renounce his own animal needs and desires and give himself up to love for all human beings, where the only bliss is.

Through humility and self-renunciation, one should strive for perfection; and social progress comes only through the moral improvement of the masses.

The meaning of life is in some higher power apprehended through reason and conscience, and this is the vital essence of all religions. The existence of manifold militant faiths yields first the belief that all faiths are delusions; but then we see that though "our expression may differ, the essence must be the same—we are both of us men" (Tolstoy [1904] 1934, 332). Since genuine religion is the meaning of life and one's relation to God is fixed by every man individually, faiths enforced by a church hierarchy or a state are false.

From Christ's command to "love thine enemy," Tolstoy drew the doctrine of nonviolence in its most radical form. The state maintains itself by violence, and no true Christian should serve in its army or support any of its institutions. By acquiescing in the use of force, the church (and he here obviously bypasses Dostoevski, who does not blame the Orthodox church) has betrayed the Christian idea; saying "state church" is like saying "hot ice."

Applying this religious anarchism internationally, Tolstoy thundered at the "stupid doctrine" of patriotism, which is "a rude, harmful, disgraceful, and bad feeling, and above all—is immoral" (Tolstoy [1900] 1911, 252). Viewing history as the movement of people from lower to higher ideas, Tolstoy called patriotism an obsolete notion, because men have attained a consciousness of the "brotherhood among men of different nationalities" and because peoples (not governments) live in friendly and peaceful commercial and cultural relations. It is perpetuated by government officials, military men, and glory-seeking rulers who profit from wars or the threat of war. When people realize this, the governments will crumble:

> Understand that salvation from your woes is only possible when you free yourself from the obsolete idea of patriotism and from the obedience to Government that is based on it, and when you boldly enter the region of that higher idea, the brotherly union of the peoples, which has long since come to life, and from all sides is calling.
>
> (Ibid., 261)

Here is universalism without any qualifying undertones.

It is clear that Tolstoy's universalism flows only from the teachings of Christ. He rejected religious sublimation in the positivist and socialist forms of world brotherhood. They are based on "utility"; they proceed from a pagan, social life-conception, that of curbing man's nature for the good of society; and they rest on a fiction—one cannot actually love a state, let alone an entity called "mankind." Tolstoy urged a "universal, divine life-conception," that which asks man to live up to his (divine) nature. Universalism comes from loving "the principle of all things—God ... whom man recognizes in himself through love ... and [man] will by the love of God love all men and all things" (Tolstoy 1894, 111).

In "What Is Art?" Tolstoy adapted his aesthetics to his new religion. The best art, to him, is that which infectiously communicates the highest moral feelings to all people. The glad feeling of communion with all men "is produced both by religious art which transmits feelings of love of God and one's neighbor, and by universal art transmitting the very simplest feelings common to all men" (cited in Simmons 1940, 540).

In practice Tolstoy did not contradict his universalist principles as Dostoevski did. His love for the Russian *narod* was expressed in sober, unchauvinistic terms: "In the Russian people, and I do not think I am biased, there is more of the Christian spirit than in other peoples" (650). He actively sympathized with the suffering Jews in Russia. In a letter to Vladimir Soloviev, the third great religious universalist of the half-century, he wrote: "the foundation of our repulsion towards the persecution of the Jewish nationality is the same: the feeling of brotherly bond with all peoples" (cited in Iswolsky 1943, 16).

Again, this point of contact becomes our point of departure. Though at one in their profession of a "brotherly bond," Tolstoy and Soloviev differ markedly in their reasons for it and in their general world views. They can be polarized on many counts, just as each of them can be polarized against Dostoevski on others.

No artist, but a theologian and genuine philosopher—rare in Russia—Vladimir Soloviev preached his universalism in the context of an elaborate metaphysical system. The primary intuition of Solovievian thought is his conception of the universe and mankind as an all-embracing unity (*vseedinstvo*). This unity is not simple and abstract but "a concrete principle containing all in itself." It can be apprehended only by a free theosophy, integrating Western empirical and rational cognition with Eastern intuition. And, in turn, this "integral knowledge" is to be integrated with daily living, to become active creation.

Soloviev formulated this view of philosophy when he was under the influence of Slavophil writers and his friend Dostoevski. He considered the active synthesis of Eastern and Western philosophy to be part of Russia's mission. Yet the principle of unity egged him onward, and Chaadaev's "Lettres" catalyzed his transition from Orthodox theology and the idea of Russia's "God-bearing" mission to his ideas of theocratic universalism and Russia's contribution to world unity. After ca. 1884 he became a quick critic of "zoölogical nationalism" and a foe of all forms of intolerance.

His new theology took form in *La Russie et l'église universelle* (*Russia and the Universal Church*) (Soloviev [1889] 1948), which had to be printed outside Russia. There Soloviev combined his ideas of unity and Godmanhood developed in his Slavophil period in an overall cosmic process favoring the Catholic church.

Soloviev believed that every being has a threefold nature: its existential actuality, its activity, and the self-conscious enjoyment of its activity through a return to its actuality. So it is, he reasoned, with God, the Supreme Being.[12] The original harmonious union of his three hypostases, however, has in reality been broken: his second hypostasis, activity, is the World-Soul (the divine essence of the material universe), which broke away by its free choice, to yield chaos (Adam's Fall). The cosmic process is the return of the World-Soul to conscious reunion with God. The absolute form and "Idea" (in Plato's sense) of this new pan-unity he calls *sophia*—the substance of the divine permeated by the principle of the divine unity.

Brought down to earth, this pins the world process as evolution through more perfect and unified stages, from mineral (just "being") through vegetable and animal to human (rational) and, finally, divine or spiritually human (the perfect state): "This highest end of man as such ... and of the human world is to gather the universe together in thought. The end of the God-man and of the Kingdom of God is to gather the universe together in reality" (Soloviev 1918, 190). Christ was the example of the God-man, and the meaning and aim of history are universal regeneration through the embodiment of Christ's spirit in all aspects of life. Christian universalism, Soloviev insisted, is not passive or negative, like Nirvana, but positive and creative: it seeks the highest self-realization through the active spiritual effort which produces the divine humanity.

The tool, of course, is love. Love has a threefold unifying task: the completion of individual man through true and eternal union with woman; the reintegration of social man through formation of the complete and stable community; "the reintegration of universal Man by the restoration of his intimate and living union with the whole of Nature" (Soloviev [1889] 1948, 212). We are bidden to see man's growth only insofar as he is rooted in the whole of humanity. Each single being (person, class, nation) acting in isolation from the divine-human sum of things is acting contrary to truth and its practical expression, justice:

> Each wants [the Kingdom of God] for himself and for everyone, and is only able to attain it *together with every one*.
> The world purpose is not to create a solidarity between each and all, for it already exists in the nature of things, but to make each and all aware of this solidarity and spiritually alive to it.
>
> (Soloviev 1918, 199, 204, italics Soloviev's)

An organization is needed to coordinate the individual and collective aspects of this process. This is the universal church, which serves as the objective correlative of divine-all-human unity. Following the dogma of Petrine succession, Soloviev made Catholicism the "priestly institution" of the church and pleaded with Orthodoxy to reunite with it. On the other hand, close alliance of church and state is necessary to assure Christian justice. Soloviev explained that it is the historic destiny of Russia to provide the universal church with the political power necessary for the salvation of Europe and the world.

We must remember that Soloviev was not thinking of political or spiritual dictatorship when he chooses the pope and czar as pillars of the new world union. He had always in mind the ideal of *sobornost*, union through freedom and love. He obsessively proclaimed "free theocracy" and "free theosophy."

In a comprehensive ethical treatise based on these ideas, *Justification of the Good*, Soloviev established an unconditional moral norm from the principle that man should make himself and everyone else more perfect to achieve the Kingdom of God. This is "the absolute worth of each individual, in virtue of which society is determined as the inward and free harmony of all" (266). *True* Christianity embodies this; it is universal both in the absence of external limitations (national, denominational)[13] and of internal ones (true Christianity is inseparable from intellectual enlightenment, social progress, etc.). Its challenge to all peoples is the improvement of institutions toward the "free union of all in the perfect good" (275).

Three collective evils oppose this. They are the immoral relations existing: (1) among nations; (2) between society and the criminal; (3) between social classes. The last can be rendered moral by the social recognition of a minimum economic level to secure a worthy human existence to each and of the moral components of every economic activity. The second is solved by rejecting retributive punishment but accepting the use of violence to prevent an evil.

Soloviev's consideration of the first evil presents a detailed and extensive inquiry into political universalism. Since the creative work of a nation is of universal value, no nation regards itself as the purpose of its own life, and the individual has no right to put service of his nation's material advantages above the demands of universal morality. Nevertheless, national differences are real, and patriotism is a natural and basic moral feeling. Soloviev concluded that we must still love our own nation but "love all other nations as [our] own" (with a love not psychologically, but ethically, equivalent to national self-love) (299).

With pragmatic sense that cuts through his florid mysticism, Soloviev found grounds to justify military defense in war. Fulfillment of one's moral duty to realize the social good cannot be done in isolation but only through those groups determined by the historical life of humanity. The group at this stage is the fatherland organized as a state; hence one has a moral duty to defend and perfect one's country until humanity as a whole can be morally organized.

The true unity of nations is, for Soloviev, not a single nationality but an all-embracing one. Here again is his metaphysical concept of positive unity or uni-totality, which characterizes human reason at its highest level of awareness (integral knowledge), and *sophia*, the Divine Wisdom.[14] His grounds for speaking of the unity of humanity are three: the common descent of all men; their universal communicability, in spite of different languages; and the fact that history is intelligible only universal-wise.

In the moral organization of humanity, no nation can prosper at the expense of others; hence, extolling one's nation as the chief good is unpatriotic. The true patriot will serve the true good of his nation; that is, the nation in humanity. Soloviev prophesized: collective man, or humanity divided into various levels of groups, will be organized in the ecumenical church, in which each finds the inward completion of his liberty. And "the cycle of sacraments, like the cycle of universal life, is completed by the resurrection of the flesh, the integration of the whole of humanity, the final incarnation of the Divine Wisdom" (Soloviev [1889] 1948, 214).

At the end of his life, Soloviev's disillusionment made him discard his dreams of world theocracy. He gave up his artificial constructions and despaired of realizing God's wisdom on earth. In an apocalyptical outburst in 1899, *The Three*

Conversations, he predicted the victory of Antichrist and misery in the world; but, after a long struggle, he showed the defeat of Antichrist and the long-awaited union of the churches. The universalist bug could not cease to bite.

V Conclusion

The Orthodox believer and passionate doubter who heightened the world's self-awareness through exposing its tragic dualism and left his own intense national-universalism as evidence; the foe of church and state whose rational quest for life's meaning became a radical renunciation of self in behalf of an amorphous humanity; the lay theologian who saw the ultimate realization of self through its expansion to God humanity via a Rome-headed church—have they anything in common besides a love for mankind? Is there enough similarity among them to suggest an "ethos" which may be contrasted with that of the Enlightenment?

The reaction of these authors to the thoughts of Nicolai Fyodorov suggests where to look. All three were significantly impressed by *The Philosophy of Common Action*, his project for universal salvation, and expressed warm approval of his ideas (cf. Berdyaev 1948, 209). In Fyodorov's work, *the sense of responsibility of each for all and the apocalyptic impulse to realize God's Kingdom on earth reached maximum intensity*. These two ideas subsume the thought of all the Russian religious universalists; indeed, they pervaded the thinking of many others of the intelligentsia in anti-religious guise, when the fact of the church gave the lie to these Christian hopes.

Fyodorov was the incarnation of these concepts. His extreme compassion for human suffering led him to oppose in earnest the most certain of man's sorrows—death. He preached that people must cease fighting one another and unite to conquer the irrational forces of nature: high collective human activity which harnessed technology would be able to do miracles, even raise the dead! This is the common task, to realize the brotherhood of man in time as well as in space. And, true to his breed, Fyodorov said that the task ought to begin in Russia, whose people are least corrupted by godless civilization.

This, too, is familiar; *the challenge to man is to surpass himself spiritually*, to seek moral perfection, Godmanhood. *The challenge is thrown to all humanity, but especially to the Russians*. The path to perfection is through *humble immersion of the ego in service for all, in all-embracing love*, and the way is illumined by the *love of the Christian God*.

The tone of the religious universalists is not that of the philosophes. There is no discussion of an isolated man, invested with certain inalienable rights, or of an abstract essence of human nature. There is no consideration of the individual apart from his moral duty to and participation in humanity—each is answerable for all. Tolstoy declared that "an intellectual, effeminate, idle person will always prove that personality has its inalienable rights" ([1887] 1934, 82). Soloviev drew the distinction with handy clarity.

> The Declaration of the Rights of Man could only provide a positive principle for social reconstruction if it was based upon a true conception of Man

himself. That of the revolutionaries ... or of their spiritual forbears, the Encyclopedists ... was well-known: they perceived in Man nothing but abstract individuality, a rational being destitute of all positive content.

([1889] 1948, 7)

It was, of course, this "abstract individuality" which gave the philosophes grounds for collapsing the irrational barriers which had thwarted the full realization of men's potential and had caused social discord. The artificial nature of traditional religion, of class privileges, and of ethnic prejudices was revealed in this light; the human being was exalted and his secular fraternity with all men announced.

The writings of the philosophes carried an appeal to reason, to middle-road, bourgeois reason. The rights of man, just as the natural laws of morality and religion, were to be apprehended by any man's natural reason. Their rational analyses of social problems stood on their own, ignoring the stuff of revelation, of mysticism, and of passion.

This suggests two further contrasts with the Russian triad. The Russian religious universalists refused to consider the brotherhood of man on a secular, humanistic, or positivistic basis. They had each gone through periods of atheism and were familiar with the nonreligious ideals of social harmony; but they insisted upon returning to God as the only meaningful source of brotherly love and social progress. Soloviev's quip points up their views: "The Russian nihilists have a sort of syllogism of their own—man is descended from a monkey, consequently we shall love one another" (cited in Berdyaev 1948, 106).

But more: they did not conceive of man's improvement in minimal, bourgeois terms. Their reactions to the "anthill" solutions of the radical intelligentsia were no less revolutionary than the schemes they attacked.

Berdyaev pointed out the Russian passion for wholeness, for a totalitarian outlook, an absence of critical skepticism and rational fragmentarianism in their thinking. This was manifest in their fusion of philosophy with the whole of life; the completeness with which they gave themselves up to various outlooks—Hegelianism, Slavophilism, nihilism. It was in the deep Orthodox tradition which lays claim to the whole of life, spiritual and temporal; in *sobornost*, the submission of the individual will in the mass, finding truth and love in the congregation; in the spirit of *narodnichestvo*, of finding fulfillment through merging with the common people.

This disposition appears in the maximalist and eschatological flavor which the works of the Russian religious universalists impart. Their thirst for salvation is an expensive one to satisfy. It is Dostoevski's obsession with messianism; his visions of future world harmony; his paradise of free, suffering, expiating spirits, the suggestion of which reaches giddying intensity in *The Grand Inquisitor*. It is Tolstoy's absolute ascetic submission to his interpretation of the Christian teaching and his demand that his fellows behave like gods. It is Soloviev's integral knowledge-life, his infatuation with the apocalyptical union of a perfected humanity with God.

The Russian tendency toward totalitarianism finds substantive as well as temperamental expression in these three writers. Their universalism seems to be based on a mystical intuition of oneness, while that of the philosophes comes more from recognition of the essential equality of a multiplicity of individuals. The fact that Dostoevski acted so contrary to his universalist principles indicates that they were not made of concrete, particular attitudes but were simply abstractions of a mystical feeling of oneness, his "living life." Tolstoy's renunciation of self for immersion in the common life of humanity suggests a negative, passive oneness. We have already discussed the all-pervading intuition of unity of Soloviev.

Despite their differences of approach and values, the philosophes and the Russian triad have a significant minimum consensus. They have a fundamental belief in the absolute worth of each human being, however differently conceived. They were unanimous in attacking cruelty, capital punishment, and war in cultures where these activities were nominally accepted. They dissolved (though for Dostoevski on a purely ideal level) those notions which alienate man from man because of membership in an outside group.

For all of them, man's family is humanity; his home, the world.

Notes

1 The distinction is taken from Boehm's (1931) article on "Cosmopolitanism."
2 Here is an excerpt from Ikhnaton's hymn (*Encyclopaedia Brittanica* 1949, XII, 79): O sole God ... Thou didst create the earth according to thy heart ... Men, all cattle, large and small, All that are upon the earth ... The foreign countries, Syria and Kush, The land of Egypt, Thou settest every man into his place Thou suppliest their necessities. The tongues are diverse in speech, Their forms likewise and their skins are distinguished.
3 For example, "Le Cosmopolite ou le citoyen du monde," by Monbron; "Le Cosmopolite ou les contradictions," by Chevrier (cited in Boehm 1931).
4 Condorcet advocated a universal language for the dual purpose of enhancing communication among men and for making more precise the objects of human understanding.
5 Most of the Russians stopped at a negation of the validity of the old beliefs (cf. Haumant 1913, chap. xii).
6 Koyré comments: "It is interesting to note in passing how little our author has forgotten the formulas which had enthused his youth. De l'homme et du citoyen!"
7 Another manifestation of "mission" thinking was the *Raskol*, or schism, which occurred within the church in the 1660s. Adoption of foreign rites by the imperious Patriarch Nikon provoked an extreme reaction among many clergy and people who had come to consider the traditional liturgy as sacred and symbolic of the mission of the third Rome. These "Old Believers" expressed an attitude of anti-innovation and xenophobia which the Slavophils inherited.
8 It is interesting that the first articulate Russian universalist should have derived his Western inspiration from the foes of the philosophes, the French traditionalist thinkers Bonald and De Maistre. They fought against the dangerous principle of individualism and praised the historical traditional institutions as giving meaning and unity to society.
9 Bakunin wore all the contradictions of Russian thought. He combined an anarchistic hatred for all authority with a demand for strict organizational discipline; he juxtaposed his ideals of decentralized democracy with the need for a postrevolutionary dictatorship. Present with his radical internationalism of later years was a steady current of anti-Semitic and anti-German feeling.
10 The discrepancy between Khomiakov's ideal and the actual church was shown by the fact that this "free society" did not tolerate his works.

11 The *mirs* were peasant communes, whose ideology was that of *krugovaia poi* (common responsibility). They conceived property as God-given and hence to be worked for the common good. They carried out periodic redivision of the land and were collectively responsible for damages and taxes. The *mir* was also idolized by the Westerners but because of its economic advantages and because it evinced an innate Russian propensity for socialism.
12 Soloviev thus connects the nature of the Trinity with absolute ontology. Indeed, the trinitary principle pervades many parts of his theology and metaphysics.
13 Soloviev on denominations: "If we affirm [Christianity] first in its denominational peculiarity, we deprive it of logical basis and moral significance, make it an obstacle to the spiritual regeneration of mankind" (1918, 273).
14 All-embracing unity figures interestingly in Soloviev's conception of a universal language, which would not be a single tongue but an inclusion of all the existing languages.

6

THE SOCIOLOGY OF MORALITY IN THE WORK OF PARSONS, SIMMEL, AND MERTON

Although a subfield called sociology of morality—of "moral phenomena," more aptly—may seem a new departure for sociologists, the topic has in fact been central to sociological inquiry since its pre-disciplinary days. From the genial precursor of sociology, Adam Smith, and it's official baptizer, Auguste Comte, to virtually all the movers and shakers of the subject, sociologists have pursued a wide array of questions regarding the forms, contents, genesis, functions, and changes of moral phenomena.

To some extent, this pursuit can be seen in the drive to establish the very discipline of sociology, which included determined efforts to get beyond "economism," a position expressing the abstractions of atomic naturalism and marginal utility theory. With a large eye to the founding figures of Pareto, Durkheim, and Weber, this case was made famous in 1937 by Talcott Parsons in *The Structure of Social Action* ([1937] 1968). The same was true no less in work by earlier figures such as Auguste Comte, John Stuart Mill, John Dewey, W. I. Thomas, Robert Park, and William Graham Sumner—figures who Parsons largely ignored at the time of writing *Structure*.

Broadly speaking, critiques of economic thinking proceed from four directions. One emphasizes the hold of traditional habits and routines that preclude the utilitarian calculus so central to economistic thoughtways. This emphasis characterizes, for example, the work of John Dewey, for whom most human conduct is guided by ingrained, habitual response, and by Max Weber, who wrote of "the great bulk of everyday action to which people have become habitually accustomed" (Weber 1968, 25). In countless instances, tradition and habit have disposed humans to pursue lines of action that most definitely fail to satisfy their needs for their survival and well-being.

Another line of thought questions the rationality postulate of economism by noting the reservoir of unconscious motives and emotional impulses that derail calculations of interest. Diverse formulations of this critique appear in much moral philosophy—the passions were at one time more prominent in moral discourse than were "interests" (Hirschman 1977)—and figures like Hume and Schopenhauer delved into them deeply. These ideas found dramatic elaboration in the work of Sigmund Freud and Carl Jung and their followers.

A third line of criticism stems from those who reject the abstractness of analyzing separate individuals and, instead, consider the myriad ways in which individual conduct is shaped and organized by collective structures. This type of critique was voiced by Auguste Comte and extended by Emile Durkheim. Following Montesquieu's attack on Hobbes, both disparaged economists for thinking that individuals, by themselves, were able to organize their decisions and actions (Levine 1995, chap. 8).

The fourth—and perhaps the most charged critique of economism—has taken the form of emphasizing the moral dimension of human action. This concern was shared by nearly all the figures mentioned above. For all that, little has been done to analyze the universe of social theory with an eye to elucidating this dimension of human conduct—to construct what we may call, for reasons to be discussed below, the Moral-Evaluative Complex.

When we look for originary sociologists whose treatments of morality were most differentiated and best developed philosophically, the names of Georg Simmel and Talcott Parsons come to mind. Both Simmel and Parsons had productive careers in which the topos of morality stood out frequently. Following and to varying degrees influenced by them, Robert K. Merton further enriched the discourse by playing a role complementary to both. All that said, it must not be assumed that the thoughtways of either Parsons or Simmel contained a single consistent way of treating morality. Indeed, ideas about morality changed so much in the course of their respective careers that one can only get a fair grasp of what they thought by tracing the evolution of their ideas. To that challenging task, I now turn.

Talcott Parsons: From Voluntarism to Multidimensional Determinism

Of the motives that promoted young Talcott Parsons to publish his first major opus, *The Structure of Social Action* ([1937] 1968), the wish to demonstrate the crucial constitutive role of moral considerations in human action was a dominant inspiration.[1] This motif was prefigured in a paper published two years before *Structure*, "The Place of Ultimate Values in Sociological Theory" (Parsons 1935). The use of "ultimate" in the title represented a Weberian concern (*letzte Werte*) about ways in which fundamental convictions mediated by religious traditions affect the most mundane details of daily action. The paper leads right out with a proclamation of what would become an animating assumption of *Structure*: "The positivistic reaction against philosophy has, in its effect on the social sciences, manifested a strong tendency to obscure the fact that man is essentially an active, creative, evaluating creature" (282).[2] In support of that claim, the paper makes four points:

1. Understanding human conduct requires that objective accounts of actions be complemented by accounts of the subjective dimensions.
2. The preeminent mode of capturing the subjective dimensions involves attending to mean-ends calculation.[3]
3. Scientific knowledge can be called on to explain the choice of means, but not that of ends; the latter entails a "voluntaristic" dimension.
4. Both the ultimate justification of empirical ends and the substance of trans-empirical ends require some kind of transcendent notions, notions that positivism cannot accommodate due to its insistence on empirical justifications for all truth-claims.

By the time *Structure* was published, these four modalities had been refined. *Structure* incorporates the normative factor into an explicit model of action. Moreover, it distinguishes that model from a number of competing alternatives, and it moves to a sharper conception of norms. This includes distinguishing between objective accounts of norms as facts in a situation and subjective accounts in which norms figure as ideal elements that stand as ideals to be realized through active effort.

The book's argument opens with a diagram that illustrates the point: all action is driven by interests but also regulated by normative elements. The schema with which Parsons portrayed diverse theories of action turned heavily on the latter variable. He signified it by the letter *i*, defined as "normative or ideal elements." A major part of the book's argument was contained in the nine chapters of Part II, devoted to showing how the work of three of the four main figures in his account (Marshall, Pareto, and Durkheim) felt constrained to supplement the economistic model of action—consisting solely of a situation, conditions, means, knowledge, and ends—with a normative component. The fourth main figure, Max Weber, was shown to have repudiated economistic assumptions pointedly *ab initio*.

To be sure, Parsons' notion of voluntarism received almost no direct attention in the work that sought to establish it as the touchstone for all future social theory. It was draped casually over his lengthy arguments about the place of normativity in action. No matter how loudly he proclaimed his allegiance to the notion of voluntarism or felt that he was rescuing the principle of human agency, Parsons failed to give it serious attention in *Structure*. In contrast to the fastidious manner in which he treated other core concepts, such as action, positivism, and utilitarianism, he never defined the term explicitly and treated it in a vague and at times contradictory manner. As a result, "commentators have been divided over whether Parsons's 'voluntarism' stands for choice, freedom of choice, freedom, free will, purposiveness, subjective decision making, subjectivity, activity and creativity in conduct, autonomy from material conditions, or antideterminism" (Camic 1989, 89). What is more, once *Structure* was published, the notion of voluntarism never again appeared in any of Parsons' publications. Parsons signaled his intent in this regard: at the conclusion of the treatise he indicated that since he had now clinched his argument about action, the notion of voluntarism had become superfluous and could be dropped (Parsons [1937] 1968, 762, n. 1; Levine 2005b).

Instead, from the very year after *Structure* onwards, Parsons came to treat morality as instantiated in what he came to call "institutionalized norms." Analyses of professions in general, and the medical profession in particular, comprised his watershed work here. Thus, he used the variable of distinct institutionalized norms to account for differences in the orientations of businessmen and medical doctors, not the differences in the motives of those who choose to enter those vocations (Parsons [1939] 1954).

Parsons' work on the professions led to a generalized theoretic framework whose central concept became *boundary-maintaining social systems organized about sets of normative role expectations*. This work culminated in his first substantive synthesis, *The Social System* (Parsons 1951). In perhaps no major sociological work since Sumner's *Folkways* had the phenomena of moral norms figured so centrally in sociological analysis. In place of defensive rhetoric about the rightful place of moral considerations deployed in *Structure*, this target composition takes the significance of norms as a given and situates them as one of three constitutive elements in all action, along with psychological need-dispositions and cultural symbols. *The Social System* proceeds to make that element the centerpiece of analysis—treating systems of norms as the equivalent of social structure, analyzing diverse types of norms, and in a searching exposition that has barely been improved on in general theory to this time, laying out a schematic analysis of how norms are complied with, sanctioned, deviated from, altered, and overthrown. This phase of Parsons' work includes the effort to integrate the models of Freud and Durkheim regarding the formation of conscience.

Perhaps the best-known precipitate of this period was the schema of pattern variables, set forth to offer a comprehensive listing of alternative patterns of value-orientation. Although Parsons delineated these alternatives, he meant to do it only in the sense that social structures can embody one or the other of each pair of values. In the third phase, Parsons developed the notions of double interchange, the AGIL paradigm, the cybernetic hierarchy, and the media of interchange. The shift from voluntarism to a structural determinism comes full circle. The view of morality as an orientational and structurally constitutive concept becomes subordinate when identifying the functions of moral evaluative systems and other subsystems of action. The systemic functions of adaptation, goal-attainment, integration, and pattern maintenance drive the establishment of institutionalized norms rather than the vagaries of random cultural choices.

Yet barely had that node been formed when Parsons embarked on another departure, the model of societal evolution. This phase anchored the normative structures of societies in a process of systemic differentiation across world history. Although Parsons had dismissed the idea of social evolution in his first major work in 1937—an idea which remains anathema to most social anthropologists—he sought three decades later to reclaim it in ways that avoided the objectionable features of the earlier view: unilinearity, uniformity, and the valorization of evolutionary progress.[4] In his reformulation of evolutionary theory, Parsons emphasized the importance of different "stages" of evolutionary development, stating that "we do not conceive societal evolution to be either a continuous or a simple linear process, but we can distinguish among broad levels of advancement without overlooking the considerable variability found in each" (1966, 26). Broadly speaking, he distinguished three evolutionary levels—primitive, intermediate, and modern—identified by the scope of their "generalized adaptive capacity." By implication, he held that each evolutionary stage harbored a distinctive set of normative structures, a kind of claim most resonant with Durkheim.

In the final phase of Parsons' work, two innovations pertinent to the sociology of morality stand out. The first appeared in his effort with George Platt to analyze the American university. This effort offered a paradigm to identify and correct the manifestations at all four levels of the universe of action to a single action modality. This they designated as the Cognitive Complex offering a model for the normative sphere, which can be designated as the Moral-Evaluative Complex.

The other innovation is his testamentary model of the Human Condition. This model presented the most complex and inclusive synthesis of all components of action, and its environments. Incorporating what Parsons had long called the cybernetic hierarchy, the Human Condition paradigm located the entire complex of moral phenomena in a cosmic context, indicated the diverse ways and points where normative elements figured in the total scheme of things.

This concise overview suggests many points of departure to further inquiry, both into the Parsonian legacy and into an evolving sociology of morals. Two long-term trends stand out. One is the progression from a vague notion of the moral dimension of action to a complex, differentiated analytic scheme. The other marks a journey in which an initial emphasis on agency and voluntarism recedes progressively in favor of an increasingly complex objective analytic framework. That journey, we shall see, appears precisely the opposite of that traversed by Simmel.

Georg Simmel: From Multidimensional Determinism To Existential Voluntarism

Notably, Parsons excluded Simmel from the short list of European authors treated in *Structure*, an omission that has prompted investigation and debate. The reasons for that omission need not concern us here.[5]

What does concern us is the fact that Parsons began his lifelong journey into the normative dimensions of action with a call for a "voluntaristic theory of action." To a certain extent, this emphasis appears to be the opposite of Georg Simmel, who began with an emphasis on natural forces as the source of morality and capped his career by locating the source of binding morality in the tumultuous creativity of the individual will. Simmel's work on this subject is divided into three phases.

The first and only full-scale treatment of morality by Simmel appeared in his early two-volume monograph, *Einleitung in die Moralwissenschaft* (Introduction to the scientific study of morals) ([1892–3] 1991). Described by contemporary reviewers as "acute, ingenious, subtle, suggestive, and almost uniformly interesting" and "one of the least dogmatic treatments of ethics in existence" (Sidgwick [1892] 1994, 434; Thilly [1893] 1994, 637), the work is so lengthy and dense that only a sample of its insights and suggestions can be included here.

The *Einleitung* opens with a comment on the current state of the field of ethics. Like Durkheim's first major publication, *De la division du travail social* ([1893] 1984), and in the very same year (1893), Simmel's text claims that the contemporary study of morality requires the formation of a new discipline. Durkheim started his tract by announcing that it will be "above all an attempt to treat the facts of moral life according to the method of the positive sciences" ([1893] 1984, xxv); this requires a discipline that eschews both metaphysical methodology and the work of positive sciences that attend to other orders of phenomena. Similarly, Simmel began by asserting that the "plethora of moral principles and the contradictions within them and in their representations shows immediately that ethics has not yet found the certainty of methods which in other disciplines produces a harmonious juxtaposition and increasing accumulation of achievements," and thus it seems ready to move beyond the stage of abstract generalities, moral preachings, and wisdom literature to that of proper empirical treatment ([1892–3] 1991, 10).

Accordingly, what Simmel proposed is a complex field of ethics composed of three subdisciplines, formed to investigate moral phenomena by means of: (a) a psychological analysis of strivings, feelings, and attitudes that can be counted as moral or immoral; (b) the social scientific analysis of the causes or effects of the forms and contents of communal life that relate to individual morality; and (c) the historical analysis of how these moral phenomena developed from primitive to more modern forms.

As propaedeutic to such an emerging discipline, the *Einleitung* seeks to criticize the apparently basic concepts (*scheinbar einfachen Grundbegriffe*) with which ethics commonly works. It proposes to do so by revealing (1) their complex and multivocal character; (2) how the abstractions generated from them have turned into potent psychological forces; (3) how they can be linked with opposed principles that possess equal credibility; and (4) how they are entangled with psychological preconditions and social consequences (Simmel [1892–3] 1991, 11). In any case, Simmel added, such work of positive ethics cannot be used for the purpose of providing practical moral guidance.

In executing this task, Simmel analyzed the following concepts: the Ought (*das Sollen*); Egoism and Altruism; Moral Merit and Moral Guilt; Happiness; the Categorical Imperative; and Freedom. He concluded that no particular content of the Ought can be derived from an intrinsic analysis of the idea of obligation. Already here, however, Simmel does more than confine himself to disambiguating a complicated moral notion. At numerous points, he inserts trains of thought that adumbrate directions for the psychological, sociological, and historical accounts he advocates. Thus, he discusses the psychological preconditions of feeling a sense of obligation and the psychological consequences of adhering to such an unwarrantable belief. He notes the social consequences of conformity to and deviation from obligatory norms. In addition, he presents an evolutionary account of the origin of the given feeling of obligation, which stems from society's enforcement of directives that promote its preservation, a thought akin to William Graham Sumner's idea of the mores. Over time, the content of these enforced commands transforms into the sense that one is obliged to enact them: the necessary (*das Müssen*) becomes the Ought (*das Sollen*).

In treating both Egoism-Altruism and Happiness, the *Einleitung* dissects a number of common philosophical notions of the concepts. The views he demolishes include: egoism is more "natural" than altruism; the order in which egoistic and altruistic impulses originated relates to their respective moral valence; these concepts have fixed referents, since what is altruism on behalf of one group may be egoistic when compared to a more encompassing group; an act is accompanied by pleasure does not warrant the claim that the act was undertaken for the sake of pleasure; and there is an inherent connection between happiness and virtue.

The chapter on Merit and Culpability dissolves a number of commonplace notions. It distinguishes the merit of inner disposition from the merit of acts it leads to. It criticizes essentializing concepts, such as the concept of Character, which Simmel claimed, simply amounts to a sum of life elements and offers nothing but a name for something wholly unknown. The concept of Character, he argued, exhibits three common logical failings: (1) it confounds a problem with its solution; (2) it considers something explained when it resembles many other things (akin to the Platonic error of explaining some phenomenon through its "Idea," which is only a summing of similar phenomena); and (3) it considers character as simply that which does not vary. Thereby, it constitutes an illusory term, not useful for denoting empirical phenomena. Other fused concepts in need of differentiation include Merit and Duty, since not every fulfillment of duty is meritorious, and the validity of the will, since where the will originates and its goals have separate normative weightings. What is more, other notions associated with the dichotomy of merit and guilt run the risk of arbitrarily sundering a unified phenomenon. Merit and guilt are not independently variable phenomena but rather are reciprocally determined. The same is true of supposed conceptual opposites like egoism and altruism, sacrifice and value, the moral and the immoral, and moral depravity and moral elevation.

Simmel concluded with a brief comment on freedom, which is treated in its own right. What he pointed out here is that freedom entails a notion of some constraint, which one escapes. Since moral choices involve a conflict between moral and immoral impulses, the victory of either one over the other is liberating. Philosophers from Kant on have erred by restricting freedom to the moral side. Freedom, thus, is not prior to merit and guilt, but ensues from eliminating one impulse or the other. New lines of thought get opened in the chapter on Freedom. There, we find Simmel noting that contemporary ethics tends to bypass the problem of freedom altogether, a neglect that may indeed be warranted for prescriptive ethics, which needs only to enunciate norms and ideals, but that cannot be condoned for a new empirical science of morality. That discipline would need to raise questions such as the origins of the notion of freedom, which seems to guide so much human action.[6]

In a stunning final chapter, entitled "Unity and Opposition of Ends," Simmel elevated his occasional insights on paradoxes and contradictions into a general heuristic principle. He claimed that the entire field of ethics is subject to a number of counterintuitive critical postulates: that every moral position requires elements from its opposite; that there is a greater coherence among instances of immorality than of morality; and that insofar as moral phenomena can claim some sort of unity, it cannot be located in their subserving a common ethical goal but only in performing a similar psychological function. This exposition also proposes a general evolutionary formula for the evolution of moral principles. If we go back further in historical development, the narrower the circle we investigate, the more we find the appellation of morals restricted to narrowly circumscribed ranges of actions identified on the basis of concrete content. Evolution proceeds by extending the moral concepts to actions that evince them in some extended, weakened, or deviant form. Thus, if morality is first equated with negating the individual's interest on behalf of the clan, the concept is broadened when one views the pursuit of self-interest as also serving the general interest. Once the concept is broadened in this way, its more recent components can be emphasized in their own right, to the neglect or even dismissal of the original concept. The developmental pattern in question is represented graphically as follows: (1) a = A; (2) a = M = (A + B); (3) a = B; (4) a = N = (B + C); etc. This process of extension and mixing can lead to contents that have nothing to do with the original one. Even so, the (vain) efforts to find a concrete similarity among the disparate components of morality, and therewith an absolute moral principle, have produced valuable relative truths regarding the ethical life; a science of ethics must include the detailed treatment of such efforts (Simmel [1892–3] 1991, 293).

Just as Parsons broached the topos of voluntarism in *Structure* with éclat only to ignore the theme after, Simmel presented his searching "Critique of Fundamental Ethical Concepts" (as the work is subtitled) in the *Einleitung* only to forget about that method and its results thereafter. Indeed, when issuing an unaltered reprint of the work in 1904, he observed simply that the work was composed at a younger age and had been superseded by his later thinking, although he did not deny that the book continued to have merit. Even so, many of the distinctions, themes, and modes of logic forwarded in the *Einleitung* recur in Simmel's later work up to the time of his testamentary work, *Lebensanschauung* (*The View of Life*) (1918).

What is more, in addition to the semantic project of unpacking and clarifying the meanings of each of these commonplace terms, along the way, Simmel connected these moral principles to sociological observations that he would retrieve and develop later on. The moral sense, he claimed, originates from ideas instilled by society. Already in the early monograph *Über sociale Differenzierung* (Simmel

[1890] 1989), he had drawn on this assumption in analyzing diverse customs related to collective responsibility. The trend of moral evolution goes from lodging moral culpability collectively to making individual persons the subjects of moral codes.

When considering the social determinations of norms during the succeeding decade, however, Simmel departed from the blanket notion of "societal" determination of norms and the sense of obligation to a more differentiated representation of the social that he began to pursue in 1894 with his seminal programmatic essay, "The Problem of Sociology." In that essay, Simmel located the matrix of moral norms in diverse sociological formations. As presented in his compendium of such studies, *Soziologie: Untersuchungen über die Formen der Vergesellschaftungen* (Sociology: Investigations of the forms of association) (Simmel [1908] 1992), these appear in the chapters on conflict (Chapter 4), super- and subordination (Chapter 3), the persistence of social groups (Chapter 8), and the significance of numbers for social life (Chapter 2). In a presentation on sociability to the first meeting of the German Sociological Association two years later, Simmel set forth his final analysis of a social form and its grounding of norms.

Countering the common perception of conflict as a process that occurs at the expense of unity among conflicting parties, Simmel argued that conflict—both internal and external—is an element essential in promoting the cohesiveness of groups. In order to fight meaningfully, parties must agree on sets of norms that regulate the conflict. Beyond that, Simmel offered the intriguing suggestion that

> the intermingling of harmonious and hostile relations presents a case where the sociological and the ethical series coincide. It begins with A's action for B's benefit, moves on to A's own benefit by means of B without benefiting B but also without damaging him, and finally becomes A's egoistic action at B's cost.
> *(1971, 81)*

In the context of analyzing diverse forms of domination and subordination, Simmel offered a typology consisting of three forms: subordination under an individual, under a plurality, and under a principle. The last of these usually takes the form of law and represents a later feature of evolutionary development. For Simmel, as for Weber and others, the difference between obedience based on devotion to a person and obedience to an objective principle represents a transformation with far-reaching consequences. In this typology, Simmel treated principles in much the same way as others such as Freud, Durkheim, and Parsons treated cultural objects in need of being internalized as conscience.

A third venue for discovering ways that particular social forms engender norms may be found in Simmel's late essay on sociability ([1910] 1971).[7] By its very definition, interaction just for the sake of associating with others entails the expectation that extraneous interests, which constitute the basis for nearly all other interactions, are not to be engaged. This amounts to an aesthetic norm, as it were: it would not be appropriate to intrude instrumental motives into a purely sociable gathering. The case of sociability suggests that investigation of other interactional forms, with an eye to discerning norms immanent to them, may open up fruitful lines of inquiry.

The aforementioned examples show ways that particular associational forms can engender moral directives, often of a specific sort. In *Die Selbserhaltung der Socialen Gruppe* (The persistence of social groups) (Simmel [1898] 1992), which may be glossed as a purely functional analysis—perhaps the only such that Simmel ever composed—modalities of morality are treated explicitly with regard to their role in enabling groups to survive and persist over time. Building on the general notion of normative constraints from custom, represented in his first period, Simmel goes on here to identify morality, honor, and law as distinct types of norms where the demands of law encompass the narrowest range and those of morality the widest. Where law supports external ends through external means, morality supports internal ends through internal means and honor external ends through inner means (330–2). A comparable trichotomy appears in the essay on the significance of numbers for group properties, which offers a structural analysis that presents group custom as a mid-term, out of which morality and law become differentiated.

Simmel's final years were devoted to analyzing cultural forms rather than social forms, and to a number of philosophical inquiries. These culminated in his final work *Lebensanschauung*, which is said to represent a third major stage in his treatment of morality. This set of "four metaphysical chapters" (Simmel 1918) concludes with an essay that represents his final effort to come to terms with Kant's ([1785] 1964) notion of the Categorical Imperative, an effort he had already undertaken in Chapter 6 of the *Einleitung* and revisited in his 1906 lectures on Kant. Although full critical appropriation of this conception belongs to the domains of psychology and philosophy, one can readily connect the very availability of this model of autonomous individuated ethics with Simmel's wide-ranging analyses of the historical conditions that animate the quest for normative authentic individuality. These conditions include the emancipatory potential of the widespread use of currency and the personal freedoms promoted by what Louis Wirth, following Simmel, would gloss as urbanism as a way of life.

The foregoing barely indicates how Simmel's diverse writings stand to yield an abundance of ideas for an encompassing sociology of morality.

Robert K. Merton: From Anomie To Normative Ambivalence

Although Robert Merton may be the only student of Parsons for whom Simmel offered a cornucopia of seminal ideas,[8] his forays into the sociology of morality were stimulated initially more by Durkheim than anyone else. In the later work, however, Merton came to develop a perspective that increasingly resembled Simmel's.

The title of one of Merton's earliest publications featured a central concept of Durkheim's sociology of morality, anomie. Although in Durkheim's usage, the concept harbored a raft of ambiguities, ambiguities that were exacerbated in Merton's varied appropriations of the term (Levine 1985, 55–72), "Social Structure and

Anomie" (Merton [1938] 1968) directed the attention of sociologists to the potent influence of normative structures on human action and invited them to a productive research program that made use of current scientific methodologies. To be sure, much of the research inspired by that seminal paper had more to do with differential material opportunities in the situation of action, but it led as well to projects in which Merton applied the notion of normative structure to the professions and thereby spotlighted certain moral tensions under which professionals live.

Exemplars of these departures include "The Normative Structure of Sciences" (Merton [1942] 1973), which afforded a now classic paradigm of the complex of norms that govern the professional scientists—communalism, universalism, disinterestedness, skepticism, and, a later addition, originality.

From an initial commitment to revealing the moral structure behind institutions, an interest sparked by his tutelage under Parsons in the mid-1930s when Parsons himself was starting to explore the normative structure of professions, Merton paid increasing attention to internal contradictions that problematize conformity to norms, in line with the central syndrome of "social structure and anomie." His conceptualization of the "status-set" and the "role-set" (Merton 1973, 113–22) highlighted contradictions among diverse normative expectations that may not be readily visible. More pointed contradictions came to the fore in papers such as "Priorities in Scientific Discovery" (Merton [1957] 1973), which illuminated the conflict between normative goals and social rewards for conformity to them. The "Priorities" paper examines how the norm of originality evokes strivings that result in actions that contravene the established norms of science such as openness and communalism. Similar tensions appear in phenomena such as priority disputes among scientists; ways that famous scientists receive disproportionate credit for their contributions while lesser-known scientists receive less credit than their contributions merit—a phenomenon that Merton dubbed the Matthew Effect.

This attention to contradictory normative outcomes culminated in Merton's late development of "sociological ambivalence." This notion enabled him to conceptualize patterns of action in terms of socially structured alternatives presented in the form of binary oppositions. For example, he argued that scientists feel obliged (both) to publish quickly and to avoid rushing into print, to value humility as well as take pride in originality; physicians are socialized (both) to show sympathy as well as detachment; business leaders are expected (both) to project a sharply defined vision of their firm's future and to avoid narrow commitments which distance their subordinates, to provide special facilitates so departments can perform well, *and* to subordinate departmental goals to those of the whole organization (Levine 1978, 1278).

For Merton, then, this meant that social roles should no longer be analyzed as coherent sets of normative expectations, but as clusters of norms and counter-norms that alternatively govern role-behavior. To be sure, the notion of socially structured alternatives appears in Parsons' conception of the pattern variables and elsewhere. However, while Parsons wants to characterize social relations in terms of the dominant pattern alternatives that they embody, Merton stresses the significance of continuously operative counter-norms that alternate with dominant norms in defining social roles. This slight difference is big with theoretical implications. It means that opposition to a dominant norm need not be construed as deviant behavior, expressing some sort of alienated disposition, but rather as normatively valorized conduct. It thereby normalizes ostensible deviance, intensifies the compulsivity of behavior that veers to one of the normative poles, produces more openings for the identification of social conflict, and more readily leverages tendencies toward social change.

Toward Integration

The foregoing indicates that efforts to systematize a foundation for the sociology of morality would benefit from close attention to the work of the three thinkers examined here. My summary of some of their many contributions to a sociology of morality provides openings for evolving a paradigm for the field. The time may be ripe for constructing a Moral-Evaluative Complex cognate with what Parsons designated as the Cognitive Complex. At the very least, this chapter may serve to codify an array of plausible claims and suggestions yielded by their seminal forays.

Notes

1 Although *Structure* has often been thought to mark the starting point of Parson's publishing career, it actually followed a substantial series of significant published papers (Camic 1997).
2 As must not be forgotten, the ways that Parsons used the concept of positivism (and utilitarianism) reflect historical misunderstandings that have produced confusions based on semantic conflations. The term positivism, as Comte and his followers have defined it, designates only a methodological principle, not a particular view of human action (and indeed, Comte's view of motivation included the elements of valuation, sentiment, and altruism—another term he coined—as well as instrumental rationality). See Levine ([1957] 1980, xii–xv).
3 The epigraph to this volume consists of a quotation from Max Weber: "Jede denkende Besinnung auf die letzten Elemente sinnvollen menschllchen Handelns ist zunlichst gebunden an die Kategorien 'Zweck' und 'Mittel.'" (Any thoughtful reflection on the ultimate elements of meaningful human action is initially bound to the categories of "ends" and "means.")
4 Since some readers may be inclined to dismiss this exposition on grounds that employ the notion societal evolution is necessarily suspect if not illegitimate, the author emphasizes the importance of those revisions. In making them, Parsons was aided substantially by a seminal paper of Robert Bellah, "Religious Evolution" (1964)—and in fleshing out his evolving conception, by the assistance of Victor Lidz. Bellah's (2011) volume on religious evolution provides the most comprehensive realization of this conception to date.
5 The question has been discussed in a number of publications, including Levine ([1957] 1980, 1991b, 1994a, 1994b), Lidz (1993), and Alexander (1993).
6 For an important pioneering treatise in this vein, see Patterson (1991).
7 Late in the sense that it was the last of Simmel's original treatments of forms of association, and reprinted in his 1971 reprise of the sociological enterprise.
8 Besides Merton, who acknowledged his deep indebtedness to Simmel, one may include work by two of his prominent students, Coser (1956) and Caplow (1968). For a full account of Simmel's influence, see Levine et al. (1976a, 1976b).

7

THEORY AND PRAXIS IN PARSONS AND MCKEON

Richard McKeon and Talcott Parsons were two of the most powerful voices of the academic world in the twentieth century.[1] In themselves, their oeuvres remain continuously generative, but considered together, they stand to offer a fresh approach to certain vexing problems of contemporary thought. Although intellectual biographies of the two men reveal striking parallels, the philosophies which they created bring notably different slants to the interpretation of culture. If those different philosophies are brought together in a complementary way, I argue, they can shed light on the perennially problematic character of the relationship between theory and praxis.

Why McKeon and Parsons?

Like Emile Durkheim and Max Weber, Richard McKeon and Talcott Parsons were contemporaries who took no documented notice of one another yet whose works were mutually relevant. McKeon lived from 1900 to 1985, Parsons from 1902 to 1979. Both men received their undergraduate education on the East Coast—at Columbia University and Amherst College, respectively—and proceeded to pursue a critical portion of their graduate studies in Europe: McKeon at the University of Paris for three years (1922–5) and Parsons at the Universities of London and Heidelberg for a year each (1924–6). The early careers of both men were marked by strife and ambiguities of status. Such loud objections were raised when President Hutchins proposed the appointment of McKeon to the Department of Philosophy at the University of Chicago in 1930 that, for some time, McKeon refused to let himself be considered further there. When he did finally come to Chicago in 1934, it was through appointments in the Departments of History and Classics.

Although Parsons received his doctorate in economics and began to teach at Harvard in the Department of Economics, his intellectual inclinations led him to affiliate with Harvard's controversial new Department of Sociology in 1930. His appointment was backed by the chairman, Pitirim Sorokin, but the initiative was turned down by President Lowell, a decision reversed only after energetic intervention by supporters of the young Parsons. However, as Parsons' work developed in ways that Sorokin did not appreciate, the chairman came to turn against him, first by keeping him at the rank of instructor after an initial three-year appointment and later by opposing his promotion to tenure—which again was saved only through friendly colleagues outside the department.

After these turbulent beginnings, both men established themselves by the late 1930s at the institutions where each would spend the rest of his life as a prominent scholar, a powerful teacher, and a devoted citizen. In addition, both came to play significant roles as administrators, roles in which they would become renowned for instituting rare and innovative multidisciplinary programs. As Dean of the Humanities Division at the University of Chicago, McKeon established four interdisciplinary committees including the Committees on the History of Culture and on the Analysis of Ideas and the Study of Methods. Parsons established and long presided over Harvard's famed interdisciplinary Committee on Social Relations. Despite their predilection for interdisciplinary work, moreover, both men received the biggest awards within their home disciplines. McKeon served as President of the American Philosophical Association, Western Division, in 1952, and later as the APA Paul Carns Lecturer; Parsons was honored as President of the American Sociological Association in 1949.

The intellectual biographies of McKeon and Parsons also exhibit striking parallels. The early works of both men concentrated on recoveries and fresh interpretations of significant classical figures. McKeon focused on medieval philosophers such as Spinoza and, in particular, Aristotle; and Parsons on Werner Sombart, Alfred Marshall, Vilfredo Pareto, Emile Durkheim and, most notably, Max Weber. From early on, the work of both men included a mission to battle against naive positivist assumptions about science—this in the 1930s, long before it became fashionable to do so. Both also strongly objected to economistic theories of action by arguing for the interpenetration of cultural ideals with economic motives.

Perhaps most remarkable is the fact that each developed a succession of categorical schemes for organizing the universe of Western culture, initially in the form of dichotomies, then in trichotomies, and finally in quadripartite schemes that evolved in ever more involuted and exponential ways. McKeon began with an opposition between holoscopic and meroscopic methods in the late 1930s; proceeded to develop a semantic schema anchored in the tripartite distinction among logistic, dialectic, and problematic methods in the postwar years; then developed through the 1950s toward the complex four-by-four matrix illustrated in his book *Freedom and History* (1990, 250, 253). Parsons similarly began with a presenting dichotomy, between what he called positivistic and idealistic theories of action, in the 1930s; shifted to an analytic framework anchored in the three-part distinction among cognitive, cathectic, and evaluative orientations in the postwar years; and thence, through the 1950s and beyond, moved toward the complex four-by-four matrices illustrated in his books *Action Theory and the Human Condition* (1978, 382), and *The American University* (1973, 436). The scholarly credibility of both men stemmed from their pioneering work on classic authors and their analyses of substantive problems, like the bases of literary criticism or the meanings of freedom and history for McKeon, and the physician-patient relationship or the origins of fascism for Parsons. Many of their students remember them chiefly for their later fourfold schemas for organizing the universe. For McKeon, this included four commonplaces (things, thoughts, words, and deeds); four semantic variables (principles, methods, selections, and interpretations); four universal arts (interpretation, discovery, presentation, and systematization); and four modes of thought (assimilation, discrimination, construction, and resolution). For Parsons, this included the four subsystems of action (behavioral organism, personality system, social system, and cultural system); the four functions of all action systems (adaptation, goal attainment, integration, and pattern maintenance); and the four media of interchange (money, power, influence, and activation of commitments).

In a volume of essays on Parsons that were published in 1991, the editors conclude: "Parsons is one of the few genuinely modern and global minds of the twentieth century" (Robertson and Turner 1991, 17). That is surely true, and Richard McKeon is just as surely one of the few others. Although several other twentieth-century thinkers could be described as quintessentially modern, I can think of none who have been so resolutely global as these two. They were global in four senses. First, they were catholic in their intellectual sweep: McKeon ranged widely as well as deeply across all branches of philosophy from metaphysics, philosophy of science, and logic through moral and political philosophy and aesthetics and on to literature, education, and the history of culture. The scope of Parsons' investigations touched nearly every subfield of sociology from small groups, socialization, and medical sociology to large groups, organizational analysis, stratification, and sociocultural evolution. Beyond sociology, his learning and creativity ranged from biology, cybernetics, psychoanalytic psychology, and anthropology to economics, political science, and religion. Second, both provided a global perspective on world history, McKeon with his sweeping interpretations of the history of Western culture, Parsons with his daring reintroduction of a perspective of societal evolution. Third, both had a flare for architectonic issues; they stand almost alone in the twentieth century for turning repeatedly to questions regarding the global organization of the intellectual disciplines. Fourth, they were ecumenical in the sense of promoting international scholarly discourse; both played significant pioneering roles in linking American thought with European traditions and then in working during the Cold War years to build bridges between Western scholars and colleagues in the Soviet bloc.

Finally, both men left highly ambiguous legacies, legacies that remain "essentially contested." Both have aroused detractors who consider their lifetime reputations inflated and hold that little of their work will endure. Others claim that the detractors either have not read or certainly not understood their works, and that in due course these profound pioneers will come to be appreciated. Followers of McKeon claim he anticipated by decades, and in more sophisticated form, positions associated with deconstructionism and related movements of recent years, and Walter Watson (1991) has suggested that McKeon's writing seems written for future readers rather than for his contemporaries; while in the volume on Parsons mentioned earlier, Mark Gould argued that Parsons' *Structure of Social Action* of 1937 was published "sixty years ahead of its time" (Robertson and Turner 1991, chap. 5).[2]

The Semantic Project and the Voluntaristic Project

Behind the comprehensive philosophical schemas that McKeon elaborated, Watson has identified a core generative idea: "the idea of pluralism, that the truth, though one, has no single expression," and that philosophers "can be unified in communication and co-operation out of the need of consensus in a common ideology" (Watson 1991, 1; see also McKeon [1969] 1998). Like McKeon, Parsons strove to develop comprehensive schemas for analyzing the diversities of human experience. And beneath Parsons' theoretical edifices, one can also identify a core generative idea: the notion that human action is doubly animated, by dispositions to pursue goals through instrumentally rational adaptations and by dispositions to follow moral guidelines that ultimately express symbolic ideals (Alexander 1983).

These contrasting generative ideas are issued in philosophies of culture in which notably different conceptions of culture were embodied. For McKeon, the central axis of cultural variation was cognitive. Whichever categories he used to analyze culture, and in whatever direction his analysis turned, McKeon's take on culture turned mainly on the various cognitive forms through which philosophers and others apprehend the world. He anchored the sources of values in the truths and hypotheses about the world found in the "framework and conclusions of the natural sciences, the social sciences and the human sciences" (McKeon [1969] 1998, 431). Nearly every time that McKeon broached a discussion of some moral or political value, he treated the topic by examining differing cognitive representations of the value in question. Thus, in his luminous discussions of the concept of freedom, he analyzed the different meanings it assumed when treated by the dialectical method, the problematic method, or the logistical method (McKeon 1952), and showed how an initially ambiguous definition of freedom could be made unambiguous through semantic analysis of the principles, methods, and interpretations through which it is configured (McKeon [1966] 1998). Such analyses typically concluded by arguing that persons or communities can agree on common courses of action while holding different beliefs about the world.

What social scientists who study culture may find neglected in McKeon's work is a systematic analysis of the ways in which different value-orientations animate culture. And what McKeon omitted constitutes precisely the dimension that Parsons made the linchpin of his philosophy of culture. In an early essay, Parsons wrote: "The positivistic reaction against philosophy has, in its effect on the social sciences, manifested a strong tendency to obscure the fact that man is essentially an active, creative, evaluating creature" (1935, 282). This formulation displays Parsons' proclivity to equate human agency with a commitment to normative orientations. Thus, when analyzing the great systems of culture, Parsons concentrated on the types of value-orientations embodied in various societies, such as the particularistic-achievement value pattern of traditional China (1951, 195–8) or the value system of contemporary United States, which he described as "instrumental activism" (1989). The same was true when he analyzed microstructures, such as the roles of the physician, the parent, or the businessman.

In following his proclivity to emphasize value-orientations, some critics have argued Parsons did not pay the cognitive dimension its due (Warner 1978).[3] Thus, despite the array of meanings Max Weber associated with the concept of rationality, when Parsons discussed rationality, he limited it solely to its technological and economic usages; that is, to the form of instrumental rationality. This is not to say that Parsons did not make significant contributions to understanding the cognitive cultural institutions; simply consider his pioneering analyses of science, ideology, and philosophy in *The Social System* or the analysis of what he called the Cognitive Complex in *The American University*. Nor is it to say that McKeon failed to illuminate the role of normative symbols in promoting cohesion within communities or the rich diversity of meanings of terms like justice and freedom. The point here is that although both thinkers appear to be presenting comprehensive philosophies of culture, they end up treating culture in a somewhat one-sided manner, with McKeon making the cognitive dimension foundational to all else at the expense of the normative, and Parsons doing the reverse.

This tendency to reduce the cognitive or the normative dimension of culture to the other leads to a peculiarity that both philosophies have in common. McKeon, for all his celebration of human reason, offered us no criteria for evaluating the cognitive forms he so brilliantly analyzed; and Parsons, for all his celebration of human agency, gave us a philosophically impoverished conception of practice and the ways it can be informed by reason. For both of them, the domain of rational choice, understood not in the circumscribed sense employed by economists but in the classical sense of choice informed by reason, appears to be neglected. The central task of this paper is to suggest ways to remedy that neglect by pooling resources supplied by the two of them, with results that point to hitherto unexplored terrain.

Practice and the Theory of Action

Two of the announced goals of *The Structure of Social Action*, the grand synthesis which climaxed the early work of Parsons and propelled his subsequent work, were to rekindle belief in the efficacy of human reason and to restore appreciation for the role of ideals and norms in directing human conduct. The irony is that Parsons never linked these two objectives by explicitly discussing the relationship between reason and moral choice. The closest he came to attending to the question of the use of reason in directing action was when he analyzed the problems of the sociological profession (Parsons 1986), where he identified a need to separate the pure discipline of sociology, with its distinctive theoretical and research tradition, from sociological "practice" (his quotation marks). Such practice consists of the application of the discipline's findings to activities like helping disturbed people or enhancing industrial productivity. Parsons advocated the institutionalization of a role wherein professionals could work full-time as applied sociologists. Accordingly, he urged the profession to set up special structures to mediate the applied functions in order to protect the integrity of the pure discipline while maintaining high standards for its applications. Parsons presented his position on this matter without engaging in explicit philosophical argument; he simply presumed the importance of preserving the integrity of pure theoretical work and that the practical contribution of sociology would take the form of its "application."

This conception assumes a radical division within sociology between pure theoretical work and applied practical work, and it assumes that in this division, the theoretical work is cognitively superior to the practical and should be completed prior to its application. The model for this conception is that of physiology as a pure theoretic discipline in relation to medicine as its applied form, or between physics as a pure discipline and engineering as its applied form. One of the few voices within sociology to question this conception was that of Morris Janowitz ([1968] 1991), who glossed this view of the relation between sociology and practice as one that embodies an "engineering model." Over the past century this outlook has come to be accepted by the majority of professional sociologists, so in his remarks on the profession, Parsons was simply giving voice to a widely shared point of view.

Anyone schooled in the thoughtways of Richard McKeon would know better than to accept such an assumption uncritically. Although Janowitz was not so schooled, he had been influenced by McKeon's onetime mentor John Dewey. From Deweyan pragmatism, Janowitz derived an alternative he called the "enlightenment model," which blurs the distinction between pure and applied sociology and sees the sociologist not as an outside expert, but as part of the social process. Had Janowitz delved more deeply into Dewey's arguments, he might have been led to maintain that the notion of a cognitively privileged and antecedently secured body of theory was a superstitious relic, an obstructive vestige of the quest for certainty pursued by Western philosophy since Hellenic titles. Had Janowitz, not to mention Dewey, enjoyed access to the distinctions available from McKeon's semantic analyses of philosophic systems, he might have broached a still more differentiating critique. But even the limited degree of dissent which Janowitz expressed in his espousal of an enlightenment model was little heeded by the sociological profession. The engineering model probably remains the dominant orientation among professional sociologists to this day. I now consider what a portrayal of the relation between theory and practice that departs from the work of Richard McKeon might look like.

Six Views of the Theory-Practice Nexus

What is the right way to conceive of the relation between theory and practice? The import of McKeon's philosophy is that such a question must be asked, but it is absurd to expect there can be only one valid answer for it. Both terms are multiply ambiguous, and both their meanings and their proper relationship depend on certain generative assumptions that possess some inexpugnable degree of arbitrariness. What is more, when carrying out some inquiry about them, it is best not to restrict their meanings by imposing some rigorous definition in advance but to let their varying meanings unfold in the course of using them and seeing how they are used in different ways.

So instructed, I direct my inquiry to recovering the fundamental alternative ways of conceptualizing practical knowledge in relation to theoretic knowledge.[4] I find that relationship to take three distinct forms. Theory can be construed as *foundational* for practice, as *disjunctive* from practice, or as *inseparable* from practice. Each of these forms exhibits two primary variants. In examining these six views of the theory-practice nexus, let us begin with what is closest to us, the conception articulated by Parsons which is so widely shared that I call it the SPS position: the position of standard professional sociology.

The SPS position holds that theoretical knowledge is required to provide a rational foundation for practice in that it supplies scientifically warranted means to employ in pursuit of stipulated goals. Its classic formulation in modern philosophy is Kant's notion of the hypothetical imperative: if you want x, then you must do y. Max Weber's essays on objectivity and ethical neutrality contain the classic exposition of this position for modern sociology. Weber argued that although the goals of action could not be set by reason, pure science was needed for rational action by virtue of its capacity to provide not an authoritative selection of the best means toward one's goals but an analysis of the costs and benefits of various alternative means. This use of reason—as a calculus of optimal means—was what Parsons referred to as *instrumental rationality*, and in his own theory of action, it proved to be the only type of rationality he seriously considered.

There exists, however, another mode of using reason in which theoretical knowledge figures as foundational for practice. This mode might be designated as *diagnostic rationality*. In the mode of diagnostic rationality, theoretic reason provides ends for action by establishing standards of well-being for persons or collectivities. Here the analogy with physiology/medicine is taken not just to indicate the best means for attaining a goal, such as repairing a broken bone or relieving an aching back, but as a model for establishing criteria of a healthy organism. Theoretical science establishes limits within which an organism can survive and/or function adequately, such as by age and gender, and by normal temperatures and blood-pressure levels for various species and its subtypes. The practical application of this knowledge works to diagnose given specimens of the species to determine their level of health.

Within the social sciences, diagnostic rationality was pioneered by Auguste Comte. Comte insisted on regarding society as a natural being and advocated basing directives to action on prior theoretical knowledge about society's natural course of development. Armed with that knowledge, statesmen could assist society in reaching its normal state with the least pain and disruption. A century ago,

Freud and Durkheim both attempted to generate diagnostic criteria for directing therapeutic interventions with personalities and with societies, respectively. Both Freud and Durkheim used the medical model to legitimate a quest for scientifically grounded' knowledge of normal and pathological conditions in human conduct. Through studying social systems of a certain type, Durkheim argued, one could arrive at formulations regarding what conditions were normal to its existence and essential to its functioning.

In contrast to these views that base rational practice on a previously secured foundation in theoretical knowledge, there stands a quartet of positions that challenge the view of the theory-practice nexus. These positions also hold that efforts to reduce practical knowledge to a process of applied theory are misguided at best. Philosophers who articulate these four positions are Aristotle, Kant, Marx, and Dewey. Two of them see theory as a separate and distinct entity but not as an appropriate guide for practice, while the other two regard a disjunction between theory and practice as illegitimate.

The great architect of the disjunctive conception of theory and practice was Aristotle. McKeon helped generations of scholars grasp the several respects in which Aristotle worked to distinguish the theoretical sciences (*epistemai theoretikai*) from the sciences of human action (*epistemai pratikai*)—of ethics, economics, and politics. Those distinctions need to be made, Aristotle said, because every science needs to limit its attention to a certain class of things in order to demonstrate their essential attributes.

With respect to their subject matters: insofar as they deal with substances, the theoretical sciences contend with things that exist by nature, while the practical sciences work with a different class of things—*ta prakta* (things done). Actions do not occur by nature, they are made by humans (as are *ta poieta* [things produced], which form the subject matter of yet another group of disciplines, the productive sciences [*epistemai poietikai*]). Things existing by nature differ from human actions in two fundamental respects. Natural substances have an internal principle of change, whereas in actions, the principle of change is external to them in the will of the actor. What is more, the properties of natural substances are invariable, whereas human actions result from deliberate choice and so are variable.

The sciences of action differ from the sciences of natural substances in their methods as well as in their subject matters. The methods employed in studying natural substances include the establishment of true generalizations by means of induction and the demonstration of valid consequences by means of deduction. The propositions of natural sciences take the form of necessary universals because the essential characteristics of natural substances are invariable. For several reasons, the form taken by inquiry in the practical sciences diverges from that taken in physics. Since human actions are based on choice, not on natural necessity, their properties cannot be so securely grasped. What is more, because people differ so radically about what they consider good, the variety of opinions people hold should be taken into account when inquiring into the nature of good action. Finally, since the circumstances of action differ from situation to situation, knowing the best thing to do demands, above all, knowledge of particulars: what counts in practice is not general rules but knowing what to do to the right person at the right time to the right extent and in the right manner.[5]

Methods geared to demonstrating universal propositions are therefore out of place in the practical sciences. The method suited for determining the right course of action is what Aristotle called deliberation (*boulesis*). Inquiry proceeds by examining the diverse opinions people hold about an issue, and its successful resolution depends on traits of good character possessed by the deliberating parties. Deliberative excellence involves the selection of worthy ends and the determination of suitable means through sound reasoning in a moderate amount of time. The conclusions of deliberative inquiry cannot be expected to reach the precision and certainty attainable by the natural sciences, and it is the mark of an educated person to realize this.

Another difference between the two kinds of sciences concerns the faculties needed to prosecute them. The generalizations of natural science come from exercising the faculty Aristotle called intuitive reason (*nous*). Showing the logical consequences of those generalizations involves what he called scientific knowledge (*episteme*). On the other hand, deliberations about the good life involve a different sort of mental ability designated as *phronesis*, which may be translated as practical wisdom or prudence. In deliberating about laws and policies, a special variant of this, which he termed political wisdom (*politike*), is needed. In contrast to the states of mind that generate theoretical knowledge, *phronesis* is concerned with the "ultimate particular fact."[6] Perhaps we can refer to the kind of reason Aristotle claimed for practice as *deliberative rationality*.

Finally, the ends, or purposes, for which the two kinds of science are pursued also differ radically. The motivation for studying natural substances is to understand the world, for the sheer aesthetic pleasure and for the relief from ignorance such understanding affords. By contrast, the reason one studies human actions is for the sake of learning how to live well and how to cultivate the dispositions that promote good action, which is to say how to pursue the *aretai*, or excellences.

Kant also holds to a principled separation between the domains of theoretical and practical philosophy, but he does so for reasons that in many respects are the reverse of Aristotle's. For Kant, too, theoretical and practical knowledge differ in their subject forms, ends, and methods, but Kant fills these distinctions with radically different contents. Where Aristotle found the subject of practical science to be variable human actions, Kant found it to be a kind of law of freedom. Aristotle faulted theory as a guide to practical decision-making because of its universality and because the essence of practical wisdom is to understand particulars. Kant faulted knowledge of human conduct from a theoretical perspective as a guide to practice because merely theoretic knowledge of what humans in different societies actually do can not be universal enough to provide categorical imperatives for action. Where Aristotle found the method of practical philosophy to be a necessarily imprecise form of deliberation about variable things, Kant found it to involve a kind of reasoning that can yield apodictic certainty. Where Aristotle considered the end of practical philosophy to be the pursuit of happiness, or at least *eudaimonia*, Kant considered it to be knowledge of how to live in accord with duty. Kant's practical reason can thus be glossed as a kind of deontological rationality.

Although Aristotle and Kant took pains to distinguish the knowledge involved in rational practice from theoretical knowledge, both of them deemed it important to preserve theory as an independent and dignified domain. Aristotle lauded the pursuit of theoretic contemplation as the highest form of human excellence, and Kant celebrated the theoretical domain which Copernicus revolutionized and Sir Isaac Newton championed. In the views of authors like Marx and Dewey, however, to protect a separate, distinct, and privileged domain of theory is to promote obfuscation and mystification.

Although Marx acknowledged the historical existence of a distinct domain of theoretical knowledge separate from practical concerns, he considered that domain detrimental to human well-being. The division of labor is the great source of human alienation, and the division of labor really takes on this alienating form only at the point when mental work gets separated from physical labor. From that moment onward, intellect flatters itself that it has hold of something supremely important. Theoretical work becomes the activity of an elite group that is exploitative in several ways: by deriving support from the exploited labor of working-class people, by detracting mental energies from attention to the economic and social miseries of the populace, and by buttressing the position of an exploitative upper class.

For Marx, then, the disjunctive conception of theory/practice contributes to human self-alienation. Since true consciousness can only be consciousness of existing practice, there can be no legitimate basis for a principled separation between theory and practice. Rational practice begins with an acknowledgment of the true human need for eating and drinking, and clothing and housing. It follows with expressing oneself creatively in work—and any intellectual activity that does not minister to the satisfaction of these needs represents false consciousness of some sort. One might refer to the use of reason implicit in Marx's philosophy as sensuous rationality. Abstract theories of society are useless, distracting, or manipulative mystifications. "Social life is essentially *practical*. All mysteries which mislead theory into mysticism find their rational solution in human practice and in the comprehension of this practice" (Marx, cited in Tucker 1972, 109).

Like Marx, John Dewey interpreted the idea of a separate domain of pure theory as the residue of an elitist social structure. He, too, believed that the mysteries of pure theory find their resolution in human practice. But Dewey regarded the effort to establish a list of absolute human needs as itself a kind of alienation, just another byproduct of the age-old, all too human wish for certainty. Dewey eschewed any and all efforts to secure tentative foundations, including those lodged in a reified conception of practice or in antecedently established notions of history and societal structure.

In Dewey's view, theory is simply a name for a special kind of practice, so the quest for a theoretical knowledge either prior to or segregated from practice must be rejected as a reflection of human fears and uncertainties. Accordingly, Dewey aspired to develop a logic of inquiry that reveals the underlying unity of theory and practice. In science, as in daily life, action proceeds from undertakings that transform a problematic situation into a resolved one. In daily life, as in science, action gets initiated in situations marked by indeterminacy or conflict, in which difficulties prompt efforts to formulate problems, suggest hypotheses, and carry out activities designed to test those hypotheses.

What Dewey found harmful about disjunctive and foundational notions of the theory-practice nexus is not so much their ideological functions in upholding privilege but their effect in preventing the great resources of scientific intelligence from being harnessed for improving human experience. Against the notion of mind as a spectator beholding the world from without in a joyous act of self-sufficing contemplation, and against the notion that theory can disclose the characteristics of antecedent existence and essences, and therewith determine authoritative standards for conduct, Dewey propounded the view that reality itself possesses practical character and that this character is most efficaciously expressed in the fruition of intelligence. This notion of reason in practice is one he would call pragmatic rationality.

Playing with Pluralism

Inspired by the spirit of McKeon's approach to historical semantics, if not employing the terms of his schemas, the foregoing reflections challenge the hegemonic view of standard professional sociology as represented by Parsons. They subject the notion that pure sociology should inform practice through the logic of instrumental rationality to a fivefold critique.

From the viewpoint of diagnostic rationality, the SPS conception of the theory-practice nexus can be faulted for failing to provide norms about normal or healthy states. For example, it might lead one to apply propositions about group process to eliminating the authority of leaders, without considering whether or not authoritative leaders comprise a normal and healthy part of group functioning. From the viewpoint of deliberative rationality, that conception can be faulted for neglecting the importance of particulars in action and the imprecise nature of practical decisions—for example, looking for universally valid processes to heighten morale in organizations without considering the nuances of local life and the difficulties of verbalizing certain aspects of interpersonal rapport. From the viewpoint of deontological rationality, it can be faulted for shortchanging the ability of reason to provide normative injunctions independent of empirical circumstances using instrumental calculations to optimize the elimination of allegedly inferior peoples without considering whether there is not a rationally prescribed duty to resist such objectives. From the viewpoint of sensuous rationality, it can be faulted for deflecting attention from urgent social needs, spending millions to do research on poverty instead of on programs to alleviate poverty through job training and job creation. From the viewpoint of pragmatic rationality, it can be faulted for deriving its problems, concepts, and methods from antecedently formulated theories, when appropriate concepts and methods can only be identified as plausible responses to problems that emerge in indeterminate or conflictual situations. One example is when one brings a set of standard procedures demonstrated to enhance communication among staff members when the chief presenting problem in their office is a lack of time to deal with crises in their families.

This kind of work—identifying shortcomings in a position by appeal to the insights of plausible alternative positions—can be construed as any of the others with critical arguments from the remaining five. Yet, this is not the only way in which McKeon's work can be utilized, for it opens up at least two more advanced ways to employ a pluralistic vision. In these other modes, the point is not to engage alternative perspectives or principles in order to open up new ways of looking at a commonplace issue, but to see how those different positions relate among themselves. As George Kimball Plochmann has observed, "essay after essay of [McKeon's] begins with some variation on the theme that there are great discrepancies in the traditional philosophies, and it is important to lay them out in order to resolve them" (Plochmann 1990, 92). I shall call them, first, the mode of cyclical history, and second, following Watson's (1985) usage in *The Architectonics of Meaning*, the mode of "reciprocal priority."

McKeon exhibited the cyclical mode chiefly when representing the broad historical shifts of attention to different subject matters in Western cultural history. Originally shown in the opening pages of *Freedom and History* (McKeon 1952, 11–12),[7] he traced a series of epochal changes starting in the Hellenic period when philosophers debated about being—when the atoms of Democritus, the Ideas of Plato, and the substances of Aristotle were considered existent things which provided principles for science and had some bearing on morals and politics. In the succeeding Hellenistic epoch, philosophers tired of the inconclusive debates about being and shifted their focus to the nature of thought. Stoics, Epicureans, Academics, and Skeptics sought their basic principles in the criteria of knowledge, criteria by which truth or probability might be achieved. Under the spreading Roman rule, philosophers found epistemological debates as unfruitful as their predecessors had found metaphysical disputes and themes to examine how people talk and how people act. At the same time, Sextus Empiricus proceeded to analyze the signs used in various sciences, and Cicero appealed to consequences in practical action. The coming of Christianity reawakened interest in doctrines about being, a concern codified by St. Augustine. Then Boethius shifted attention to the problem of knowledge, after which Cassiodorus and Isidore of Seville engineered the linguistic turn and the court of Charlemagne revivified interest in philosophy by attending to problems of practical action. This cycle of shifts in subject matter, from being to thought to words and deeds, took place five times in the history of the West. It took place most recently in the cycle beginning in the seventeenth century, when modern science began with a new interest in the nature of things, after which Kant reoriented philosophy to the problem of knowledge, leading to our century with its interest both in the nature of symbols and the patterns of action and experience.

The cyclical mode offers an ideal type for a conjectural history of shifts of attention and emphasis. The operative principle is the notion that a certain approach gets cultivated until its fruitfulness is exhausted and its omissions become too glaring. How might one adapt such a conjectural grid to the vicissitudes of approach to the theory-practice mode in sociology during the past century? It began with some strong statements of diagnostic rationality—Durkheim's about normal and pathological states, Thorstein Veblen's about stage-appropriate conditions, and Pareto's about optimal equilibria. These were replaced by a concern for using social science to organize publics and inform public opinion, which can be seen in the statements of Dewey and Park from the 1920s. During the 1940s and 1950s, sociologists attained an unprecedented level of professional respectability and shifted to an appeal to instrumental rationality based on their specialized expertise. The 1960s saw a good deal of revolt against this engineering model and a renewed appeal to Marxian doctrines against dislocated instrumentality. The shortcomings of directly sensuous rationality became apparent in the 1970s and 1980s as writers like Jürgen Habermas came to emphasize deliberative rationality; others insisted that the horrors of Nazi genocide be confronted and invoked the need for deontological rationality.[8]

In addition to relating different approaches in terms of this model of cyclical manifestations, McKeon offered a model by which any given perspective could find some kind of place for the main thrust of the others. This kind of mutualized accommodation has been represented aptly by Watson's felicitous phrase, "reciprocal priority."

In the mode of reciprocal priority, one position is taken as central, and the others are confronted, redefined, and assimilated in accord with its perspective. So if we were to take the position represented by what I have called instrumental rationality, we could, in principle, find some way of accommodating each of the other five. Thus, from the viewpoint of instrumental rationality, diagnostic rationality might be criticized as purporting to advance scientific grounds for what are in fact conventionally based norms, but the norms it suggests could be used as goals for directing the analysis of means. Deliberative rationality would be criticized for leaving too much to opinion, since rigorous scientific methods are now available to assess various outcomes. However, this does not mean that the precision of physics can be expected in measuring human affairs, so their results must be stated in probabilistic terms. There is no reason why those results cannot be discussed by an informed public in open democratic process. Deontological rationality would be attacked for ignoring immoral consequences in its quest for rationally grounded motives for action, but its efficacy in setting the normative ground rules for honest inquiry and open discussion would be acknowledged. Sensuous rationality would be faulted for failing to appreciate the complexities of action situations and human dispositions, but its caution about getting lost in alienated procedures could be appreciated. Pragmatic rationality would be hailed as a close ally. It would perhaps be faulted only for failing to appreciate that to tie optimal actions so closely to the particularities of situations is to undermine the quest for generalizations about factors that structure the contexts of action.

Confronted with a plurality of positions about the relationship between theory and action—or anything else—then, the philosophy of Richard McKeon opens up the three options we have just considered: to use the other positions to generate criticisms of the one chosen, to see them in a cyclical progression as giving rise one to another, and to use a chosen position to translate others so as to assimilate their congenial features while rejecting their incompatible ones.

The work involved in pursuing these options can demand a great deal in maturity of mind and strength of intellect. But there is some sense in which one responds to this work with amusement, regarding it as some sort of game—which is why I have called this section "Playing with Pluralism." There remains, however, something ultimately unsatisfactory about it; namely, its apparent difficulty in providing any rational ground for choosing one position over another. McKeon's philosophy seems to be excellent for clarifying the cognitive alternatives in our culture, and certainly consistent with the criticism of degraded versions of those alternatives, but provides no criteria for selecting one alternative or another.

Selecting a Mode of Thought

Indeed, that does seem to be the prime weakness for which this philosophy has been faulted. The only advice McKeon ever gave about which approach to select was his reported comment that one picks an approach "that feels most comfortable" (Plochmann 1990, 91). His indifference in this regard parallels Max Weber's advice regarding ultimate values: only hearken to your inner demon. But what if you have no clear demon; what if two demons are warring in your breast; what if you suspect that your demon is inappropriate due to changing circumstances; what if new prophets appear or forgotten truths are recovered; what then?

McKeon's failure to specify criteria for selecting a cognitive approach may be connected with his relative inattention to the normative dimension of culture. This can be clarified by considering some features of Parsons' theory of action. In an earlier phase of work on culture, Parsons analyzed cultures with respect to the general value-orientations they embodied, values to which he gave such names as universalistic-ascription and particularistic-achievement patterns. In later work, he came to focus on the generic needs of boundary-maintaining systems of action, needs which he came to refer to in terms of the functions of adaptation, goal attainment, integration, and pattern maintenance. Different value-orientations, then, came to be viewed as differentially relevant to one or another of these generic system functions.

Through the same logic that relates the selection of values to the functions of action systems, one can also find criteria with which to assess the differential relevance of diverse cognitive approaches. Let us return to the authors whose views we sketched above and encapsulate their respective approaches to the theory-practice question by referring to the different meanings they ascribe to practice.

For Aristotle, practice refers to a human process involving choice, and the choices are made with respect to some end or purpose. Since all human activities aim at some good, and the higher or more general good directs the lower or more particular goods, the chief task of practical philosophy is to articulate the ideal ends of human action. In *Ethics*, this turns out to be the cultivation of the *aretai*, or human excellences; in *Politics*, the establishment of laws will promote justice as well as the cultivation of excellence. Durkheim saw a similar agenda for sociology. Although he differs from Aristotle in rejecting the notions of common opinion as a point of departure for discourse about the good, he aspired to use his social science in practice by establishing conceptions of the normal and the pathological that will provide the reasonable ideals toward which human decisions should be oriented.

For Kant, practice also refers to human action that is subject to choice. Kant's emphasis, however, is on the subjection of those choices to imperatives that guarantee freedom—of the inner exercise of will in ethics; of the external exercise of will in jurisprudence. The task of a philosophy of practice, accordingly, is to ground the principles which generate ethical and juridical notions.

The meaning of practice changes considerably in Marx. For Marx, practice refers to the satisfaction of human sensuous needs. The task of a philosophy of practice thus is to show how those needs are historically met and frustrated, and what must be done to overcome those obstacles to their complete satisfaction. Dewey also connected practice with the satisfaction of human needs, but what Dewey understood by practice differs from what Marx meant by the term. Practice for Dewey consists of efforts to cope with anything that impedes the enjoyment of experience, whether it be of a material or an intellectual character. Dewey's formula for practice is couched not as the satisfaction of needs, but the solving of problems. That formula would also cover the kind of practice entailed in Max Weber's notion of instrumental rationality.

The question now before us is whether it is possible to determine if one of these meanings and its attendant agenda is superior to another. I have argued that it is not possible to do so without departing from the limits of McKeon's philosophy, but that such a determination could be derived from the conceptual resources of Parsons' theory of action. An immediately transparent way to do so would be to make reference to familiar Freudian schema for analyzing the parts of the personality. The part of personality that presents bundles of imperious needs that clamor for satisfaction Freud called *das Es* (the id). Another part deals with the solution of problems posed by the relations among the different parts of the personality and its relations with the reality outside the individual, *das Ich* (the ego). Yet another part confronts the individual with duties and norms that are to be obeyed, *das Über-ich* (the superego). Finally, what he sometimes designated as a part distinct from the superego, what Freud called the ego-ideal, provided general ideals for the person to follow.

While Parsons accepted this schema for the analysis of psychic structure, he interpreted it as a refraction at the level of the personality system of the four-function schema that pertains to all systems of action. The ego deals with the function of adapting to reality in order to attain goals. The id provides general motivation to resources available to energize action. The superego is concerned with normative integration, and the ego-ideal with pattern maintenance. What Parsons offers to a philosophy of culture, then, is a way of connecting different dimensions and systems of cultures with the satisfaction of different kinds of systemic needs. At the global level of culture, he connects the functions of adaptation with science, of goal attainment with art, of integration with ethics and law, and of pattern maintenance with religion.

Returning to the construal of meaning at the personality level, we could say that Aristotle's concern with excellence and Durkheim's with standards of health and normality represent alternate approaches to the specification of ego ideals, which afford alternate ways to fulfill the function of pattern maintenance. Kant's concern with the specification of norms corresponds to the superego of the individual, fulfilling what Parsons called the function of normative integration. Marx's identification of practice with the satisfaction of needs corresponds to one ego-id interface, that involving the function of goal attainment; while Dewey's identification of practice with problem-solving and the SPS position correspond to another ego-id interface, the identification resources within the personality and the general system function of adaptation.[9]

Parsons' schema thus suggests a rational way to select one of the cognitive modalities so brilliantly typologized by McKeon. If the system problem concerns adaptation or resource generation, use instrumental or pragmatic rationality, for that is the kind of reasoning that specifies the costs and benefits of alternate means. If the problem has to do with goal attainment, use sensuous rationality, for that is the kind of reasoning that applies to whether or not resources have been effectively mobilized to satisfy needs. If the problem concerns illustration, use deontological rationality, for that is the type of reasoning related to compliance with obligatory norms. If it has to do with pattern maintenance, use deliberative or diagnostic rationality, for that type of reasoning clarifies the ultimate values which govern the system's orientation.

It should be clear that the above suggestions are offered in an illustrative and exploratory mode. Whatever the status of these particular suggestions, I hope the way of thinking they configure indicates what might be gained by connecting the analyses of values Parsons found embodied in action systems with the diversity of cognitive orientations McKeon identified in philosophical outlook.

Notes

1 An earlier version of this essay was presented at the *Conference on Pluralism and Objectivity in Contemporary Culture: Departures from the Philosophy of Richard McKeon*, The University of Chicago, March 13–14, 1992. For assistance in its revision, I am indebted to Craig Calhoun and Doug Mitchell.
2 Beyond debates about their enduring value, the works of both men have been beset by controversies regarding the extent to which their oeuvres are unified or not. Watson depicted this matter in the form of a double paradox: McKeon's work proceeded by stages, inspiring students who distinctively manifested the emphasis of each stage, yet McKeon claimed his work was the same throughout, only to contradict himself by referring at other times to its continual development and novelty. Similarly, Parsons had

followers who worked chiefly with the ideas of one or another stage, some of whom accused him of betrayal for abandoning earlier positions as he evolved new ones. Parsons himself claimed that there was an essential unity in his lifelong effort to develop a comprehensive theory of action, although as his theory evolved, he kept referring to what he called radical new insights and fundamental breakthroughs in this theory.

3 However, Alexander (1983, 460–2), offers trenchant argument to show that Warner overstated this criticism.
4 Although the taxonomy that follows is my own, not McKeon's, the type of thinking it embodies has clearly been inspired by McKeon.
5 Aristotle, *Nicomachean Ethics*, 2, 6, 1106b20–24; 2, 9, 1109a25–29.
6 Ibid., 6, 1141b 14–22, 1142a 23–28.
7 See also "A Philosopher Mediates on Discovery" (McKeon [1952] 1987).
8 Levine (1995) applies this cyclical mode in another context—to interpret a sequence of shifts in the types of narrative used by sociologists over the past century—including Parsons' *The Structure of Social Action*—to represent the history of their disciplinary tradition.
9 On this point, my gloss on the Freudian schema cuts across that of Parsons.

8

FREUD AND UESHIBA

Pioneers of Therapeutic Human Interaction

Conceptual understandings about the martial arts lag behind what we do in practice. In spite of the historic shift from viewing martial arts training from techniques of accomplishing something to ways of being—available concepts fail to do justice to what we know from the experience of training and teaching budo. We know, for example, that we do not practice aikido as separate individuals but almost always in connection with others. And yet, when we think about the essence of the aiki experience, we typically do so with an eye to the improvement of personal character through becoming more accomplished *nage*s.[1] Although that perspective is of course valid, exclusive reliance on an individual-centered perspective overlooks the special properties of the *interactions* involved in this joint practice.

If that is so, we might take a moment to consider the *uke-nage* transaction as an instance and a metaphor for general interhuman relations. To examine that transaction fully requires shifting from perspectives centered on individuals to perspectives centered on interactions—from viewing aiki transactions as processes of mutual communication rather than as something that one person does to another.

An interactional model of the aiki transaction can take different forms. I propose two of them. For one thing, aiki transactions offer a paradigm of therapeutic relationships of all kinds. In this paradigm, *uke* is seen as sick, as a patient. In developing this interpretation I draw, in particular, on the insights and models of Talcott Parsons regarding the "doctor-patient" relationship. In a different vein, I conceive *uke* as an example of the role of dynamic creator. Pursuing this notion will take us toward a paradigm that seeks to combine elements from Lao Tse, Friedrich Nietzsche, and Martin Buber.

My remarks, then, fall into three sections: (1) shifting away from focus on single individuals to discourse about social interaction; (2) interpreting aiki transactions as parallel to patient-doctor relationships; and (3) viewing aiki work as modeling the interactions between creators and receptors.

Paradigm Shift: From Individuals as Such to the Interaction of Parties

To ground my advocacy of a shift from an individual-centered to an interactional perspective on aikido, I need to call on a different sort of *waza*: the history of social theory. This history directs us to observe that the greatest part of human thought assumes that the proper subject of philosophical, spiritual, and scientific investigations about humans should be the concrete individual. That assumption appears in three major venues.

1. We find, in all cultures, a program of human improvement directed to the individual. In this perspective we find doctrines that regard the person as an entity to be shaped by right discipline; or ennobled by purifying practices; or edified by proper enlightenment; and the like.
2. In Western moral philosophy, we find a tradition of thought, originating with Thomas Hobbes, that bases its analyses of social phenomena on a concept of the individual as an organism moved by desires, pursuing utilities, and guided by interests. Sometimes referred to as "utilitarianism," this perspective has gained renewed currency with the ascendance of "economism" in the past few decades.[2]
3. Finally, we find a view of the human individual that derives from philosophers like Rousseau, Goethe, Emerson, and Nietzsche—the individual as a subject whose nature is to be expressed, whose personal growth is to be cultivated, and whose creative urges are to be satisfied. This view is sometimes formulated as an effort to promote the cultivation of individuality, a form of modern individualism that has been contrasted with the libertarian individualism championed by thinkers of the Enlightenment (Simmel [n.d.] 1957).

In reaction to these formulations centered on individuals, voiced above all by thinkers of the British and German traditions, a number of French thinkers counterposed the notion of "society" as a phenomenon whose natural properties and moral values could not be reduced to those of individual actors. Foremost among these thinkers were Montesquieu, Rousseau, Comte, and Durkheim. These thinkers of the French tradition espoused what has been referred to as a notion of "societal essentialism" (Levine 1995). (Modern debates between proponents of societal essentialism and those of what has been called "atomic naturalism" recapitulate older metaphysical debates between nominalists and realists.)

This opposition between the individual and society dominated nearly all of Western social thought. There have, however, been two striking exceptions, which emerged toward the end of the nineteenth century. In Germany, philosopher Georg Simmel interposed between those polar terms the notion of "interaction," a domain that had properties, he insisted, that were distinctive and *sui generis*. In the United States, John Dewey and G. H. Mead collapsed the distinction in favor of a notion of socially constituted and societally constituting selves. For Mead, the crucial ingredient of this process was the acquisition and use of language. Both the ability to participate in social interaction and to construct a self-conception, Mead argued, depends crucially on the ability to grasp and internalize the meaning of external objects as symbols. This central process suggests a formulation that works better in German than in English: the birth of dialogue (*Gespräch*) out of the spirit of language (*Sprache*).

Reaching back to Mead's seminal work, Jürgen Habermas retrieved the notion of a form of rationality that he called *dialogical*, which he contrasted with the monological rationality that had previously formed the subject of philosophic discourse (Habermas 1984). Well before Habermas, however, the notion of dialogue had been thematized and made central by Martin Buber, whom I regard as one of the philosophers most closely attuned to the Aiki Way. Buber's intellectual development traverses the shift in paradigms of which I have been speaking. He began as a devotee of Nietzsche, from whom he acquired the ideal of intense transcendent experience. Buber became, as his biographer Paul Mendes-Flohr aptly put it, an "*Erlebnis*-mystic." At the University of Berlin he joined the Neue Gemeinschaft, a fraternity dedicated to pursuing the "Dionysian worldview" which Nietzsche celebrated.

At the same time, Buber's studies with Simmel at the University of Berlin planted seeds for a transition away from an exclusive focus on the individual self. Simmel's insistence that psychologistic explanations of interaction are inadequate, converted Buber to a perspective in which the interhuman (*das Zwischenmenschliche*) figures centrally. The first step of this transition appears in Buber's introduction to Simmel's essay *Die Religion* (1906) published in *Die Gesellschaft*, a series which Buber edited. In this introduction, Buber endorsed Simmel's view of the discipline of sociology, employing Simmelian terms like *Formen der Beziehung, Wechselwirkung, Vergesellscghaftung* (forms of relation, interaction, association) and affirming Simmel's ontological point:

> *Das Zwischenmenschliche* is that which occurs between (*zwischen*) men; in *some ways it is not unlike an impersonal, objective process*. The individual may very well experience *das Zwischenmenschliche* as his "action and passion," but somehow it cannot be fully ascribed or reduced to individual experience. For *das Zwischenmenschliche* can only be properly comprehended and analyzed as the synthesis of the "action and passion" of two or more men.
> *(Cited in Mendes-Flohr 1989, 38–9)*

For Simmel, the concept of *forms of association* served to carve out a distinctive domain for the new academic discipline of sociology. Reproducing Simmel's argument in 1906, Buber affirmed: "Sociology is the science of the forms of *das Zwischenmenschliche* ... [forms such as] super- and subordination, cooperation and noncooperation, groupings, social rank, class, organizations and all types of economic and cultural associations, both natural and normative" (cited in Mendes-Flohr 1989, 39).

In spite of this new ontological vision, Buber did not endow social interaction processes with any particular moral or spiritual qualities. He continued to locate transcendence in the sphere of *Erlebnis*, of personal life experienced with the utmost intensity and integrity. Indeed, it was his enthusiastic engagement in the war spirit that brought to Buber, as to so many other German intellectuals of the time, an unprecedented intensity of transcending experience.

What turned Buber away from his war enthusiasm and his idealization of intense personal experience was a traumatic exchange with his close friend Gustav Landauer in May 1916 (in his new family home at Heppenheim, not far from Schweinfurt). Landauer was one of the few German intellectuals who opposed the War strenuously. After his visit with Buber, Landauer wrote a letter in which he excoriated Buber for the moral lapse of indulging in militaristic sentiments. Mendes-Flohr has argued that Landauer's critical letter occasioned a *volte-face* in Buber and wrote:

> In Buber's writings subsequent to the spring of 1916, we notice three new elements: an explicit opposition to the war and chauvinistic nationalism; a reevaluation of the function and meaning of *Erlebnis*; and a shift in the axis of *Gemeinschaft* from consciousness (i.e., from subjective-cosmic *Erlebnis*) to the realm of interpersonal relations.
>
> *(1989, 102)*

From that time on, Buber expanded his conception of interpersonal relations in ways that connected it with the wish for transcendence. He came to sacralize what Simmel's lectures had identified simply as a sociological form.[3] He came to find in the relation between "I" and "Thou" an instantiation of ultimate values. In 1914, according to Mendes-Flohr,

> Buber, the *Erlebnis*-mystic, spoke of religiosity as a tendency in man that seeks to actuate God's realization; by securing the creative integrity of one's personality one acts to renew the cosmic harmony. In 1919, Buber defined religiosity as the human disposition that affects the realization of God through the establishment of authentic relations: "Whenever one man joins hands with another, we feel [God's] presence dawning (*aufkeimen*)."
>
> *(1989, 115)*

In sum, Buber had come to find in *das Zwischenmenschliche* the venue for self-transcendence that he had previously sought in Nietzsche's appeal for a peak experience. In this, he later recalled, he was harking back to Ludwig Feuerbach. For Feuerbach, he noted, man

> does not mean man as an individual, but man with man—the connection of *I* and *Thou*. "The individual man for himself," runs his manifesto, "does not have man's being in himself, either as a moral being or a thinking being. Man's being is contained only in community, in the unity of man with man—a

unity, however, which depends only on the reality of the difference between I and Thou."

(Buber [1938] 1965, 147–8)[4]

Buber's journey thereby brought him to a point of fusing the interactionist model of Simmelian sociology with the self-transcending ecstasies of Nietzsche. The way to such heights was to be obtained by a concentrated, open, and genuine kind of communication between two subjects. Buber's notion of genuine dialogue between two committed subjects offers precisely the kind of model of open communication that we strive to attain in the practice of aikido.

The possibilities of such interhuman encounters are endless, just as possibilities of *uke-nage* communication are endless. I turn now to examine two sets of possibilities that are manifest in aiki interactions, forms resonant with our experiences in everyday life. One of those possibilities is evoked when the person who initiates the interaction presents himself as or is perceived to be sick.

Uke as a Patient, *Nage* as Healer: Aiki Interactions as Therapeutic Work

There are precise parallels between the therapeutic transaction and the aiki transaction. This effort draws inspiration from three sources. First off, I was struck by how many of those who were initially drawn to the work of Aiki Extensions were themselves psychotherapists or bodyworkers with therapeutic consequence. A number of practitioners claimed to be securing therapeutic results by using aikido techniques or at least aikido-inspired ideas. Indeed, some of them reported accomplishing more by doing aikido with their patients than through any standard therapeutic techniques in which they had been trained.

Within the non-aikido community of therapists, moreover, I took note of the growing import of those who construe the psychotherapeutic situation in terms of interpersonal process. An earlier proponent of this approach, Jacob Moreno, inventor of sociometry and psychodrama, had in fact acknowledged an explicit indebtedness to Georg Simmel, and a number of psychologists were inspired by the pioneering work of Harry Stack Sullivan, who defined the therapeutic experience as essentially constituted by interpersonal relationships.

In pursuing these leads I was struck by parallels between the founders of these two practices, Sigmund Freud and Morihei Ueshiba, and Figure 8.1 schematizes a few of these parallels. Both men successfully completed rigorous training in conventional disciplines in young adulthood and then, in their early forties, had breakthroughs associated with intense emotional experiences that led them to found new disciplines and to renounce early martial ambition fantasies (Levine 1985). They were also charismatic figures whose new disciplines—and prophetic postures—inspired international movements which they headed. Moreover, Freud and Ueshiba continued to evolve beyond their mature breakthroughs, remaining active and productive well into their eighties. Both had disciples who trained with

Charismatic Founder	Sigmund Freud (1856–1939)	Morihei Ueshiba (1883–1969)
Cultural Context	biologism	martialism
Disciple	head of school head of ryu	director of institute leader of organization
Local Head	supervisor	sensei
Role of Teacher	analyst	sempai/nage
Role of Student	patient, client	kohai/uke
Secessionists	Jung Adler	Tomiki, Tohei

FIGURE 8.1 Parallels between Psychoanalysis and Aikido

them along the way and went on to transmit the teachings of that phase as *the* orthodox teaching. They were survived by a number of disciplines whose competitive strivings introduced dissent in what they each hoped would survive as unitary movements (Beaulieu 2005).

Parallels in their substantive teachings are no less striking. Freud and Ueshiba both propounded an ethic based on nature and respect for the natural propensities of humans rather than on some transcendental conception. Conceptions of natural energetic forces grounded their teachings. Jonathan Lear's words about psychoanalysis apply to aikido: "Psychoanalysis works both against a devaluation of empirical life and for a reintegration into the flow of life of patients who have been thrown off their middle" (Lear 2000). Both Freud and Ueshiba identified the sources of human aggression and martial combat in the psychic disposition of humans rather than in culture and social structure. Both illuminated ways in which inner discord gives rise to external discord. Both devised training programs to alleviate inner discord, programs that focused on a slow process of becoming more integrated (inner harmony) as a way to promote external harmony as well as personal freedom.

Above all, I suggest, both of them invented practices whose meaning they did not fully comprehend, practices which evolved nontrivially through efforts of later practitioners. Others have wondered about this. Psychoanalytic theorist Edgar Levenson confessed that

> analysts of all persuasions continue to treat all of their patients with a considerable degree of success ... and yet are hard put to know exactly how to talk about what it is they do when they do what they know how to do. This ineffable competence can be defined as the *praxis* of psychoanalysis.
>
> *(1983, 6)*

And one of Ueshiba's students, Anno Sensei, wondered if what the Master created had not evolved beyond budo, or martial arts, altogether (Anno 1999).

Levenson himself attempted to identify the obscure secret of good therapeutic praxis. He described it as a "deep structure of cognition ... [whose] efficacy, no different from that of other forms of propagandizing influence, depends on its resonance to deep structures of thought" (Levenson 1983, 89). In contrast, I want to suggest that there is *an unconscious structure built into the interactional structure of the therapist-client relationship*, one that is cognate with what Talcott Parsons identified half a century ago as the unconscious structure built into the doctor-patient and many other kinds of socially reintegrative relationships. I believe that both Freud and Ueshiba, through their intuitive genius, created structures whose true significance has only begun to be visible through generations of work since their mature formulations.

During the 1950s, Talcott Parsons came to theorize in different ways the logic of what he termed double-interchange paradigms. The template for this schema came from the depiction of interactional flows of the economic system. Figure 8.2 shows the familiar schema of this flow in economic exchange, where one party offers labor or its equivalent for goods or their equivalent. For Parsons, this schema of double interchange offered a template for exchanges among subsystems of action at all levels. He did so unaware that Simmel himself had posited the advantage of doing this when he suggested that "most relationships among men can be considered under the category of exchange" ([1907] 1971, 43).

Prior to presenting this general model of systemic interchanges, Parsons had offered a cognate schema of interchanges in his analysis of the system of medical practice in *The Social System* (1951). In that work and related writings of the period, Parsons analyzed the virtually subliminal structuring of responses of doctors and patients. He did so along lines he would employ later when discussing comparable dynamics in the socialization of children. The net effect of all this was to highlight the unwitting structuring of processes by which the motivations of persons with needs for social integration could be mediated by occupants of roles with resources suited for that task.

With just a little reflection, one can see how closely the elements of the paradigm of medical practice resemble the elements of the *uke-nage* interaction system. Figure 8.3 brings out the main aspects of these parallels.

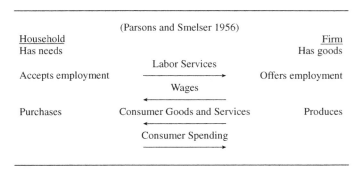

FIGURE 8.2 Double Interchange in the Economy
Source: Parsons and Smelser (1956)

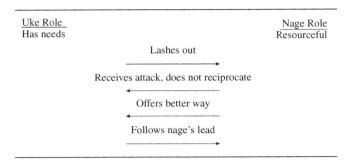

FIGURE 8.3 Double Interchange in the Aikido System

What this represents is that the script for *uke*, like that of the patient, is to express his feelings openly. In aiki practice, this is manifest in the advice to "attack sincerely." That is the "basic rule" of the psychoanalytic interview, just as it is a basic rule of aiki practice. In response, the task of the therapist/*nage* is to accept that expression, without getting upset, letting himself be hurt, or reciprocating. The therapist/*nage* then moves to resolve the situation by guiding the client/*uke* in a tonic direction. In response to that, the client/*uke* takes responsibility for changing his patterns by moving in that new tonic direction. This basic schema has been refined in many ways by experienced therapists, just as experienced senseis have a repertoire of increasingly subtle ideas.

Before discussing them, let us step back a moment and note that in order to adapt all of these double interchange paradigms to real situations, one more thing must be added: a starting point or a presenting situation. For the therapeutic situation, two conditions have been identified. One is the setting of the therapeutic interview. It must be defined by ritually demarcated boundaries in time and space, a condition that affords a safe and secure therapeutic "playground" for the client, as Freud himself called it. In aikido, the "playground" in which the *uke* and *nage* carry on is similarly constituted, through the ceremonial marking of boundaries in time (bowing in and bowing out of class) and space (bowing on and bowing off the mat).

The other condition concerns the state of being of the therapist, who is expected to embody a higher degree of integration and whose mind is to be marked by "evenly hovering attention." Similarly, the *nage* in aikido is expected to strive for a "centered" state of being and to maintain a mental attitude marked by "soft vision." In that frame of mind, both therapist and *nage* can actually initiate the interaction with a "leading" move. The therapist can "lead" the client to open up with a remark such as "you seem upset today" or simply "how are you feeling?" The alert *nage* can sense a coming attack and extend an arm to draw out the imminent energy that the *uke* itches to deliver.

Once the interaction begins, a number of subtle responses are likely to be involved. It is hard to imagine the sense of freedom, self-acceptance, self-confidence, and growth that may come in the wake of the *uke*'s feeling free to express anything she wishes, or the *uke*'s freedom to attack with full sincerity. There is also an added boost for the client/*uke* on those rare occasions when they get through to one of the therapist's/*nage*'s vulnerable spots. In addition, that the client can be listened to compassionately, that the *uke*'s attack can be graciously received, comprise elements of anticipatory gratification and of actual relief and self-enhancement that may do much to restore confidence in the possibility of genuine I-Thou connecting. It can also be a matter of satisfaction and growth for the therapist and the *nage* to realize that they in fact possess the capacity not to reciprocate their antagonist's deviant bid and that they have the power to refrain from treating him the way that everyone else normally does.

That much accomplished, it remains for the therapist/*nage* to resolve what was potentially a difficult problem in a tonic manner. The challenge for them is to avoid making responses that are either exploitative or that involve an improper degree of familiarity. That done in turn, it remains for the client/*uke* to follow their lead in a positive manner, albeit remaining on the lookout for openings and weaknesses in the therapist/*nage* to make use of as they see fit. It is not productive if they simply wimp along when the therapist/*nage* manifests weaknesses of leadership and shows openings. If the client/*uke* should resist this lead, however, the therapist/*nage* will be challenged not to oppose their resistance but to blend with those resistances and to soften them.

Each transaction takes place in a broader context of ongoing interactions. It behooves the therapist/*nage* to restore attention to the larger context, to mark the boundaries of successive engagements, and to set the terms of continuous work. It is up to the client/*uke* to integrate what has been learned from each transaction and to get ready for proceeding to the next step.

Uke as Dynamic Creator, *Nage* as Creative Receptor: A Six-Stage Paradigm Drawing on Lao Tse, Nietzsche, and Buber

Instead of viewing *uke* as a patient, as a pathological actor in need of healing, we can reframe the role of *uke* in a more positive manner. Suppose we carry out the reframing process radically—that we view *uke*'s ostensible aggression as an expression of energy that is to be welcomed for the good it can bring. Such a shift can lead to a reframing of the entire aiki transaction that might unleash a great deal of human potential. The paradigm that I visualize for this interpretation has six components, as seen in Figure 8.4.

This paradigm stays closer to the aikido experience as we know and seek to cultivate it. The paradigm amounts to little more than an effort to take the basic moves that we practice and to extend them directly into everyday responses. At one and the same time it stands as a guide to training and as a guide to life generally.

It commits us, to begin with, to find the center of our being in ways that keep us open to the worlds within us and around us.

It reminds us, since we are prone perpetually to lose our center, to study more effective ways to regaining center.

Handeln	Action	Manner	Role	Breathing
1. Sein	Being	Centered and open	Expecting nothing, ready for anything	Continuous deep breathing
2. Schöpfen	Initiating	Energetically	Uke 1	Exhale 1
3. Engagieren	Engaging	Harmoniously	Nage 1	Inhale
4. Lösen	Resolving	Appropriately	Nage 2	Exhale
5. Anpassen	Adapting	Creatively	Uke 2	Exhale 2
6u. Zuruckprallen	Rebounding	Easily	Uke 3	Inhale-exhale
6n. Beherrschen	Controlling	Zanshin	Nage 3	Inhale-exhale

FIGURE 8.4 New *Uke* Paradigm

It encourages us to align with the yang energy entailed in every creative process, albeit in a way that favors that extension with the yin of subtlety and control.

It alerts us to be receptors of creative inputs, treating them neither as threats, nor as annoyances, nor as demons.

It bids us to offer honest and insightful responses to creative initiatives, such that any destructive or misleading elements they may contain can be redirected into more benign channels.

It coaches us to be flexible and to learn from obstacles or things that do not work, viewing them not as "mistakes" but as a normal part of the creative process.

It tells us to regain our balance after every exchange, returning to a state of readiness to learn, to create, to enjoy, and to be.

Conclusion

The aiki schemas of *uke* as patient/*nage* as therapist and *uke* as creator/*nage* as receptor are two among many. I invite you on your own to extend this mode of analysis to other forms in which you may be engaged: parent-child, husband-wife; leader-followers; mediator-client; enemy combatants. I believe that it is valuable for us to execute comparisons of this sort with a double aim in mind: to show how aikido practice can deepen our capacities for such experiences off the mat and to suggest how awareness of those applications can enrich our training experiences on the mat.

In setting forth these ideas I hope to have responded to the question with which I began: what can we say about the nature of the Aiki Way, which we try to pursue?

Insofar as we are patients—and we are all patients—it disposes us to reach out when we are in need, to ask for help, and to do so in a sincere and direct manner; and then to respond respectfully and in good faith, yet not blindly, to solutions to our problems offered by those who listen to us.

Insofar as we are healers—and we are all healers—it inclines us to listen with compassion to requests for help without giving in to illegitimate responses that may be proffered, to learn how to make contact with another while staying attuned to the center of our being, and to develop resources that can be useful in resolving issues that others present from time to time.

Insofar as we are creators—and we are all creators—it inspires us to express our deepest feelings with courage, honor, and awareness and to regard obstacles along the way as important components of the entire creative process. "In the hands of a master," one of my music teachers once observed, "the limitations of a medium become its virtues."

Insofar as we are receptors—and we are all receptors—we learn to savor the various responses of our partners in ways that show we take them seriously but will not be taken in by gestures that seem misleading or harmful to themselves or us or anyone else.

The Way of Dialogue, which Martin Buber elucidated on from his devotion to the inspirations of Nietzsche and the profound teachings of Lao Tse, can be enhanced through the somatic practices fashioned by Morihei Ueshiba O'Sensei. I find this point restated with exemplary economy by one of the newer members of Aiki Extensions, David Rubens of London, who wrote in a personal communication: "One of the blessings of aikido, at least as I have found it in my life and as you have shown in your work with Aiki Extensions, is that it creates a completely effective shortcut to creating connections between people." If *aiki waza* is indeed a *michi shirube*, that is not such a bad *michi* to be heading toward.

Notes

1 See Shibata (2004) on problems associated with the term *nage*.
2 Ciepley (2006) offered a searching account of social and ideological forces behind the resurgence of economistic world views in the United States over the past half-century.
3 In the *Die Religion* essay, however, Simmel pointed the way to Buber's sacralized dialogue by tracing in certain types and moments of interhuman experience the seeds for what becomes objectified as religion.
4 Buber took this quote from Feuerbach's *Grundsätze der Philosophie der Zukunft* (*Principles of Philosophy of the Future*). This was published in 1843, two years after his most famous publication, *The Essence of Christianity*. The earlier work provided fodder for Marx's famous attack in Thesis VI, where he excoriated Feuerbach by asserting: Feuerbach resolves the religious essence into the human essence. But the human essence is no abstraction inherent in each single individual. In its reality it is the ensemble of the social relations. Feuerbach, who does not enter upon a criticism of this real essence is consequently compelled: (1) To abstract from the historical process and to fix the religious sentiment as something by itself and to presuppose an abstract—*isolated*—human individual. (Cited in Tucker 1972, 109) It is ironic to compare Marx's words of 1845 to those of Feuerbach in 1843 just cited. The original Feuerbachian text cited by Buber follows: Der einzelne Mensch für sich hat das Wesen des Menschen nicht in sich, weder in sich als moralischem, noch in sich als denkendem Wesen. Das Wesen des Menschen ist nur in der Gemeinschaft, in der Einheit des Menschen enthalten—eine Einheit, die sich aber nur auf die Realität des Unterscheids von Ich und Du stützt. ... Selbst der Denkakt kann nur aus dieser Einheit begriffen und abgeleitet werden (Feuerbach [1843] 1903, 318). In retrieving these words, Buber went on to observe: "Feuerbach did not elaborate these words in his later writings" (Buber 1965, 148).

9

DEWEY AND HUTCHINS AT CHICAGO

> The purpose of school education is to insure the continuance of education by organizing the powers that insure growth.
>
> – *John Dewey (1916)*

> The object of a university is to emphasize, develop, and protect the intellectual powers of mankind.
>
> – *Robert Maynard Hutchins (1934)*

> What is needed for free minds is discipline, discipline which forms the habits which enable the mind to operate well. Nothing better can be said on this subject than the concise statement of John Dewey. "The discipline," he said, "that is identical with trained power is also identical with freedom."
>
> – *Robert Maynard Hutchins (1943)*

The University of Chicago's contribution to the general education movement took place over the course of a century. At the heart of the educational tradition that developed there, one finds the convergent ideas of John Dewey and Robert Maynard Hutchins.

This claim must seem odd to one who knows something about their personal differences and public hostilities. Prior to the culture wars fueled by Allan Bloom's provocative 1987 book, *The Closing of the American Mind*, no curricular controversy captured the American public's attention so dramatically as that between those two towering innovators. In the one corner, Dewey, an engaged philosopher, embodied, drawn to aesthetic epiphanies, conciliatory to a fault—the grand prophet of concrete experience; in the other, Hutchins, an administrative celebrity, solitary, standing in the West, aloof, aesthetically indifferent if not tone-deaf—a grand apostle of abstract intellection.

Beyond differences of character, they found themselves as head-on antagonists in academic politics. As incoming president of the University of Chicago in 1929,

Hutchins sought personnel changes in the Department of Philosophy. His initiatives immediately antagonized the department's leadership, which was then in the hands of Dewey's close colleagues, James Tufts, and George Herbert Mead, both of whom were about to retire. Hutchins' proactive efforts to bring Mortimer Adler, Scott Buchanan, and Richard McKeon into the department upset Tufts and Mead and fostered the perception that Hutchins was antagonistic both to Mead and, more generally, to the work of the pragmatists.[1] Although Hutchins wanted to palliate these tensions, particularly with Mead,[2] the conflict left lingering animosities, especially since it led to Mead spending the final year of his life in distress.

This episode may have contributed to the famous flare-up between Dewey and Hutchins half a dozen years later. Despite Hutchins' subsequent praise for Dewey's work ([1934] 1936, 39), in two successive issues of *The Social Frontier* starting in January 1937, Dewey leveled a critique of Hutchins' book *The Higher Learning in America* that attracted much attention. His review faulted Hutchins for (1) his alleged "contempt for science"; (2) divorcing higher learning from contemporary social life, and divorcing intellectual work from experience; (3) insisting that the elements of human nature are fixed and constant and that the truth is everywhere the same; (4) relying so heavily on Plato, Aristotle, and Aquinas; and (5) for a conception of rationality that assumed the existence of "fixed and eternal authoritative principles as proofs that are not to be questioned" (Dewey 1937a, 1937b).

With characteristic wit, Hutchins pleaded, "Mr. Dewey has stated my position in such a way as to lead me to think that I cannot write, and has stated his own in such a way as to make me suspect that I cannot read" (Hutchins 1937, 137). In short compass, Hutchins proceeded to cite passages that handily refuted the charges of being against science, of promoting withdrawal from the world, of authoritarianism, and of relying too much on Plato et al. Dewey in turn accused Hutchins' response of adopting the method of legal forensics, thereby evading what Dewey claimed was the central critical issue: "the place of experience, practical matters, and experimental scientific knowledge in the constitution of authentic knowledge, and consequently in the organization of the subject matter of higher education" (Dewey 1937b, 167).

It must be said that the animus in the exchange originated with Dewey's distortions of Hutchins' position.[3] Hutchins *never* endorsed the view of truth as a fixed body of doctrine that was secured by an elite and imposed dogmatically upon hapless students. He consistently upheld the values of science and scientific observation, the notion that what was considered true was subject to continuous change, and, as he expressed it in *Education for Freedom*, the assumption that intellectual principles, "like all knowledge, are derived from experience [and] are refinements of common sense" (Hutchins 1943, 62).

Aside from Dewey's manifold misreadings and Hutchins' slight evasiveness, both men had a point, insofar as neither clarified the misunderstandings that produced their ostensible differences of opinion.[4] What is more, on one important issue they appear to have been truly polarized: on the question of the philosophical basis for defending democracy, each of them viewed the other's position as dangerous.

Interpreting Hutchins' call for attention to a value hierarchy as a way station toward authoritarianism, Dewey peppered his otherwise civil critique with insinuation by denial: "I would not intimate that the author has any sympathy with fascism" (Dewey 1937a, 104). For his part, Hutchins attacked positivistic naturalism, which many readers took to be an indirect attack on Dewey, as an abandonment of reasoned discourse in support of democratic values, thereby presenting a relativistic way station toward fascism. In all this back-and-forth, the perception of antagonism was heightened by the fulminations of Hutchins' erstwhile comrade Mortimer Adler, who famously accused academics like Dewey of promoting a kind of morally bankrupt position more dangerous to democracy than Nazism—a serious distortion from the other side, as Dewey himself attacked empirical naturalists no less severely for abdicating the need to ground moral judgments on rational discourse (Westbrook 1991, 519–23).[5]

In fact, the two were much closer than Dewey allowed. They shared numerous assumptions and commitments; both of them were passionate advocates of democracy; and they even opposed U.S. involvement in the looming World War II on the grounds that it would threaten democratic freedoms.[6]

On a number of other issues, moreover, differences between the two educational philosophers amounted to very little. Although Dewey objected to Hutchins' assumption of a universal human nature, his own *Human Nature and Conduct* ([1922] 1988) presumed a certain universality. And while Dewey famously criticized Hutchins for looking to Plato, Aristotle, and Aquinas, he himself (as Hutchins noted [1937, 137]) had praised the same three authors for their exemplary grasp of the science and social affairs of their times. What is more, insofar as they ostensibly differed in their views of the relative educational importance of concrete experience and intellectually challenging texts, this difference may be linked in part to Dewey's virtually exclusive preoccupation with primary school grades, and Hutchins' preoccupation with early collegiate grades.

With respect to their more general educational visions, whatever apparent differences remained between them seemed trivial. Indeed, the ideas they had in common generated a continuous tradition of academic reforms at the University of Chicago, an institution with which both developed intense emotional involvements.[7] In Dewey's rejoinder to Hutchins' defense, he praised Hutchins' book as being highly significant for its "vigorous exposition of the present confused state of education in this country" (Dewey 1937b, 167) and for raising a basic issue in the philosophy of education. Had he been able to reflect on the University's first full century of curricular development, he might have appreciated the extent to which he and Hutchins had been pursuing a similar radical and visionary quest for educational reform.

Dewey as Educator

Both Dewey and Hutchins came to Chicago from the East, where virtually nothing in their early work suggested the kinds of iconoclastic positions they would come to espouse there. Dewey's Chicago sojourn began in 1894 and lasted a decade, during which he completed the transition, started at Ann Arbor, from trying to straddle three interests—neo-Hegelian idealism, physiological psychology, and political activism—to a formulation of pragmatist philosophy and social psychology where those three elements contributed to an emerging synthesis. The Chicago Laboratory Schools formed a principal outlet for this synthesis, embodying Dewey's view that student learning, institutional reconstruction, and civic democracy are mutually constitutive.

At Chicago, Dewey came to formulate the educational ideas for which he would become famous. His work there became a gathering point for fresh departures in educational thought, for which the innovative university founded by William Rainey Harper provided a benign milieu. Like Dewey, Harper pioneered ideas and arrangements that were at odds with academic conventions, and he went out of his way to support the lab school experiments. Although Harper never had the necessary budget to provide adequate support for the lab school (or anything else, for that matter), he tried his best to help. For example, in the spring of 1899, when the school faced a deficit of one-tenth of its annual costs, Harper made a special appeal to potential donors and contributed $100 of his own (equivalent to about $2,300 in 2006 dollars).[8]

Dewey's educational philosophy embodied a pointedly sociological vision. It was not by accident that three of his students—Charles Horton Cooley, Robert E. Park, and William I. Thomas—went on to become some of the foremost figures of American sociology of the early twentieth century. All four of them voiced concerns about the levels of social disorganization engendered by the rapid changes associated with modern science, technology, industry, and urbanization. For Dewey, these concerns issued in a lifelong project to reform the learning experience at all levels.

One may condense Dewey's complex concerns about the links between education and modern society into two points. For one, the unparalleled growth of objectified knowledge and technical skills led to programs of training that were increasingly in danger of being split off from connection with one another and with the experience of everyday activities. For another, the expansion of society and the eruption of novel social problems created unprecedented demands for individuals educated for thinking and communicating about these problems in democratic forms. Both sets of changes meant that conventional modes of instruction, in which students were passively lectured at and required to memorize by rote, had become dysfunctional.

For Dewey, the reconstruction of society and the reconstruction of education were aspects of the same process. The capacity to solve social problems required the intellectual ability to perceive problems, identify their features, and entertain diverse options for their solution. In order to promote such habits at all levels of learning, Dewey maintained that new forms of teaching were needed, forms in which curiosity and imagination were awakened through direct encounter with puzzling experiences. Thus, instead of being confronted with formal lectures about the abstract properties of substances, students would engage in spinning and weaving, activities through which they would run up against questions that would prompt them to investigate such properties. Performing such investigations again and again would afford the discipline that led to the development of robust powers. In Dewey's words,

> since really to satisfy an impulse or interest means to work it out, and working it out involves running up against obstacles, becoming acquainted with materials, exercising ingenuity, patience, persistence, alertness, it of necessity involves discipline—ordering of power—and supplies knowledge.
> *(Dewey [1915] 1990, 38)*

These skills could not be gained in isolation. They could be acquired only in social settings that did not suppress impulses but instead directed those impulses into creative channels. The structure of this learning was constituted by forms of communication that were open, mutually respectful, and mutually responsive. Learning thus deeply relied on powers of communication, the same powers that were requisite to public deliberation in a democratic society. Beyond that, Dewey argued, the very process of communication itself has an inexorably educative effect on all parties involved.

Examine all school levels, then and to a great extent now, and you will find precious little of this sort of learning. Over much of the educational world, Dewey's plaint written in 1916 still applies: "Why is it, in spite of the fact that teaching by pouring in, learning by passive absorption, are universally condemned, they are still so entrenched in practice?" (1916, 38). That is because those who support, direct, and teach in these schools have been habituated to inherited patterns, whereby each generation unthinkingly reproduces the paradigm of teaching—a process of delivering facts—that it grew up with. This pattern has now been reinforced by the plethora of standardized tests that determine students' futures, tests that today are increasingly being prepared for by forced attention in the classroom and by commercially packaged and seductively propagated supplementary programs.

Dewey's antidote for such archaic systems, which mindlessly pursue goals frozen in yesteryear, consists of an effort at reconstruction wherein educators subject their programs to searching reviews. These reviews reconsider the goals of each educational program, in the context of the entire trajectory of educational programs, and work to find the best means for attaining those goals. This is a never-ending process, since both the stock of knowledge and societal conditions are continuously changing.

What is more, innovation in one part of a program may require adaptation in other parts. This becomes evident only when attention is focused on curricular coherence. For Dewey, no piece of the curriculum should be considered in isolation, either synchronously or over time. This approach contrasts with the curricular bricolage whose pieces derived randomly from different genealogical eras, a state that Dewey depicted in the remarkable chart reproduced as Figure 9.1. To rid schools of rampant waste, educators need to remove all the parts that impair coherence.

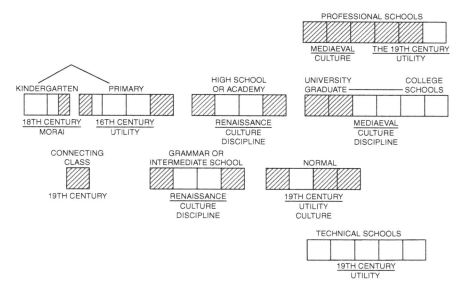

FIGURE 9.1 Dewey's Chart of the School System
Note: Clusters represent component parts of the school system. Blocks within each cluster indicate the time students spend in each stage. Shaded blocks donate an overlap of time and subject matter. Captions show historical periods and ruling ideals. The line bridging the first two clusters indicates continuity in pedagogy (Dewey [1915] 1990, 65).

In Dewey's account, the kindergarten emerged as a site for moral instruction; primary school reflects the practical, skills-based priorities of the sixteenth-century "popular movement"; grammar school originated to teach Greek and Latin, for acculturation more than discipline. Technical and normal schools arose, respectively, in response to changing business conditions and the related need to train teachers. The resulting system is disjointed. Its parts arose in distinct periods for the sake of different goals and "have never yet been welded into one complete whole" (Dewey [1915] 1990, 70).

Dewey urged a turn toward coherence in curricular planning along two dimensions. Along the horizontal dimension, he wanted to make school an "organic whole" rather than a composite of isolated parts: "All studies arise from aspects of the one earth and the one life lived upon it. We do not have a series of stratified earths, one of which is mathematical, another physical, another historical, and so on" (91). He sought to connect academic studies with everyday life, so what the student learns at school willy-nilly reflects the unity of lived experience.

Yet more daunting, Dewey envisioned coherence along a vertical dimension so that educational programs formed a continuous progression from kindergarten through graduate school. This meant identifying developmental stages, adapting curricula to what is appropriate to each period of personal growth, and fitting the curricula to one another in a coherent manner. Thus, stage one (4- to 8-year-olds) involves material connected to social and personal interests informing immediate motor outlets—teaching through "play, games, occupations, or miniature industrial arts, stories, pictorial imagination and conversation" (106). Stage two (8- to 12-year-olds) involves material connected to "rules of action—that is, of regular means appropriate to reaching permanent results" rather than merely personal ends. The third stage involves specialization through the use of independent powers and skills in "distinctive studies and arts for technical and intellectual aims" (107).

In addition to his emphasis on attuning curricular materials more finely to what was appropriate to each developmental stage, Dewey also stressed the fact that no two students are identical. Each one presents a particular profile of needs, interests, blockages, and talents. For this reason, education for autonomy, creativity, and community must find ways to address individual differences. It cannot rely on standardized inputs that are applied mechanically to an entire cohort. It cannot set up objectified goals—whether preparation for a remote future, an unfolding of presumed native faculties, an instillation of specific disciplines, or a recovery of some canon of past achievements—that depart from the essential goal of education: enabling individuals to reorganize their current experience in ways that equip them to direct the course of future experience (ibid., chaps. 5, 6).

None of the issues in question is simple or easily decided. They require the same kind of energized thought that any tough investigative problem entails. That is why, Dewey argued, an important part of the mission of a great university must be to conduct programs of research and evaluation regarding all aspects of educational technique and content. All educational programs mounted by a university, from kindergarten through doctoral, must become experimental in a nontrivial sense.

As the massive changes in society require changes in how students are educated, and these changes in turn require changes in systems designed to educate them, so the reconstructed teaching institutions will entail changes in the larger society. An attitude of openness to learning, support for ability to define problems and imagine alternative solutions, communication about them in a mutually respectful discursive network, and the enrichment of experience that all this entails will form the lineaments of the new democratic society. These goals would require public support for a restructuring of universities in several respects: precisely the reconstruction that Robert Maynard Hutchins pioneered. It would, in words that Hutchins celebrated, become a "learning society."

Hutchins as an Unwitting Deweyan

The academic reforms Hutchins pioneered after becoming President of the University of Chicago in 1929, and the rhetoric with which he sought to promote them, look as though they were derived straight from Dewey's educational theories. Like Dewey, Hutchins initiated his discourse on American education by attacking its lack of clear direction and its discordant and wasteful organization: "The most striking fact about the higher learning in America is the confusion that besets it" (Hutchins [1934] 1936, 1). The forces that directed American education appeared to consist of commercial pressures, consumerist whims, professorial predilections, and public opinion. The system appeared rampantly disordered because it lacked an ordering principle. This situation was doubly tragic, Hutchins thought, because it deprived students of the possibility of developing their human powers and deprived society of citizens equipped to facilitate intelligent social change.

In order to help students cultivate those powers and to prepare them for promoting informed social changes, universities would have to devote special resources and energies to the task of creating a program designed for those purposes. The key ingredients included a faculty dedicated to the task as well as materials and methods organized to accomplish it. Instead of letting professors teach whatever they chose, they would be expected to teach in a program designed with specific educational goals in mind. Instead of letting students sign up for whatever courses they wished, they would be expected to follow a carefully constructed, coherent course of study. Instead of following the old custom of offering students textbook summaries of facts, faculty would offer them serious texts that engaged their intelligence and forced them to think. Instead of following the custom of teaching through lectures that more or less repeated the textbook packages, teachers would engage students in stimulating discussions of problems.

In pursuing the ideal of a coherent program of study suited for students in accord with their developmental stage, Hutchins sought to institute a curriculum of general education that would run from the beginning of the junior year of high school to the end of the sophomore year of college. This curriculum would be self-contained and could mark the end of formal instruction for most students. The materials for this curriculum would be books that have attained the stature of classics, books that raise perennial questions and are contemporary in every age. These books are essential to general education because they are needed both to understand the foundations of all subjects and to comprehend the contemporary world. In order to read such books intelligently and critically, students would also learn the arts of reading, writing, thinking, and speaking by means of the study of grammar, rhetoric, logic, and mathematics. Given a curriculum of this sort, which is serious, coherent, and comprehensible, students would find it attractive rather than intimidating or inaccessible. Reporting on his work in teaching classics to young people, Hutchins quipped,

> Mr. Adler and I have found that the books are more rather than less effective the younger students are. Students in University High School have never heard that these books are too hard for them. ... They have not had time to get as miseducated as their elders.
>
> *(1943, 15)*

Like Dewey, Hutchins did not imagine that creating such a curriculum would be simple or easy. For one thing, little is known about the best way to organize the curricular materials and the best ways to teach them, taking into account the differences among students. To provide such understanding, as he proclaimed already in his inaugural address of September 1929, universities would need to establish programs of focused research regarding education. "If this were not so," he observed soon after,

> I should recommend [the College's] abolition. ... [For] few institutions in our area can do what we can do in collegiate education, and that is to experiment with it with the same intentness, the same kind of staff, and the same effectiveness with which we carry on the rest of our scientific work.
> (Hutchins 1930, 12; see also Hutchins 1931)

Even with the best of information, moreover, such a curricular project would face serious resistance. Much of it would stem from the persistence of old habits among the teaching faculty: not many professors of today, Hutchins complained, are ready to change the habits of their lives. Meanwhile, they are bringing up their successors in the way they were brought up, so the next crop will have the habits they have had themselves. And their love of money, misconceptions of democracy, false notions of progress, distorted ideas of utility, and the anti-intellectualism to which they all lead conspire to confirm their conviction that no disturbing change is needed.

It was with such ideas in mind that Hutchins proceeded, in the first two years of his presidency, to restructure the University in such a way as to support initiatives to design a coherent curriculum and a faculty especially devoted to creative teaching; to separate administratively the undergraduate college as a division distinct from the divisions devoted to research and graduate training; and to support initiatives to carry out focused research on learning at this level.[9] Over the next two decades, the faculty of the College would engage in extraordinarily creative work in designing such a program of liberal learning.

After leaving the University in 1951, Hutchins continued to develop his ideas about learning in a democratic society. At a time of growing public nervousness, he spoke out boldly against attempts to curtail the University's rights to free expression and inquiry. At a time of growing anti-intellectualism and of the stupefying effects of television, he articulated afresh his vision of the ideal university and the ways in which it could promote and enhance the elements of a "learning society."

In these and other ways, the critiques and the visions of Hutchins and Dewey appear remarkably similar. The parallels between them become transparent when presented in the form of a schematic concordance, as shown in Table 9.1.

The Hutchins-Dewey Debate

Given the consensus between Dewey and Hutchins on so many key points, their well-publicized antagonism of 1936–7 becomes all the more remarkable. Indeed, some truly striking differences in their views about education never really came to the fore. In two areas not mentioned in the *Social Frontier* debate, one can identify marked differences of emphasis, if not position, in their beliefs about education.

TABLE 9.1 Dewey-Hutchins Concordance

Points of convergence	Dewey	Hutchins
Critiques of American education	a. Confused b. Degraded by mindless conventions d. Hodgepodge curriculum e. Remote from life experience	a. "Beset by confusion" b. Corrupted by "materialism" c. Curricular incoherence d. Fails to prepare students for life
Societal need for educational reform	a. Need for adaptation to changed conditions b. Sustaining democracy	a. Need for social change directed by intelligence b. Support for democracy
Pertinent reforms	Eliminate waste Reconstruct through adapting means to ends	Don't squander two more years of college than other countries have; squeeze out waste, water, and frivolity
Aims of education		
a. Powers	a. Independent use of powers	a. Development of human powers
b. Freedom	b. Plato on the slave as one whose actions express another's ideas, not his own	b. Freedom as condition for knowing and achieving the order of goods
c. Moral improvement	c. Moral conduct as unifying and culminating end	c. Enhanced morality
Means	a. Don't just transmit information	a. Information as such is not meaningful
b. Engage students actively	b. Active experience instead of passive absorption	b. Active engagement with issues to replace textbooks, listening to lectures
c. Give experience in solving problems	c. Focus on searching for solutions to genuine problems	c. Give practice in thinking about problems, vocational skills in on-the-job training
Coherence of curricular structure	a. Integrated learning; coherent general curriculum b. Integrated learning; coherence across the life cycle	a. General education curriculum contra anarchic elective system b. Student completes solid general education in sophomore year

Points of convergence	Dewey	Hutchins
"Progressive" education as license is harmful	Valorize impulsivity, but only to reconstruct habits	Locks up the growing mind in its own whims and difficulties
Sociality of education as means	Education a social process, not a function of isolated individuals	Education as participation in dialogue
Sociality of education as end	Communication as both means and end of education	Education as way to promote social consciousness, conscience
Respect for young students	Celebrates abilities, powers of the young	Freshmen can do independent work; liberal education can be completed by college sophomores; young students like to tackle tough classics
Individualized programs	Important to tailor educational structures to situation of individual students	Individualized education affordable if schools allocate resources wisely
Conduct university research on education	Use precollegiate schools as laboratories for university study	Need for focused research on education in a great research university Scholarship should aim to reveal highest human powers
Toward a learning society	Learning in school as continuous with a learning society	Universal learning as the highest goal of democratic society
Chicago as exemplar	Chicago's lab schools as model	Chicago's 1942 BAs a lodestar

Soon after their debate, Hutchins achieved notoriety by abolishing football, which led to the famous image of his antipathy toward athletic activity, whereas Dewey emphatically affirmed the educational value of attention to bodily well-being.[10] While art formed a central part of Dewey's curriculum and later philosophical discourse, Hutchins proclaimed that the University should cultivate intellectual powers and not focus on powers of artistic creativity.[11] One could still play up the different roles they assigned to reading books, with Dewey much more disposed to emphasize a certain amount of hands-on practical experience.

When these distracting points are bracketed, points of difference between them reduce to different formulations of broadly similar positions. Despite the notorious polemics between them, it proved possible for educators who aligned themselves with both Dewey and Hutchins to develop educational ideas that embodied the convergent principles they espoused.

This is not to say that the University of Chicago has remained staunchly true to the ideals of Dewey and Hutchins. Forces of the market, which both of them decried as inimical to education, have made serious inroads against the gains that they promoted. Ironically, whereas for Dewey the subject of geography should stand at the center of pre-collegiate learning, the University revoked the departmental status of its historic Department of Geography in 1986. Moreover, whereas for both of them a crucial component of the University's work should be carried out in its Department of Education, the University decided to dissolve its historic Department of Education in 1996. And while granting a monopoly to consumerist appetites remains one of the most insidious obstacles to liberal learning for both of them, the University of Chicago subsequently became publicly identified with the hegemony of economistic thinking. Both of them decried the lack of coherence in curricula at all levels. The University's College has found it increasingly difficult to strive for curricular coherence, without which "the course of study goes to pieces because there is nothing to hold it together" (Hutchins 1943, 26). During the first century of its existence, however, the University created an unparalleled wealth of resources for the enterprise of liberal learning, and it has by no means squandered all of them, even today. This is a story that must be told, again and again.

Notes

1 Although Hutchins, Adler, and Dewey had very high regard for one another's intellectual powers, a certain ambivalence did color their relations from time to time. As early as 1924, when Adler was Dewey's student at Columbia, Adler read a paper at a philosophy conference in which he criticized Dewey's conception of philosophy for leaving out the suprahuman dimension of experience. On that occasion, Dewey uncharacteristically pounded his chair and abruptly left the room. Even so, three years later, Dewey went out of his way to write a complimentary review of Adler's first book, *Dialectic* (Adler 1977, 49); and, at various points, both Hutchins and Adler expressed their admiration for the work of the pragmatist philosophers.

2 When Mead and others threatened to resign, Hutchins responded that "he fully recognized the right of a department to pass on its personnel," that he would not keep Adler or Buchanan in the department if the others wished, and that he would raise department

salaries according to Tufts' recommendations. When shortly thereafter Mead resigned and fell ill, Hutchins told Mead he was distressed by the latter's resignation and had delayed communicating the resignation to the board of trustees, hoping for a reconciliation.

3 Knowledgeable persons have expressed wonderment at this uncharacteristically contentious outburst by Dewey, who in nearly all other engagements was the very model of a pacific, unruffled, gentle man. Indeed, this contentiousness persisted in subsequent exchanges with Hutchins and his defender Alexander Meiklejohn through 1945 (Martin 2002, 452–8). Beyond some lingering feelings about the 1931 episode with the Philosophy Department, the following seem to account for it: the fact that the two universities Dewey had been most closely tied to, Columbia and Chicago, were in the forefront of what was seen as a return to traditional forms of liberal learning; the instigation provided by Dewey's young followers at the journal *Social Frontier*, a medium for radical, progressive educators associated with Columbia's Teachers College; and possibly Dewey's lifelong struggle against religion triggering an aversion to figures Hutchins quoted, such as Augustine and Aquinas. Issues regarding the appropriate intellectual defense of democracy, discussed later in this chapter, probably aroused the most passion. These plausible interpretations were suggested by Philip Jackson in oral communication, March 3, 2003.

4 The exaggeration of differences and the escalated antagonism between Dewey and Hutchins may be taken as a case in point to illustrate how hard it is even for brilliant and well-educated people to engage in undistorted communication, even when the parties in question are prominent proponents of the value of dialogue.

5 For a discussion of the broader context of the democracy debate, see Ciepley (2001).

6 Both appealed to the disaster of World War I chiefly by citing the effect it had on eroding democratic freedoms. "It is quite conceivable that after the next war in this country we should have a semi-military, semi-financial autocracy ... [and] the suppression of all the democratic values for the sake of which we professedly went to war" (Dewey 1939, 11). "When we remember what a short war did to the four freedoms [freedom of speech, freedom of worship, freedom from want, freedom from fear], we must recognize that they face extermination in the total war to come" (Robert Hutchins, "Untitled, re: Our present society," 10 March 1940, Folder 4, Box 25, Robert M. Hutchins Papers, University Archives, Special Collections, Joseph Regenstein Library, University of Chicago, Chicago).

7 Biographical parallels between their relationships to the University include the youthful age at which they came to it—Dewey at 35, Hutchins at 30; the aura of special excitement that surrounded their arrival at the University; and the traumatic circumstances of their departure (Dewey after 11 years, Hutchins after 22), when those who had opposed or offended them tried strenuously to keep them from leaving.

8 Harper's support for Dewey has been hidden under the perception of an antagonistic attitude that led to Dewey's departure. In fact, what upset Dewey was an administrative misunderstanding regarding his wife's lab school appointment, for which Harper was not responsible, and Harper tried ardently to get the Deweys to stay at Chicago.

9 In 1929 Hutchins secured a sizable grant from the General Education Board to pursue such research.

10 Here as elsewhere, differences between them have been subject to exaggerations that distort their true beliefs. Dewey quite objected to conventional physical education as practiced in the United States; Hutchins, while publicly disdaining physical exercise, was himself an avid tennis player. Beyond that, the "Hutchins College" developed some distinctive forms of athletic work. In its famous Humanities 1 course, it also gave students distinctive opportunities to create paintings, poetry, and music (Ward [1950] 1992, chap. 3).

11 Hutchins insinuated that making music, sculpture, or painting did not qualify as a "university discipline" (1936, 93–4).

PART III
Dialogues Involving Pointed Conversations

10

HOBBES AND LOCKE

Scholars of diverse persuasions regard Thomas Hobbes (1588–1679) as a foundational figure for modern social science. Strauss described Hobbes' political philosophy as "the first peculiarly modern attempt to give a coherent and exhaustive answer to the question of man's right life, which is at the same time the question of the right order of society," and hailed him as "the first who felt the necessity of seeking, and succeeded in finding, a *nuova scientia* of man and State. On this new doctrine, all later moral and political thought is expressly or tacitly based" (Strauss 1936, 1). Sorokin named Hobbes as the first of a brilliant group of philosophers who created "'the Social Physics' of the seventeenth century, which, at least in its plan and aspirations, has not been surpassed by all the mechanistic theories of the nineteenth and twentieth centuries" (1928, 5). Parsons identified Hobbes as founder of the utilitarian tradition, one who "saw the problem [of order] with a clarity which has never been surpassed, and [whose] statement of it remains valid today" ([1937] 1968, 93). I now go further and advance the claim that all the philosophical traditions that undergird the disciplines of modern social science—anthropology, economics, political science, psychology, and sociology—consist of elaborations, revisions, or replacements of the Hobbesian conception of social science.[1]

The Hobbesian Assault on Aristotle

The full import of Hobbes' achievement cannot be grasped without setting it in a context of dialogical confrontation with Aristotle. This is not to say, of course, that Aristotelian views of practical philosophy held sway in Europe for two thousand years until Hobbes came along. Aristotle's corpus was virtually forgotten for three centuries after his death. When it did come to light in the first century BC, it aroused opposition from the practical-minded Romans and later from Christian thinkers. Aristotle's writings did not even get translated into Latin for more than a millennium after their rediscovery, through the introduction of his texts by Averroes. *The Politics* arrived in the West by a different route, from Byzantium, and was translated at the request of Aquinas in 1250. Aristotle's political ideas gained currency through their use as support for republican ideas in the Italian city-states of the early Renaissance, most notably in the work of Marsilius of Padua. Only by the fourteenth or fifteenth century could one identify Aristotle as the authoritative voice of secular European moral philosophy, but that is when the quest for a secular ethic began.

The critique of Aristotle as the preeminent authority in secular, moral, and political thought may be said to have begun with Machiavelli's declaration that guides to action should no longer be based on the "imagined republics and principalities" of the past, but rather on the hard-nosed truth about how human beings actually live. It was consummated by Hobbes' full-scale effort to erect a secular ethic on wholly new philosophical foundations in the 1640s.

This was no work of a rebellious youth. Until his early forties Hobbes stood faithful to the philosophy of Aristotle, a stance reflecting his classical education at Oxford. Prefacing his first publication—a translation of Thucydides in 1628—Hobbes affirmed the common belief that "Homer in poesy, Aristotle in philosophy, Demosthenes in eloquence, and others of the ancients in other knowledge, do still maintain their primacy: none of them exceeded, some not approached, by any in these later ages" ([1843] 1966, VIII, vii). The following year, however, Hobbes experienced geometry for the first time, in what has been described as an intellectual "conversion" during a visit to France. Euclid offered him a powerful new entree to truth. On a later visit to the Continent, which included a pilgrimage to Italy to visit Galileo, he became attracted to the latter's audacious views that motion is the natural state of bodies and that bodies continue in motion to infinity unless impeded. These views contradicted the Aristotelian doctrine that rest is the natural state of bodies. Hobbes also embraced the Galilean notion that the natural universe consists of a vast field of atomic motions, replacing Aristotle's conception of natural phenomena as a collection of substances constituted by essential qualities and ends. Applying these ideas of Galilean physics to psychological phenomena led Hobbes to challenge Aristotle. In his *Little Treatise* (1637), he reinterpreted sensation in terms of the interaction of external bodies with sense organs. He went on to develop a view of human action as impelled by unlimited desires and perpetual motion rather than the tendency toward a state of rest and fulfillment.

Moved by the promise of geometric method and mechanistic psychology, Hobbes aspired to use the ideas of this new science to transform all of moral and political philosophy. These thoughts brought him to the point where he regarded the political and ethical teaching of Aristotle as "the worst ... that ever was" (Aubrey 1949, 255).[2] His plan was to take the form of three treatises—first on the body, then on man, and last on the state. Upset by the growing civil strife in England in the late 1630s, however, Hobbes proceeded to draft the last treatise first. By doing this, he hoped to use forceful new modes of argument to persuade his fellow citizens to obey the law and, thus, put the finger on lawless killers and conspirators by refuting the vicious doctrine that it is all right to rebel against kings.[3]

Much has been made—and rightly so—of the significance of Hobbes' new substantive moral doctrines. Those attentive to his work have generally concentrated on his secular reasons for justifying the absolute authority of political sovereigns, albeit in discussions that tend to ignore the moral constraints Hobbes imposes upon sovereigns at the same time as he exempts them from legal restraints. Strauss (1936) has also argued that the truly revolutionary feature of Hobbes' moral philosophy lies in its displacement of the elitist ethic found in Aristotle's celebration of the aristocratic virtues of magnanimity and valor by an egalitarian ethic that championed the virtues of justice and charity. However, for the story of the sociological tradition I am telling, what must be stressed is the set of principles Hobbes devised for shaping a discipline of practical philosophy. We can best consider those principles by contrasting them with the Aristotelian principles Hobbes was replacing.

Nature

Like the Greeks, Hobbes sought to construct a purely secular rational ethic and to do so on the basis of what is natural. His laws of morality turned out to be "laws of nature." To be sure, he also referred to these laws as commands of God, possibly to protect himself against charges of atheism, but the logic of his arguments flows independently of any theological strictures.[4] Nevertheless, what Hobbes understands by "nature" differs radically from Aristotle's *physis*, such that this shift in metaphysical assumptions radically transforms the whole program of moral philosophy.

Where Aristotle considered nature to be the essential quality in a universe of substances that tend toward rest, Hobbes came to view nature as an inherent force in a universe of atoms existing in perpetual motion. Like Aristotle, Hobbes regarded human passions—the appetites—and human faculties—like reason—as natural phenomena. Unlike Aristotle, Hobbes thought they exhausted the universe of such phenomena. The human world is constituted as a great field of interacting impulses, just as the mechanical world is constituted as a great field of interacting atoms. Their force is so strong that they perturb the workings of the only other natural phenomenon humans evince, reason. Analysis of these interacting motions, based on the natural propensities of atomic individuals, constitutes the alpha and omega of Hobbesian social science.

For Hobbes, the primary motions were twofold: "a perpetual and restless desire for power after power" ([1651] 1909, ch. 11, par. 2, 77), and the avoidance of violent death, which proceeds from "a certain impulsion of nature, no less than that whereby a stone moves downward" ([1642] 1972, 115). The first impulse derives from the uninhibited expression of various natural appetites; the interaction of individuals animated by this desire for power produces an anarchic condition, the war of all against all. This condition in turn activates the second natural impulse, self-preservation. This impulse aligns with reason and motivates men to covenant among themselves to instate a sovereign who can impose civil peace.

Hobbes restricts what is natural in humanity to a field of strong appetitive forces and a relatively feeble faculty of reason. This eliminates two other phenomena that Aristotle also assumed to be natural: the propensity of substances to actualize their potential in a certain direction and the tendency of humans to organize themselves in enduring associations. Discarding the latter assumption makes the polity entirely a work of art, not a natural formation. Suggesting that humans have a natural tendency to actualize themselves toward the good means that analysis can focus only on the presumed givens of human conduct, not on imagined ideal end states.

Semantic shifts can take one of three forms: a shift in the generic meaning of the concept, in the identification of phenomena that get described by the concept, and in the qualities associated with the concept. The way the meaning of "nature" changed from Aristotle to Hobbes is so momentous because shifts of all three kinds take place simultaneously. Hobbes replaced the classic notion of nature as signifying the essential quality and character of something with the more abstract sense of an inherent force that directs the world. As applied to human phenomena, he withdrew the attribution of natural from social formations and thereby restricted it to individual human behavior. Further, he specified the self-regarding appetites and the faculty of reason as natural, eliminating individuals' developmental ends, which Aristotle had regarded as inherent in their nature. So momentous a complex of shifts had ramifications throughout the philosophy of Hobbes and of those influenced by him. Not least of these ramifications were the associated shifts in conceiving the relation between theory and practice.

Theory and Practice

Throughout his systematic treatments of moral and political philosophy, Hobbes based his expositions on the ideas and methods of natural science. Since it was the power of geometric argument that originally had inspired these analyses, geometry provided the model he sought to emulate in constructing his sciences of man. In a moment of enthusiasm for the model, he exclaimed:

> Were the nature of human actions as distinctly known as the nature of *quantity* in geometric figures, the strength of *avarice* and *ambition*, which is sustained by the erroneous opinions of the vulgar as touching the nature of *right* and *wrong*, would presently faint and languish; and mankind should enjoy such an immortal peace that … there would hardly be left any pretence for war.
>
> *(Hobbes [1642] 1972, 91)*

There were three respects in which Hobbes can be said to have tried to make moral philosophy like mathematics. As the above passage indicates, one was to employ distinct and univocally defined terms for discourse, in marked contrast to Aristotle, who acknowledged the plenitude of meanings that commonplace terms about action bore. He sought to incorporate those diverse meanings in discourse about the good. Another was an attempt to suggest a calculus for representing quanta of good and evil, about which more will be said below. A third was to employ rigorous deductive reasoning, following what he described as Galileo's resolutive-compositive method. This method reduces political phenomena to their elements—the propensities of individuals—and then reconstitutes them through logical deduction. Thus Hobbes made the deductive aspect of natural science—what Aristotle called *episteme*, or scientific demonstration—the constitutive method of his practical philosophy. In all three respects Hobbes turned his back on Aristotle's dictum that one should not expect the kind of certainty one gets in mathematics from investigations concerning human action and, thereby, erased one of the boundaries between theoretical and practical knowledge that Aristotle had drawn.

He similarly collapsed the Aristotelian divide between the subject matters of the two branches of philosophy. Natural science dealt with the motions of bodies, so likewise the sciences of man dealt with the motions of bodies. Not action for the sake of some good purpose, but action as the playing out of so many natural impulses comprised his practical subject matter. The point of practical philosophy for Hobbes was to follow the vicissitudes of these natural motions and to align reason with them at junctures where natural equilibria were being reset. This approach to practical philosophy made it consist of nothing other than *applied theory*. And since natural bodies were now understood as consisting of atoms in motion, not as substances actualizing their potential forms toward some end, the forms and ends of human action could be disregarded. Hobbesian practical science, no less than Galilean physical science, eliminated the search for formal and final causes by directing attention exclusively to the search for material and efficient causes.

Grounding Morality

Hobbes, like Aristotle, projected a vision of the good society that also theorizes about the source of human moral dispositions. For Hobbes, however, the good society does not deal with arrangements for realizing the highest potentialities of humans, but rather restricts itself to the ways and means of creating a state free from warfare. The practical problems for Aristotle were twofold: how to go on living and how to live well; for Hobbes, just living at peace suffices.

Logically, this agenda for practical philosophy gets set by assuming that practical wisdom consists of the applied theory of nature. Criteria of the good then derive from affirming the naturally given needs and rights of individual human actors. Since Hobbes' theory of the natural human condition holds that the free play of human appetites leads inexorably to the war of all against all, the central dilemma of action must be to secure a stable equilibrium or order. The touchstone of morality becomes obedience to the laws of an absolute sovereign. Moral laws are laws of nature, the first of which is to seek peace, but to provide defenses for oneself in the absence of peace. Since morality gets channeled exclusively into a concern for survival and stability, the touchstone for personal morality becomes a disposition to abide by the laws and manners of civil society. Therefore "all the virtues are contained in justice and charity" (Hobbes [1658] 1972, 70). Such laws of nature are defined as the dictates of right reason: they are inexorable consequences of aligning natural reason with the passion for self-preservation.

The secular ethic propounded by Aristotle involved a complex mixture of ingredients: realized potentials for excellence, voluntaristic decisions, proper use of language, public discourse, well-constituted societies, wise laws, suitable habits, and satisfied appetites. From this complex, Hobbes abstracted one element—the satisfaction of natural desires—as the cornerstone of his entire ethical edifice. He proceeded to transform moral philosophy by adopting a new method based on geometry and mechanics; he developed a new view of nature, based on a conception of atomic elements in motion; and he devised a new way of posing the question of morality, based on resolving the dilemma posed by free play of natural appetites. In so doing, he constructed a framework of assumptions that were to undergird the major philosophical efforts to construct sciences of human phenomena in Britain for the next three centuries. At the same time, he stripped moral philosophy of a number of Aristotelian assumptions—about the natural character of social associations, the importance of voluntarism for moral judgment, the disjunction between theoretic science and practical knowledge, the natural bases of goal-directed potentialities, the social importance of well-qualified elites, and the probabilistic character of moral judgments—that thinkers in other traditions would struggle for centuries to restore.

The Loyal Opposition: British Critics of Hobbes

Although Hobbes' writings do acknowledge a human capacity for benevolence, the human striving for self-aggrandizing power—as in his point that "man surpasseth in rapacity and cruelty the wolves, bears, and snakes that are not rapacious unless hungry and not cruel unless provoked, whereas man is famished even by future hunger" ([1658] 1972, 40)—is theoretically central in his system. Due to this disposition of human nature, the unconstrained expression of natural impulses inexorably produces an intolerable state of mutual predation.

Perhaps most readers of Hobbes would echo the judgment of Pogson Smith that "he offers us a theory of man's nature which is at once consistent, fascinating, and outrageously false" (1909, ix). The intellectual landscape of the two centuries after Hobbes is strewn with trenchant refutations of this theory. Those refutations—in Britain, France, and Germany—form the points of departure for notions that undergird the modern social sciences.

Subsequent writers in England and Scotland were quick to challenge many of Hobbes' bold substantive statements. They criticized his views on political authority as well as his image of human nature, and they focused on societal problems other than that of civil security. In virtually all cases, however, *they retained the basic principles for erecting a social science that Hobbes had laid down.*

One can schematize the Hobbesian principles in the form of postulates that provide answers to questions posed, such as how the facts of human experience are to be constructed and explained. Hobbes responds to that with what is called the

Postulate of Methodological Individualism: *Social phenomena are best explained by analyzing the propensities of the individual actors that constitute them.*

To the question of how secular thought can provide a rational grounding of moral judgments, Hobbes responds with what is called the Postulate of Normative Individualism: *Normative judgments are best grounded rationally by appeal to the naturally given needs and rights of individual human actors.* Practical wisdom thus amounts to the direct application of theoretical knowledge to moral questions.

To the question about the source of human moral dispositions, Hobbes responds with what is called the Postulate of Natural Individual Morality: *Human moral orientations derive, directly or indirectly, from natural propensities inherent in all human beings.*

Later writers in the British tradition of social thought characteristically accepted all three of these postulates while challenging Hobbes on one point or another. For about a half-century after Hobbes, these writers—principally Locke, Shaftesbury, and Mandeville—lived in England. For the century thereafter, they flourished in Scotland, forming the remarkable cluster of figures who created what is known as the Scottish Enlightenment. Following the century of Scottish ascendancy, the tradition reverted back to England. Figure 10.1 presents a genealogical outline of the British tradition of social theory. It depicts not merely a number of thinkers who lived in Britain, *but also a network of participants in a transgenerational dialogue, which constituted a tradition by virtue of documented connections with one another.*

The process of revising Hobbes' conclusions in a framework of debate loyal to the postulates he set forth began with John Locke and a group of philosophers known as the Cambridge Platonists. Although Locke did not explicitly engage with Hobbes in the self-conscious way that Hobbes criticized Aristotle, Hobbes affected Locke's thought both by giving him a target to attack and by offering him the mode of thinking by which to carry out that attack.[5] Adhering to what I have called the postulates of Methodological Individualism and Normative Individualism, Locke followed the example set by Hobbes of making the rights of individuals the cornerstone of his moral and political philosophy. However, in a stance more in keeping with the values of British political culture, which stood for curtailing the powers of sovereigns, Locke endeavored to refute the Hobbesian defense of political absolutism. In doing so, he introduced two notions that would guide centuries of British revisionism: that the human animal manifests socially benign dispositions and that human selfish dispositions can have socially benign consequences. These notions were taken up by two writers who, though mutually antagonistic, both reflected Locke's influence: the Earl of Shaftesbury and Bernard de Mandeville.

The Shaftesbury Amendment

Anthony Ashley Cooper, Third Earl of Shaftesbury, is known chiefly for a collection of essays published in 1711 under the title *Characteristicks of Men, Manners, Opinions, Times, Etc.* An elegant writer more than a systematic thinker, he gains

146 Dialogues Involving Pointed Confrontations

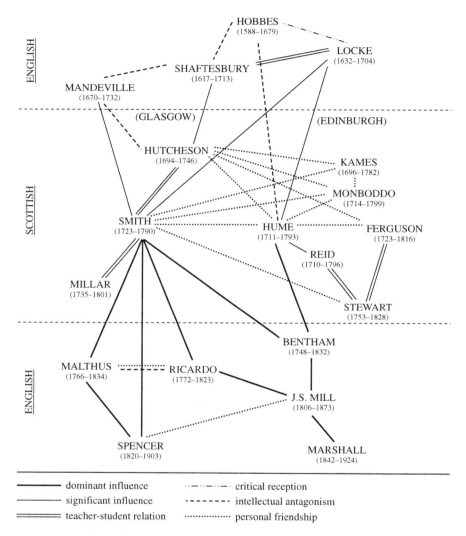

FIGURE 10.1 Links in the British Tradition

importance in our story for crystallizing one of the two main lines of revision of Hobbesian thinking. Educated privately by Locke, who was a close friend and physician of his grandfather, the first Earl of Shaftesbury, he went on to elaborate two of Locke's humanistic themes: the importance of political freedom for the improvement of mankind and a view of humanity as relatively benign in character. The latter theme is developed through a pointed attack against Hobbes' emphasis on the selfish cast of human nature, an attack supported by his identification of a number of self-transcending passions or affections, such as love, sympathy, and friendship. Shaftesbury traced them to a "social feeling" or "associating inclination" that appears naturally strong in most people ([1711] 1900, I, 72, 75). Against Hobbes he defended the natural bases of sociability by arguing that the very disposition to establish conventions presumes social sentiments: "faith, justice, honesty, and virtue, must have been as early as the state of nature, or they could never have been at all" (73). He also made reference to a naturally given moral sense, which he compared to the tuning of musical instruments—a sensibility that disposes one to find enjoyment by expressing natural social affections and prudential self-affections in the right proportions, and to shun unnatural affections like cruelty and malice (I, 258–93).

Whereas Locke had sought some rapprochement of moral philosophy with Christian theology by placing the source of morals in the will of God, Shaftesbury, though a spirited deist, championed a purely secular basis for his ethical notions. Shaftesbury not only defended human nature against its disparaging depictions by writers like Hobbes, but he also celebrated nature itself as the source of all value,[6] which earned him acclaim as "the first moralist who distinctly takes psychological experience as the basis of ethics" (Sidgwick [1886] 1954, 190). His approach was pursued by the moral philosophers of the Scottish Enlightenment, who used the notion of a moral sense to ground moral philosophy strictly on the basis of psychological facts. But his position was also seized to be made the butt of one of the keenest wits in England.

The Mandeville Amendment

Like Hobbes, Mandeville believed that coercive authority was essential to civil order, observing, for example, that a hundred equal men "under no Subjection, or Fear of any Superior upon Earth, could never live together awake Two Hours without Quarreling" ([1714] 1924, I, 347). However, Mandeville followed Locke in placing his analytic emphasis on the problem of commercial prosperity rather than on the problem of civil order. In the commercial domain, man's selfish dispositions produce socially advantageous consequences; according to the subtitle of *The Fable of the Bees*, Mandeville's most famous creation, they produce *Private Vices, Publick Benefits*. For example, vicious traits like vanity, envy, and love of luxury motivate people to buy goods and thereby stimulate the economy. Deceitful practices of buyers and sellers alike lubricate trade; even criminals serve to keep locksmiths in business and circulate wealth. Society is held together by public morality, but public morality springs from the vain and hypocritical behavior of egoists eager to gain public approbation, and therefore "Moral Virtues are the Political Offspring which Flattery begot upon Pride" (I, 51).

Mandeville assumed that all natural human propensities were exclusively oriented toward the satisfaction of self-regarding appetites. In defense of this thesis, he later took up cudgels against Shaftesbury, regarding whom he quipped: "The attentive Reader … will soon perceive that two Systems cannot be more opposite than his Lordship's and mine. His Notions I confess are generous and refined. … What pity it is they are not true" (I, 324). Mandeville placed more stock in human artifice than in human nature, and he found the incremental accumulation of experience over long historical periods crucial for developing the human skills that generate material prosperity. He invoked the doctrine of the division of labor as a principle essential for this development. This enabled him to explain the development of mankind from an originally savage state to its modern constructive capacities without recourse to an optimistic view of human nature, a position that Mandeville may have reached through his search for arguments with which to counter Shaftesbury (Horne 1978, 41).

However pronounced the oppositions among Hobbes, Shaftesbury, and Mandeville, from a more distant perspective, one cannot fail to be struck by similarities among their underlying analytic schemas.

Abstracting from the particular contents of these formulae, we find in each of them the basic tenets of atomic naturalism, a term useful for designating an ideal type that represents some core assumptions of British social theorists. Nearly all of them proceed from an assumption of certain propensities located within individuals, propensities that are naturally grounded, universally distributed, and followed in some calculating manner. From these propensities they derive the notion of a social field constituted by kinds of interactions produced by individuals so disposed; they culminate with a conception of a relatively stable order analogous to that of mechanical equilibrium produced by the aggregation of those social interactions.

Taken together, Hobbes, Shaftesbury, and Mandeville articulated the British tradition's three variant presuppositions regarding the individual-society nexus:

1. natural human propensities are essentially selfish and produce destructive consequences unless coercively checked;
2. natural human propensities are essentially selfish, but they produce positive social consequences; and
3. natural human propensities include dispositions toward social affection and moral sensibility.[7]

Over the next two centuries British social theorists used these presuppositions to construct systematic discourses and academic disciplines. One practical impetus behind their work was a need to valorize the dispositions required for a commercial society, as Mandeville had done, while still upholding some sense of human life as oriented to the realization of virtue, as in the tradition of civic humanism. Addressing this challenge became the distinctive mission of a sub-tradition known as Scottish moral philosophy. Its father was an Irish Presbyterian teacher, Francis Hutcheson, who returned to the University of Glasgow (his alma mater) as professor of moral philosophy in 1730. Five years before, Hutcheson had staked out his place in the trangenerational dialogue by declaring in his first publication that his would be a work "In Which The Principles of the late Earl of Shaftesbury are Explain'd and Defended, against the Author of the *Fable of the Bees*." Indeed, the wish to combat what he saw as the misguided doctrine of natural egoism became the driving force behind much of Hutcheson's work. In Hutcheson's view, the doctrine that held the principle of self-interest to be the spring of all human action simply did not stand up to the evidence:

> This scheme can never account for the principal actions of human life such as the offices of friendship, gratitude, natural affection, generosity, public spirit, compassion. ... In like manner this scheme can never account for the sudden approbation and violent sense of something amiable in actions done in distance ages and nations.
>
> *([1728] 1971, 117–18)*

In addition to upholding Shaftesbury's claim that, besides self-interest, humans exhibit naturally sociable and benevolent affections, Hutcheson followed Shaftesbury in establishing the disposition to make moral judgments in a naturally given faculty, the moral sense, and in making the exercise of that faculty the touchstone of moral judgment. Moral judgment thus represents an autonomous phenomenon; it cannot be reduced to self-interest, as with Hobbes and Mandeville; to the will of God, as Locke maintained; or to self-evident truth, as with rationalists like Gilbert Burnet. Errors in moral judgment get corrected by providing the moral sense with more accurate information regarding the consequences of an act for the general welfare. With this notion Hutcheson found a way to relieve the discomfort produced by Mandeville's formula of "private vices, public virtues"; for if an action, however motivated, was conducive to some sort of public benefit, then Hutcheson's utilitarian formula would indicate that it must not be considered a vice, but morally good.[8] He thereby found a way to reconcile the principle of self-love (which Mandeville had found so crucial for commercial society) with virtue.

Hutcheson also aimed to impart scientific rigor to moral philosophy. The title page of his first essay on morality advertises an "Attempt to Introduce a *Mathematical Calculation* in Subjects of Morality." That essay included a Newtonian formula that likens benevolence to the force of gravitation and so makes the strength of benevolence inversely proportioned to the distance between people ([1725] 1971, 220). It also sets forth a standard for measuring the goodness of an act—"the moral evil, or vice, of a given action, is as the degree of misery, and the number of sufferers; so that action is best which accomplishes the greatest happiness for the greatest number" (177). This standard is elaborated in his *System of Moral Philosophy* (Hutcheson 1755), which includes a chapter on how to calculate the morality of actions. Thus, however much Hutcheson aimed to refute Hobbes by defending the irreducibility of human passions for the public weal, he reproduced Hobbes' scientific project by claiming to rid the subject of morality of its usual causes of error—"the confusion of ambiguous words"—and by making moral analysis a matter of quantifying the desires and aversions of individual actors.

David Hume continued the project by applying the Newtonian method of experimental science to Hutcheson's observations about the human mind and the moral sense. Although Hume may seem to have undermined the quest for a rational secular ethic by separating judgments of fact from judgments of value, he reintroduced it by making a rationally discernible natural faculty the basis for all moral judgments, a faculty that operates by identifying what is good with the production of pleasure and the avoidance of pain. Hume advanced the utilitarian tradition beyond Hutcheson's formulation of the greatest happiness principle by analyzing its anthropological grounding in a natural sentiment of approbation of things that are useful to society. "It appears to be a fact," he argued in his *Enquiry Concerning the Principles of Morals*,

> that the circumstance of utility, in all subjects, is a source of praise and approbation; that it is constantly appealed to in all moral decisions concerning the merit and demerit of actions; that it is the sole source of that high regard paid to justice, fidelity, honour, allegiance, and chastity; that it is inseparable from all the other social virtues, humanity, generosity, charity, affability, lenity, mercy, and moderation; and, in a word, that it is a foundation of the chief part of morals, which has a reference to mankind and our fellow creatures.
> (Hume [1751] 1975, 221)

A student of Hutcheson and friend of Hume, Adam Smith, applied these ideas to questions of economic productivity and moral order. Known in his lifetime chiefly for *The Theory of Moral Sentiments* (1759), which extended the doctrines of innate social sentiments and moral sensibilities and erected a coherent theory of morality upon the analysis of sympathy, Smith gave a powerful boost to the social sciences through his other masterwork, *An Inquiry into the Nature and Causes of the Wealth of Nations* (1776). Smith's definitions of the nature of a nation's wealth and his analysis of its causes reflect the premises of atomic naturalism. The wealth of a country, he argued, is to be measured not in terms of the amount of bullion in its treasury but in terms of the quantity of goods produced each year divided by population. This measure of annual gross national product per capita registers the number of possessions enjoyed by all individuals in the society, which at the time was a revolutionary way to register a nation's wealth.

Smith identified two sources of wealth: the level of productive skill in the workforce and the ratio of productive to unproductive laborers. The level of productivity in the workforce is a function of the extent to which productive capacities are specialized, for specialization promotes manual dexterity, efficiency, and inventiveness. Specialization flows from the division of labor, which in turn gets promoted to the extent that a market exists for specialized products. Although the extent of the market depends on infrastructural factors like transportation, what ultimately accounts for markets is a natural human disposition—the propensity to trade one thing for another.

The other main factor responsible for high productivity is the proportion of the workforce actually engaged in productive labor. This depends on the quantity of capital stock available to finance enterprises that can employ workers. The amount of capital accumulation depends on a natural human disposition to save, based on "the desire of bettering our condition, a desire which ... comes with us from the womb, and never leaves us till we go into the grave" (Smith [1776] 1976, I, 362).

Left to themselves, these two naturally grounded dispositions—to better our condition through trade and through savings—are sufficient to lead any society to wealth and prosperity. Other natural propensities account for the cohesion of communities. The natural disposition to admire rank, distinction, and preeminence accounts for stable social hierarchies, while a disposition to revere general rules upholds the observance of societal norms. The human capacity for sympathy together with the naturally powerful wish for approval accounts for the moral order in society.[9] The logic of Smith's sociology follows the same pattern we witnessed in Hobbes, Shaftesbury, and Mandeville.

Natural individual propensities not only provide Smith with the principles by which social phenomena are to be explained; they also serve as the grounding of human morality and of criteria for defining the social good. Smith repeatedly praises nature for her unerring wisdom ([1759] 1982, 218, 222, 226).

The good becomes known through "what, in particular instances, our moral faculties, our natural sense of merit and propriety, approve or disapprove of" (159). The chief objects of moral approbation are those laws that safeguard the rights of individuals: their life and persons; their property and possessions; and their personal rights, or what is due them from the promises of others (84). Beyond this, the efficacy of natural dispositions in promoting public weal indicates that governments should undertake only what individuals cannot accomplish on their own: national security, administration of justice, and certain public works. Otherwise they should observe a principle of laissez-faire so that

> the obvious and simple system of natural liberty establishes itself, [such that] every man, as long as he does not violate the laws of justice, is left perfectly free to pursue his own interest his own way, and to bring both his industry and capital into competition with those of any other man.
>
> (Smith [1776] 1976, II, 208)

Notes

1 Recent scholarship has tended to play down the originality of Hobbes by situating his thought in a general movement of ideas in that period. This does not, however, diminish the centrality of Hobbes as a point of reference in the tradition.
2 The point gets expanded in the *Leviathan*: And I believe that scarce anything can be more absurdly said in natural Philosophy, than that which now is called *Aristotle's Metaphysiques*; nor more repugnant to Government, than much of that he hath said in his *Politiques*; nor more ignorantly, than a great part of his *Ethiques*. (Hobbes [1651] 1909, ch. 46, par. 11, 522)
3 The treatise on the state appeared first as *Elements of Law* in 1640; it was circulated in manuscript form and not published until 1650. Hobbes published an expanded version of part of the *Elements* in Latin as *De Cive* in 1642, which he later reworked and published in English as *Leviathan* in 1651. The treatise on the body, *De Corpore*, appeared in 1655 and the treatise on man, *De Homine*, in 1658 (although it was not translated into English until 1972).

4 Though Hobbes does not provide us with a political theory free of theology, there is nothing essential missing when the theology is taken out. ... He also makes it clear that God requires nothing of men which they would not require of each other if there were no God. Atheists, no less than other men, can discover that the laws of nature are rules which it is every man's interest should be generally observed, and have as powerful a motive for creating the conditions in which it is most likely that they will be observed. (Plamenatz 1963, 21, 16)

5 The word "Leviathan" occurs in [Locke's] Second Treatise, and there are phrases and whole arguments which recall the Hobbesian position, and must have been intended in some sense as comments upon them. Moreover, the thinking of Hobbes was of systematic importance to Locke and enters into his doctrines in a way which goes much deeper than a difference in political opinion. ... He seems to have been in the curious position of having absorbed Hobbesian sentiments, Hobbesian phraseology in such a way that he did not know where they came from: his early reading, never repeated, perhaps; or other men's books and the general discussion of Hobbes; or both (Laslett 1960, 81, 85–6)

6 "O glorious nature! supremely fair, and sovereignly good! ... 0 mighty nature! Wise substitute of Providence! ... I sing of nature's order in created beings, and celebrate the beautys which resolve, in thee, the source and principle of all beauty and perfection" (Shaftsbury [1711] 1900, II, 98).

7 These assumptions inform what Elie Halévy identified as the three logically distinct doctrines used by utilitarian thinkers to reconcile individual interests with the general utility or public interest—the doctrines, respectively, of the artificial identity of interests, the natural identity of interests, and the fusion of interests. Although these positions appear somewhat contradictory, all three are present in some form in every utilitarian doctrine (Halévy [1901–4] 1966, 13–18).

8 Hutcheson did make a distinction, however, "between actions materially good that regardless of motive, benefited the public and acts formally good that were public benefits resulting from virtuous motives" (Horne 1978, 90).

9 Smith was so committed to explaining social formations by natural propensities that he engaged in such naturalistic pursuits as studying the behavior of birds. For an illuminating account of Smith's naturalism and its grounding in the naturalistic theology of Hutcheson and other British predecessors, see Brown (1994).

11

MONTESQUIEU AND DURKHEIM

The writings of the British moral philosophers were well known to intellectuals in France and in Germany during the eighteenth century. Voltaire popularized Newton and Locke; Diderot translated Shaftesbury; Condillac worked with Locke's epistemological notions, as Condorcet did with Hume's; Quesnay followed Locke and Hume in propounding the principles of individualistic capitalism based on natural laws; and Helvétius served as the conduit through which the utilitarian notions of Hume reached Bentham. Kant has been credited for being one of the few contemporary readers of Hume's *Treatise of Human Nature* to have understood it fully—he lavishly praised Shaftesbury, Hutcheson, and Hume. Herder waxed ecstatic over Shaftesbury. Yet in neither country did the atomic naturalism of the British philosophers take root in ways that would orient sociology along the lines they had projected. Instead, their ideas came to serve as foils against which French and German philosophers would react and move in radically different directions for grounding a social ethic and modern sociological thought.

Montesquieu and Rousseau

The great theme French thinkers would oppose to the British idealization of natural individuals was the ideal of society. The Baron de Montesquieu can rightly be taken as progenitor of this theme in French thought. Later theorists in the tradition—Rousseau, Comte, and Durkheim—would name him as the seminal inspiration for the modern science of society.[1] Montesquieu too promoted the notion that by himself he had fathered something original, referring to his masterwork *De l'esprit des lois* (1748) as "*prolem sine matre creatam*," an offspring created without a mother (cited in Lepenies 1988, 1).

Montesquieu challenged Hobbes on every major point of his doctrine. He argued that since humans are always born into a society and never encountered outside of society, it is meaningless to talk about the origin of society and government, as Hobbes had done, by analyzing the raw dispositions of individual actors. Moreover, self-interest cannot be a sufficient basis for human institutions, so the possibility of good government depends on moral socialization and the inculcation of civic virtues. Finally, there can be no universal touchstone for morality; rather, what is morally appropriate must depend on a society's particular circumstances—its physical milieu, its customs, its ideas about life, and its informing spirit.

Although Montesquieu became known as a follower of Locke and a champion of "English" notions like liberty, toleration, and constitutional government, his treatment of those notions rested on distinctive positions.[2] He believed that freedom does not stand as an absolute value derivable from the properties of human nature and related human rights. Freedom instead is a social fact: it depends on favorable environmental conditions and social customs, and it manifests itself as a right to do only whatever the laws permit. And social dispositions do not stem, as British critics of Hobbes and Mandeville would argue, from naturally given social sentiments and moral sensibilities, but from socially instilled attitudes, beliefs, and habits.

One can thus find in Montesquieu's writings, albeit expressed in a literary mode and often analytically imprecise manner, the core notions of the French tradition, which subsequent thinkers would develop more pointedly. We can formulate the positions in question by contrasting them with the postulates of the British tradition. To the question of how the facts of human experience are to be constructed and explained, Montesquieu adumbrates what is called the Postulate of Societal Realism: *Society is a supraindividual phenomenon with determinate properties not reducible to individual propensities.*

To the question of how secular thought can provide a rational grounding for moral judgments, Montesquieu adumbrates what is called the Postulate of Societal Normativity: *Normative judgments are best grounded rationally by determining what enhances societal well-being.* This is known through the investigations of intellectual experts, so practical wisdom amounts to the application of theoretical knowledge about society to moral questions.

To the question about the source of human moral dispositions, Montesquieu responds with what is called the Postulate of Societal Morality: *Society is the source of moral sentiments and habits, which it instills through institutions like family, education, religion, and government.*

Jean-Jacques Rousseau has been described as "the first great thinker to pass under the spell of Montesquieu" (Peyre 1960, xv). However, if subsequent writings in the French tradition are to be viewed as a more or less continuous refinement of Montesquieu's social thought, then to some extent Rousseau must be seen as an aberration or retrogression. That was how Comte viewed him, for Rousseau reverted to the Hobbesian way of beginning the quest for a social ethic by speculating on how humans live in an imagined state of nature anterior to forming a social order.

For Rousseau, as for Hobbes, society is *not* a natural entity. But in contrast to Hobbes, Rousseau's *homo* in the state of nature is a benign, self-sufficient creature who can survive very well without civil society. Few writers in the Western tradition can match the sincerity and depth with which Rousseau depicted the "natural goodness" of man (Melzer 1990). Nevertheless, Rousseau's natural man does not possess a *moral* sense. Both morality and reason can develop only in and through society. Accepting Montesquieu's argument that humans require moral socialization in order to live together sociably, Rousseau grounded his argument on a priori speculation rather than on appeals to observed societies.

In his famous essay on the social contract, Rousseau drew a number of distinctions between the properties of human life in the state of nature and in civil society. In chapter 8 of book 1, "The Civil State," Rousseau ([1762] 1987) listed a number of changes in the human condition that come about when people pass from the natural state into the civil state. Humans in the state of nature are marked by instinct, physical impulse, inclination, stupidity, and animality, whereas in civil society these traits are replaced, respectively, by justice, morality and duty, reason, intelligence, and full humanity. Man's natural condition exhibits liberty limited solely by force and slavery to the appetites, whereas in the social state, humans acquire civil liberty, which is limited by the general will, and moral liberty, in which they enjoy self-mastery by virtue of obeying laws they themselves collectively legislate. What is more, in nature possessions are secured by force, in civil society, through ownership of a positive title. In his chapter on "The Legislature" in book 2, Rousseau added that the establishment of society under laws transforms each individual from being self-sufficient, solitary, and independent into a dependent yet integrated and moral being.

Reculer pour mieux sauter. If from the point of view of developing positive sociology, Rousseau has regressed into pure speculation about the human condition in an assumed state of nature, he has withal provided an unprecedentedly precise analysis of the societal component of human functioning. In doing this he sharpened Montesquieu's key pronouncements about the nature of society.[3] For one thing, Rousseau refined Montesquieu's notion of a society's general spirit (*esprit général*) by developing the idea of a general will (*volonté générale*), which enabled him to draw a distinction between "aggregation" and "association," and to describe the general will as *sui generis* and not derivable from aggregating private wills (*volonté de tous*). He formulated the theorem of emergent levels, which later French writers would employ repeatedly, defining society as "a moral entity having specific qualities distinct from those of the individual beings which compose it, somewhat as chemical compounds have properties that they owe to none of their elements" (cited in Durkheim [1892] 1960, 82).

Rousseau also articulated the principles of the existential and normative primacy of the collective will. Montesquieu believed that laws are based on customs and manners, political structures on climate and societal conditions. Rousseau translated this into the proposition that governments function as an agent of society, commissioned to do the bidding of the will of the people. He affirmed the moral superiority of the collective body over individual interests by calling the intrusion of private interests into public affairs "evil," and asserting that "whatever breaks up social unity is worthless" (Rousseau [1762] 1987, 55, 99).

In spite of Rousseau's idealized view of the human condition in a state of nature, his quest for a social ethic culminated with a conception of *societal well-being as the preeminent value*. He declared the social order to be a "sacred right that serves as a foundation for all other rights" (17). He proposed to diagnose the "health of the body politic" (81) by assessing the extent to which public opinions are harmonized and private interests are subordinated to the public interest. Another diagnostic criterion is the extent to which a state's citizens become populous and multiply, so he included "count, measure, compare" (67) in his advice to future social scientists looking for an objective indicator of societal health.

French Critics of Rousseau

At first the ideas of Montesquieu and Rousseau did more to shape political ideologies than to build a social science. Montesquieu's linkage of checks and balances with political democracy guided the framers of the U.S. constitution, while Rousseau's *volonté générale* inspired the makers of the French Revolution.[4] Before Durkheim could redefine them as ancestors of French sociology, the tradition would have to be thickened.

Just as in Britain the postulates of atomic naturalism accommodated widely diverse views about human nature, so in France the postulates of what I shall call societal essentialism went along with views of man that diverged sharply from those of Rousseau. In the wake of the French Revolution such views burst forth in writers who took issue with Rousseauan assumptions and the revolutionary doctrines associated with them. These writers tapped into a deeper vein of thought in the French tradition in which man was viewed as a weak and sinful creature. Montaigne in his *Essays* (1580) and La Rochefoucauld in his *Maxims* (1665) had painted man as essentially vain, stupid, self-deceiving, and vicious—reflecting strands of Augustinian moral thought embedded in the Catholic tradition.

The preeminent postrevolutionary writers, Louis de Bonald and Joseph de Maistre, reaffirmed the role of Catholicism in counteracting essential human immorality. Bonald attacked Rousseau's point about the self-sufficient individual, arguing that only society and its traditions, anchored in language, can give individual life any reality; to regain social health, postrevolutionary France would have to return to a unified political system (monarchy) and a single set of religious beliefs (Roman Catholicism). Describing himself as a spiritual twin of Bonald, Maistre actually pushed this line of thought to ferocious extremes. Maistre dwelt on the incurably wicked and corrupt nature of man, which made absolute authority indispensable. He ridiculed contractarian views, which assumed that individuals know what they want. For Maistre, humans not only have no clear sense of what they want, but they are also propelled by unlimited strivings and irrationally destructive and self-immolative urges. What is more, individuals cannot articulate their needs before entering society, for the very language they need to do so comes from society. Similarly, contracts presuppose an elaborate network of social conventions and a complex social apparatus of enforcement. Society is as ancient as man, and adequate human functioning requires the fusion of the individual in a society that is sustained by a common religion and coercive authority. Individualist strivings to pursue imagined rights or needs can only atomize the social tissue.

For his radical opposition to social contract theories, in relation to Rouessau, Maistre has long seemed like nothing but an antagonist. Indeed, Maistre derided Rousseau's concept of the legislator as intolerably confused, rebutted his conception of law, ridiculed his belief in the sovereignty of the people, and called his maxim that man was born free a "foolish assertion" (Maistre 1971, 101, 120, 123, 143). In the words of his prime British translator, "Maistre saw Rousseau as one of the arch-villains of his century of villains" (Lively 1971, 44). Nevertheless, these robust differences arise on top of a foundation of common understandings. The same commentator went on to observe:

> Yet ... Maistre shares many basic assumptions and emotional attitudes with Rousseau. ... His ultimate object, like Rousseau's, was to resolve the conflict between man's self-will and his social nature, to release the capacity for virtue frustrated by existing civilization, to reestablish a state of harmony lost through the persistent exercise of self-will. ... [This] required the willing subordination of men to authorities whose moral justification consisted, in the last resort, not in what they aimed at, but in the unity they enforced. ... Both were more anxious abut the moral quality of communal life than about the source of sovereignty, and both judged that moral quality by the degree of emotional, unreasoned involvement in the community felt by the individual.
>
> *(Ibid., 44, 42)*

While Maistre, like Rousseau, took a dim view of the prospects of modern society, Maistre posed as the last defender of a high civilization about to perish, whereas Rousseau revered Geneva as one of the last embers of freedom in a darkening world. Other critics of Rousseau, such as the Marquis de Condorcet, took a more positive view of the prospects of humanity in the age of reason and science: that *Esquisse*, often regarded as the philosophical testament of the eighteenth century, celebrates the progressive liberation of humans from the scourges of nature and social bondage through the unfolding of human capacities to observe accurately and reason soundly.

Through public education, a journal coedited with Abbé Sièyes, and his own publications, Condorcet had devoted his life to promoting the application of scientific method to human phenomena—most notably, the procedures of mathematics, including a calculus of probabilities. Condorcet embraced Rousseau's notion that individuals should submit their actions to the decisions of the general will and, like Rousseau, sought a way to institute a system that would rationalize collective decision-making for the public good. However, he departed from Rousseau's model of radical democracy, both by arguing for the legitimacy and indispensability of representative institutions and by defending the need for qualified elites to produce rational public decisions. These departures reflect his view of the general will as a vehicle for expressing the truth discoverable by reason rather than as an expression of moral right based on collective will (Baker 1975, 229–31, 243). More generally, he departed from Rousseau in affirming the value of reason and its progressive cultivation as a liberating force in human history. Condorcet hailed the emergence of "social mathematics" as a critical factor in the progress of humanity.

Henri de Saint-Simon, a marginal supporter of the Revolution, admired both Condorcet and Maistre. He shared the humanitarian rationalism of the philosophes—their espousal of scientific progress and their attacks on religious dogmas for suppressing the masses. At the same time he rejected their wholesale critique of medieval political and religious institutions. Siding on this matter with Maistre, who in turn evoked Rousseau and Montesquieu in his beliefs, Saint-Simon held that some sort of common faith was essential to sustain social solidarity and that moral beliefs had to be in accord with societal conditions. Thus, while harsh on past ecclesiastical abuses—he indicted all popes and cardinals since the fifteenth century as "heretical" for supporting the Jesuit order and the Inquisition, and he condemned Protestants for their allegedly inferior morality, faulty forms of worship, and false creed—Saint-Simon affirmed the positive role of the medieval Church in promoting political unity and intellectual and social vitality.[5]

Proceeding from convictions about the need for social harmony, the role of ideas in promoting it, and the superiority of science and industry over theology and militarism, Saint-Simon evolved a vision of the good society that inspired generations of his countrymen. Like most Enlightenment thinkers, his social ethic rested on the conviction that the good society must be in accord with what is natural in human life. From physiology, he derived a notion, which entailed a society based not on the principle of equality, but on the natural inequalities of people.[6] The way he divided up different human capacities changed. What endured was his belief in the need for social elites and for sincere deference to citizens with superior qualifications—thanks to which the society of the future would be free of class conflicts and would sanction a greatly reduced role for coercive authority and governmental action. In the feudal order these superior strata took the form of religious and military elites; in the modern era those would be replaced—gradually, to avoid the horrors of revolution and sudden change—by men of science and leaders of industry.

Given how much credibility the theologians had lost in the eighteenth century, it was important for savants to provide a new social bond. They could do so by following the trajectory of intellectual development along which each of the natural sciences had progressed, from a conjectural to a positive, or empirically grounded, basis of reasoning. Saint-Simon reproached scientists for losing themselves in mindless accumulation of isolated facts and urged them to create a general theory that could unify all scientific knowledge. Indeed, Saint-Simon became impatient with any scientific work that was not immediately directed to practical objectives, part of the foundation of his later rupture with Comte.[7] Concurring with Bonald on the importance of "systematic unity," he rejected Bonald's proposal that it be based on the concept of deism in favor of the concept of universal gravitation (Saint-Simon [1952] 1964, 18).

Following Saint-Simon's death in 1826, his chief disciples declared that the task of the future was to reconcile the ideas of Maistre with those of Enlightenment rationalists like Voltaire and Condorcet (Berlin 1990, 62). Saint-Simon had resolved the opposition between Maistre's claim of the human need for hierarchy and the philosophes' rejection of old privileges by positing a need for new elites based on scientific and industrial capabilities. He had reconciled Maistre's respect for historical context and the philosophes' belief in progress by viewing the work of earlier periods as historically appropriate contributions to the long-term development of humanity. Yet his last-minute reversion to revealed religion doubtless made some followers believe he finally reneged on the commitment to rationalism that led him earlier to describe deism as an outworn belief. This crucial reconciliation was to be achieved by Saint Simon's young associate of seven years, Auguste Comte.

Societal Essentialism

At this point, I shall examine Comte's social ethic and related sociological ideas. His ideas took shape through a remarkable synthesis of diverse and complex strands of the French tradition of sociological thought up to his time, as Figure 11.1 suggests. Comte was influenced significantly by Montesquieu, Turgot, Condorcet, Bonald, Maistre, Saint-Simon, and Rousseau. From Montesquieu he took the aspiration to promulgate laws of societal functioning; from Turgot and Condorcet, the vision of human progress powered by the perfection of man's rational faculties; from Bonald and Maistre, the importance of societal integration and moral regulation; and from Saint-Simon, the conception of new forms of temporal and spiritual elites to replace the old.

One might conjecture that at some point Comte absorbed the theorem of emergent organizational levels from Rousseau. It appears that he did not get that idea from Saint-Simon. This is noteworthy since Comte shared virtually every other major assumption with Saint-Simon. Indeed, except for Marx and Engels or perhaps Dewey and Mead, there has scarcely been any collaboration in the history of Western social theory so intimate as that between Saint-Simon and Comte.[8]

Saint-Simon recruited the impecunious 19-year-old Comte as his secretary in 1817, becoming his mentor, patron, and employer. With Comte's aid he published a series of periodicals devoted to proclaiming the virtues of the coming industrial order. Although Comte gratefully absorbed much from his benefactor for some years, he began to chafe as the relationship wore on. Their break came in 1824, over issues that were largely psychological, programmatic, and proprietary.[9] Yet, there was one important substantive question on which they diverged, a divergence that came more sharply into focus as Comte forged his own system of positive philosophy. Saint-Simon assumed the only truly certain knowledge was mathematical, an assumption Comte would criticize as "metaphysical." In that spirit, Saint-Simon advocated a unified theory of all phenomena based on the law of gravity; he appealed to such a theory to ground his new religion for humanity, which he called "Physicism," but his problem of how to reconcile Condorcet's

160 Dialogues Involving Pointed Confrontations

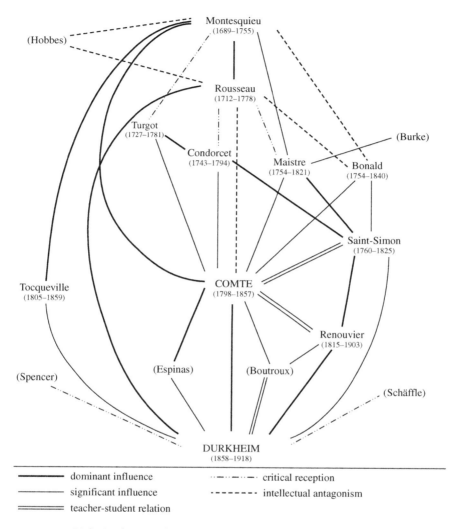

FIGURE 11.1 Links in the French Tradition

rationalism with Maistre's religionism was not solved. Universal gravitation scarcely provided an object capable of eliciting the sentiments of philanthropy that Saint-Simon required to animate his reorganized European society. This embarrassment comes poignantly to the fore in his 1808 essay on science when he, after invoking the concept of universal gravitation as linchpin for the new scientific system *"and consequently for the new religious system,"* went on to argue that the idea of God is defective and should not be used in the physical sciences, adding, "but I do not say that it should not be used in political affairs, at least for a long time; it is the best means yet discovered for motivating high-minded legislative dispositions" (Saint-Simon 1859, 211, 219). The chasm between what Saint-Simon's political community needed in the way of common beliefs and what his physicalist science could produce was unbridgeable—so much so that he finally turned to a fervent theism to anchor his social faith.

One of Comte's main contributions to the running dialogue of the French tradition was to bridge the remaining chasm between Condorcet and Maistre—between the rational imperatives of modern science and the emotional imperatives of societal order. He did so by establishing a series of claims regarding the objects of scientific study and the intellectual procedures for studying them. Opposing Saint-Simon's quest for a universal science unified under physics, Comte held that the essence of positive science was its subordination of rational propositions to empirical facts and that observations had to respect the distinctive features of different types of phenomena. Rather than assay something so "chimerical" as explaining all phenomena by a single law like the law of gravity, Comte made it the task of positive philosophy to coordinate *different* laws pertaining to different orders of phenomena.

The main thought of Comte's schematization of the sciences is this:

> All observable phenomena may be included within a very few natural categories, so arranged as that study of each category may be grounded on the principal laws of the preceding, and serve as the basis of the next ensuing. This order is determined by the degree of simplicity, or, what comes to the same thing, of generality of their phenomena. Hence results their successive dependence and the greater or lesser facility for being studied.
>
> *([1853] 2009, 44)*

Following this principle, Comte proceeded to divide all natural phenomena into two classes—inorganic and organic bodies. Inorganic bodies then get ordered, according to the principle of increasing complexity and decreasing generality, into celestial bodies, masses, and molecules—the subject matters, respectively, of astronomy, physics, and chemistry. Organic bodies similarly divide into individual organisms and species. The sciences that study any of these bodies become positive to the extent that they relinquish the futile search for ultimate causes, whether finding them in spirits or in abstract notions, and rely instead on the search for empirically ascertainable laws of coexistence and succession. Human knowledge approaches this positive condition one science at a time, beginning with the science of the most general and least complex of the phenomena, astronomy, and moving in order up the hierarchy, as in Figure 11.2.

Due to this uneven development of the sciences, there is a chronic tendency for proponents of well-established sciences to explain higher-order phenomena in terms appropriate for lower ones: for mathematicians to absorb mechanics into calculus, for physicists to absorb chemical phenomena, for chemists to absorb biological into chemical terms, and, finally, for biologists to make sociology a mere corollary of their science. Comte called this tendency materialism; today we would more likely call it reductionism. Accordingly, each of the sciences has to undergo a long struggle against the encroachments of the one preceding it. The time had

162 Dialogues Involving Pointed Confrontations

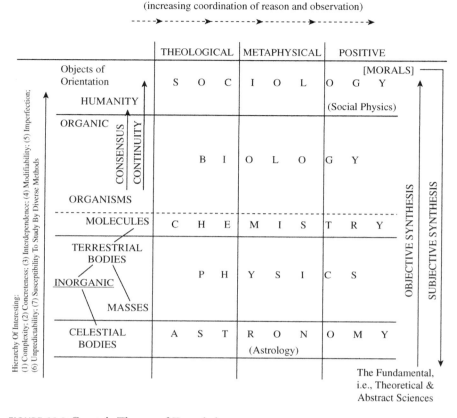

FIGURE 11.2 Comte's Theory of Knowledge

finally arrived for sociology to complete this struggle and reveal social phenomena as subjects to invariable natural laws, not reducible to those of biology or any other simpler science. This meant that in addition to the inanimate and organismic phenomena, which for Saint-Simon exhausted the phenomenal universe,[10] there was yet another, more complex order of reality whose facticity could be established and whose properties, like those of other orders of phenomena, could not be reduced to those lower in the hierarchy of beings. That reality was society.

How did Comte's positive schematization of the sciences solve the Saint-Simonian question of faith? It did so in part by making the whole question of God's existence obsolete. Although atheism had been useful during the metaphysical period for removing the last vestiges of theological belief, it prolonged the metaphysical stage by seeking new solutions of theological problems instead of setting them aside as utterly futile. Since humans can never penetrate the mystery of the essential cause that produces phenomena, the only meaningful type of knowledge to seek is that which establishes laws about the behavior of phenomena. Further, the negative spirit of atheism has greater affinity with anarchy than with union at a time when society needs to move toward an organic, solidary state.

Instead of belief in God, what can provide the cement for modern society is the idea of humanity. That idea represents no theological or metaphysical speculation, but a being whose properties can be determined. If its ultimate cause cannot be known, its reality can be demonstrated by the fact that it exhibits lawful regularities. Its reality thus justified, humanity can serve henceforth as an object for religious devotion in a positive polity. Comte's positive philosophy thus eliminates theology, as Voltaire and Condorcet wanted, but retains religion, as Bonald and Maistre wanted.

The Postulate of Societal Realism serves as the key building block for Comte's social science and his social ethic. Comte articulated it in its classic form, arguing that "society is no more decomposable into individuals than a geometric surface is into lines, or a line into points" (1875, II, 181). The master concept of the science that studies this supraindividual phenomenon is *consensus*, defined as the interconnectedness of all parts of the social system. Comte took the concept of consensus from biology, but took pains to distinguish its manifestations in human society from those in biological organisms, since the former uniquely admits *historical* linkages; that is, the gradual and continuous influence of generations upon each other. With this notion in mind, Comte formulated the governing principle of social science as follows:

> Without extolling or condemning political facts, science regards them as subjects of observation: it contemplates each phenomenon in its harmony with coexisting phenomena, and its connection with the foregoing and the following state of human development; it endeavors to discover, from both points of view, the general relations that connect all social phenomena—and each of them is *explained*, in the scientific sense of the word, when it has been connected with the whole of the existing situation, and the whole of the preceding movement.
>
> *([1853] 2009, 473)*

Once the reality of society as a phenomenon subject to static and dynamic laws had been established, a remarkable transformation took place in human thought—a transformation manifest in Comte's own transition as he moved from the *Course in Positive Philosophy* ([1853] 2009) to the *System of Positive Polity* (1875). The superiority of the theoretic function now gives way to the superiority of the practical.[11] "It is our business," Comte had advised, "to contemplate order, that we may perfect it" ([1853] 2009, II, 461). The hierarchical arrangement of natural phenomena established through the objective method gave way to a new, inverted ordering of phenomena based on what Comte called the subjective method. This subjective synthesis begins with a new discipline placed at the top of the old hierarchy: the science of morals. Morals provide systematic guidance for humans based first on attachment to the whole of humanity and to the progressive course of its development. These practical commitments henceforth direct the problems to which specialists in each of the sciences should devote their attention.

These notions indicate the way Comte links the Postulate of Societal Realism with the Postulate of Societal Normativity. Normative judgments are to be based on what enhances societal well-being, which is known through a science that determines the normal conditions of order and progress. This assumption, in turn, is linked with the Postulate of Societal Morality in that the moral dispositions needed to secure social order have to be instilled by social institutions—most notably, the family, which cultivates the social affects of "attachment" and "veneration," and religion, which cultivates the love of humanity. In Comte's view, then, society is "essential" in three senses: the term refers to a real being with essential properties, it is required as an object of attachment in order to establish moral guidelines, and it is necessary for instilling the moral values needed to sustain the social order.

The French Discipline

Due to the eccentric cast of his religion of humanity and his odd personal and intellectual conduct, Comte was ridiculed and largely forgotten for decades after his death in 1851.[12] Yet half a century later his ideas had become enshrined in one of the most powerful bodies of thought to enter the foundations of modern social science, the sociology of Emile Durkheim. That is suggestive evidence of the tenacity of national traditions and their capacity to wash out idiosyncratic expressions.

Some of Comte's ideas reached Durkheim through Émile Boutroux, his teacher at the École Normale, who favored Comte's emphasis on the irreducibility of different levels of phenomenal reality, and through the widely influential writings of Charles Renouvier, one of Comte's students at the École Polytechnique, who inspired Durkheim with an uncompromising rationalism and a determination to submit the domain of morality to scientific study. Durkheim may also have been exposed to the activity of Comte's erstwhile disciple Émile Littre, who organized a sociology society while Durkheim was in secondary school. He was also exposed to Comtean ideas through German authors, most notably Comte's erudite disciple Albert Schäffle. More directly consequential for his science of sociology was Alfred Espinas, an outspoken follower of Comte, whose dissertation on animal societies offered an exemplar for the naturalistic study of social organization. For considering social consciences "among the highest realities" and "society [as] a concrete living thing" (quoted in Deploige [1911] 1938, 125) and for studying social facts in order to construct a rigorous science of them, Durkheim felt that Espinas' book constituted the very first serious achievement of scientific sociology (Lukes 1972, 84). Espinas in turn was able to provide major support for Durkheim's sociological project by establishing the special chair, in pedagogy and social science, that brought Durkheim to Bordeaux in 1887.

Even so, Durkheim's absorption of Comtean notions reflected not just the continuing efforts of supporters to keep their master's vision alive, but also the resonance of Comtean themes with French intellectuals' widespread disposition to take literally the metaphor of society as a body. This, together with his sheer intellectual brilliance, helps account for the ascendancy of Durkheim and his school of thought over intellectual competitors like Gabriel Tarde and René Worms, both of whom shared certain Comtean notions but rejected, on different grounds, the core concept of societal essentialism.[13] Although this disposition was fortified by reactions against the French Revolution, it had already appeared before the Revolution, as in Diderot's definition of morality as that which is "conductive to the survival and cohesion of the body social" (Proust 1962, 338). Foucault has expressed the matter vividly: for the fantasy of the king's body the French came to substitute "the idea of a social body constituted by the universality of wills ... a social body which needs to be protected, in a quasi-medical sense" (1980, 55). Throughout the nineteenth century, French of all ideological hues agreed in finding the social order threatened with dissolution by the noxious growth of individualism.[14] This concern for protecting the health of the French body social was intensified by the national demoralization that set in following the defeat of France by Prussia in 1871.

Thus Durkheim's formative years were spent in an intellectual and political milieu that both encouraged him to cultivate the Comtean doctrines of societal essentialism and promised him a responsive ambience for them if he did the job well. In any event, Durkheim's appropriation of Comte turned into one of the most productive instances of dialogue in the history of Western social theory. For if it is true, as Evans-Pritchard once remarked, that "there is little of general methodological or theoretical significance in [Durkheim's] writings that we do not find in Comte if we are earnest and persevering enough to look for it" (1970, 19)—indeed, Durkheim himself always freely acknowledged the influence (Lukes 1972, 68)—this was by no means a matter of rote replication. Not only did Durkheim provide trenchant support for Comte's doctrines, but on a number of issues he transmuted Comte's positions in nontrivial ways.

Regarding issues related to the Postulate of Societal Realism:

1. Durkheim agrees with Comte that society represents a *sui generis*, non-reducible natural reality; but he

    a   advocates the study of societies and clusters of social facts, not generic "society" or humanity;
    b   inserts the domain of psychology between that of the biological study of organisms and the sociological study of societies.

2. Durkheim agrees with Comte's precept that society like all other phenomena should be studied in a positive manner, eliminating uncontrolled speculation; but he

    a   criticizes Comte's practice for being at odds with this standard, calling him metaphysical and dogmatic, and rebuking his sociology as a

"science ... brought to a conclusion with its foundations barely laid" (quoted in Lukes 1972, 69);
b   dismisses Comte's rejection of the scientific search for causes and couches his own program in terms of a search for social causes; and
c   frames sociological explanation in terms of efficient and final causes instead of following Comte's holistic method of explaining social phenomena in terms of the totality of current and preceding conditions.

Regarding issues related to the Postulate of Societal Normativity: Durkheim agrees with Comte that the theoretical determination of normal societal states can provide diagnostic standards for practical action and that one of the major criteria of societal health is the presence of adequate social solidarity, but he

1. disagrees with Comte that in modern industrial societies solidarity should be based on an extensive body of common beliefs and the suppression of individual freedoms of expression. Instead, he argues that in modern societies functional diversity requires moral diversity, and that the modern cult of the individual provides the only system of beliefs that can ensure the moral unity of such a society;
2. also rejects Comte's model of a single evolutionary trajectory for all of humanity in favor of an evolutionary model like a tree with branches heading in divergent directions, each of which possesses its own characteristic standard of morality.

Regarding the Postulate of Societal Morality, Durkheim supports Comte's notion that social institutions like the family, government, and religion are important for inculcating morality, but dismisses his notion that certain social dispositions are instinctually based. In this he reverts to a more Rousseauan position of finding a radical duality in human nature: purely egoistic dispositions grounded in the natural organism opposed by moral dispositions that come only from society. Indeed, Durkheim fills the biological side of human nature with potentially insatiable appetites that, without regulation, would lead to pathological extremes like suicide.

Durkheim similarly qualifies Comtean positions with respect to a number of more particular propositions. For example, he accepts Comte's association of the division of labor with population growth, but holds that Comte has mistaken a cause of the division of labor—demographic growth—for one of its consequences. Durkheim agrees with Comte that the division of labor produces mental overspecialization and moral parochialization, but he does not agree that this thereby diminishes societal solidarity. Moreover, he considers impossible and undesirable Comte's prescription that such differentiation be balanced through societal organs that produce consensus. Durkheim also agrees with Comte that certain intuitively bad phenomena may be socially beneficial, but Comte sees this only as the cost of progress, while Durkheim sees socially disfavored phenomena, like crime, as an inherent part of social order.

In these and other ways, Durkheim refined the relatively crude formulations of Comte and set the stage for twentieth-century sociology. Yet, there is no mistaking the central rhetorical thrust of his life's work. As I argued in a previous publication (Levine 1985, 67–8), his major monographs can be viewed as efforts to demonstrate the validity of what I have identified as the three grand postulates of the French tradition of social theory. The Postulate of Societal Realism was clearly the enveloping theme of *Suicide*, which begins by identifying an explanandum, suicide rates, as constituting a type of fact that represents, both in its constancy and its variability, distinctive properties that can be identified only at the societal level of analysis, and concludes by asserting the demonstrated superiority of explanations that adduce strictly social causative factors.

The Postulate of Societal Normativity formed the rhetorical focus of *The Division of Social Labor*. Holding that the principal objective of every science of life is to define and explain normal states and to distinguish them from pathological states, Durkheim sought in his first substantive monograph to address the question of whether high levels of specialization were morally acceptable. He did so by asking if the division of labor contributes to the well-being of society, and if those phenomena associated with the division of labor that are commonly considered objectionable represent normal or pathological conditions. Durkheim aimed, in that work, to demonstrate that moral questions could be treated in a superior manner through a positive science that would examine types of societies and determine their normal and pathological states.

Durkheim came to argue that just as society provides the object to which religious symbols ultimately refer and the forces that predispose humans to create and revere such symbolism, so society constitutes the reference point of moral beliefs and sentiments and the agency for inculcating them in otherwise nonmoral organisms.

In addition to bringing the themes of the French tradition to a kind of climactic expression, there are other respects in which Durkheim has been said to represent a summation of the French tradition. For one thing, he performed a kind of civic role by providing recognition for virtually all the participants in the transgenerational dialogue listed in Figure 11.1. For Montesquieu, Rousseau, Saint-Simon, and Comte, he wrote much to celebrate them as contributors to the French tradition.

What is more, he repeatedly identified the body of work that led to sociology as a specifically French creation. In an official report of 1895, he asserted that sociology could develop only where two conditions were obtained—an intellectual dissatisfaction with simplistic conceptions and a disposition to apply scientific method to complex objects—and those conditions existed only in France. In an article for the *Revue Blue* in 1900 he declared:

> To determine France's part in the progress made by sociology during the nineteenth century is to review, in large part, the history of that science. For it

is in our country and in the course of this century that it was born, and it has remained an essentially French science.

(Durkheim [1900] 1973, 3)

Finally, Durkheim sometimes clarified and defended his positions by contrasting them with divergent positions held in philosophy. That practice introduces a new dimension to my narrative: the dynamics of transnational dialogue.

Notes

1 Rousseau referred to Montesquieu as "the one man of modern times who was capable of calling this great [social] science into being" ([1762] 1979, 458). Comte observed that "Montesquieu must have the credit of the earliest direct attempt to treat politics as a science of facts" ([1822] 1974, 157). Durkheim averred that Montesquieu made "our science" aware of its subject matter, its nature and method, and laid its groundwork ([1892] 1960, 2).
2 Montesquieu's attachment to the ideal of liberty only came after his visit to England in the years 1729–31. Earlier, expressing sentiments Comte would echo a century later, he had belittled the advantages that free peoples hold over others and showed disdain for popular disputations and the fashionable infatuation with freedom of speech (Shackelton 1961, 284).
3 Rousseau himself implied that part of his mission was to sharpen some of Montesquieu's formulations when he observed of the latter that "this great genius often lacked precision and sometimes clarity" ([1762] 1987, 56).
4 Prerevolutionary pamphleteers like the Abbé Sièyes, National Assembly delegates deliberating on the rights of man, and engineers of the Terror alike espoused simplified versions of Rousseau's teachings. For a superb review of recent literature anent the long-debated question of Rousseau's influence on the Revolution, see Starobinski (1990).
5 These indictments actually appear in Saint-Simon's final work, "New Christianity", where he broke with his earlier rationalism to affirm the revealed character of Christianity and announced that in "fulfilling a divine mission [to recall] nations and kings to the true spirit of Christianity," the voice of God was now speaking through his mouth ([1825] 1964, 114–16).
6 Saint-Simon adapted the thesis of Bonald and Maistre that at bottom humans desire not to achieve equality with those of higher status but to express themselves in roles they were born into; in other words, people naturally desire to express their intrinsic physiological aptitudes. These aptitudes included different functional capacities—divided among knowing, willing, and feeling—as well as different levels of ability (Manuel 1962, 126–7).
7 Saint-Simon promoted technological progress as well as expanded social organization. "The philosophy of the eighteenth century was critical and revolutionary, that of the nineteenth will be inventive and organizational" was the motto of an encyclopedia of scientific knowledge he envisioned. Saint-Simon's thinking inspired cadres of engineers, including the first men to work on the Suez Canal as well as advocates of a federated Europe. The editor of Saint-Simon's *Oeuvres Choisies* (1859), Lemonnier, founded a League of Peace, from which sprang the idea of the League of Nations (Saint-Simon [1952] 1964, xxi, xxxiii, xliii).
8 "During [Comte's] formative period it is no more possible to separate the proprietary rights of Saint-Simon or Comte from their common store of ideas than it would be to perform the same task for Marx and Engels" (Manuel 1962, 259).
9 Comte resented Saint-Simon's continued assumption of a tutelary position as he approached his mid-twenties. And Comte became disturbed by his aging master's mental

condition—the intellectual stagnation, the apparent turn toward theology, the pathetic suicide attempt. The two also had different views about how to implement the positive program: Saint-Simon wanted to apply his epochal discoveries to contemporary affairs without delay, while Comte believed it necessary first to secure firmer intellectual foundations by completing the new synthesis of positive knowledge. Tensions came to a head in jurisdictional quarrels over the publication of Comte's seminal essay of 1822, "Plan of the Scientific Operations Necessary for Reorganizing Society" (Comte [1822] 1974) which incited Saint-Simon to cut him off.
10 "There are no phenomena which are not either astronomical, chemical, physiological, or psychological" (Saint-Simon [1952] 1964, 21).
11 From his first publications, Comte diverged from Saint-Simon by insisting on the distinction between theoretical knowledge and practical knowledge, and the need to constitute the latter as an application of the former. In the *Course*, Comte judged theoretical knowledge superior not only for providing a necessary foundation anterior to practical knowledge, but also regarding the dignity of its subject matter: However great may be the services rendered to industry by science ... we must never forget that the sciences have a higher destination still ... that of satisfying the craving of our understanding to know the laws of phenomena. To feel how deep and urgent this need is, we have only to consider for a moment the physiological effects of *consternation*; and to remember that the most terrible sensation we are capable of is that which we experience when any phenomenon seems to arise in violation of the familiar laws of nature. ([1853] 2009, 40) In the *Positive Polity*, he reversed this ranking, stressing the contribution of positive philosophy to practical life and submitting that "it leads at once to an object far higher than that of satisfying our scientific curiosity; the object, namely, of organizing human life" (Comte 1875, I, 46).
12 The comment by Hippolyre Taine, often alleged to be a follower of Comte, is typical: "[Comte's] mind seems in all respects to be absolute, exclusive, narrow, vigorously and irrevocably immersed in its own evolution, confined to limited horizons and to a single conception" (cited in Simon 1963, 130).
13 Clark defended Tarde's own brilliance and the superiority of his positions over Durkheim's in many instances, but argued that his work suffered because it "was out of harmony with the dominant intellectual temper of the time" (1968, 508). Specifically, Clark made reference to Tarde's values of spontaneity and disengagement, in contrast to Durkheim's Cartesian rationalism and engagement (1969, 7–18). But the central substantive divergence between the two hinged on the question of methodological individualism versus societal essentialism. It seems fair to say that Tarde's nominalism was out of harmony with Durkheim's milieu as well. While Tarde was fairly isolated socially, Worms, like Durkheim, was heavily involved in institutionalizing sociology by founding a journal, a social science library, a Paris society of sociology, and the Institut international de sociologie. However, Worms failed to galvanize an intellectual following, in good part because he abandoned Comte's tenet that society has *sui generis* properties that cannot be found at the organismic level of reality. On Comtean strains in Tarde and Worms, see Simon (1963); on the institutional ascendance of Durkheim, see Clark (1973).
14 The summary description of this situation by Steven Lukes is worth citing at length: The theme of social dissolution was a pervasive one in nineteenth-century French thought. ... It wastaken up, with differing emphases, by conservatives, Catholics, Saint-Simonians, Positivists, liberals, and socialists. All agreed in condemning *l'odieux individualisme*—the social, moral, and political isolation of self-interested individuals, unattached to social ideals and unamenable to social control; and they saw it as spelling the breakdown of social solidarity. For some it resided in dangerous ideas, for others it was social or economic anarchy, a lack of the requisite institutions and norms, for yet others it was the prevalence of self-interested attitudes among individuals. It was variously traced to the Reformation, the Renaissance, the intellectual anarchy consequent on the "negative" thought of the Enlightenment, the Revolution, to the decline of the aristocracy or the Church or traditional religion, to the Industrial Revolution, to the growth of capitalism

or democracy. Almost all, however, agreed in seeing it as a threat to social order—whether that order was conceived of in a traditionalist and hierarchical manner, or as an organized technocracy, or as essentially liberal and pluralist, or, as the socialists envisaged it, as an ideal co-operative order of "association" and "harmony." ... In short, Durkheim's notions of "egoism" and "anomie" were rooted in a broad and all-pervasive tradition of discussion concerning the causes of imminent social disintegration and the practical measures needed to avoid it—a tradition ranging from the far right to the far left. (1972, 195–8).

12

KANT AND HEGEL

Kant's Triple Revolution

No one in the history of Western philosophy pursued the quest for a rational secular ethic with more feverish intensity and altered the course of that quest more profoundly than Immanuel Kant (1726–1804). In transforming the field of moral philosophy, Kant introduced ideas and themes that inspired a library of seminal works of German social science.

Like some of the French authors who came to reject atomic naturalism, Kant began his career under the influence of British thinkers. Awed by Newton's achievements, Kant focused his early work on the sciences of nature. He lectured at the University of Königsberg on physics, mathematics, and physical geography, and wrote extensively on cosmology and natural philosophy. In the 1760s, Kant still accepted the British assumption that Newtonian science could provide grounds for a credible ethic. He praised Shaftesbury, Hutcheson, and Hume for having made the most progress in the search for the first principles of all morality. During his fifties, Kant developed a new approach to philosophical questions through the *Critique of Pure Reason* and the *Critique of Practical Reason*.

In these writings, Kant viewed himself as producing an intellectual revolution no less momentous than that of Copernicus. In effect, he begot not a single but a triple revolution. For one thing, Kant overturned the notion that all the concepts needed to represent natural phenomena could be derived by observing external events. Instead, he insisted that we have a conditioned understanding of phenomena: it must be structured by forms of intuition and categories of understanding supplied by human subjects in order to represent the things they observe.

Kant also introduced a separation between domains defined by two radically different perspectives, the world of nature and the world of freedom. The former is a world of appearance or phenomena and the latter is a world of supersensuous reality, which he called noumena. For Kant, the world of freedom, not that of natural phenomena, constitutes the ground of morality. Thus, for his third revolution, Kant became the first secular philosopher in the West to reject the possibility that criteria for the good are to be grounded on the natural properties of living creatures.

With his critiques of the 1780s, Kant staked out a position more expressive of the world view of German religious culture, which, owing to a deeply rooted strain of pietism and the teachings of Martin Luther, maintained an opposition between the constraints of nature and the experience of inward freedom and righteousness.[1] Where French social philosophers rejected the "atomic" but kept the "naturalism," Kant went further and rejected the naturalism. He located the good not in the expression of natural inclinations but in the performance of duty, which he defined as compliance with moral laws that individuals rationally and freely construct for themselves. He defined virtue neither as the expression of a natural sensibility nor as the acquisition of socially instilled habits, but as the capacity and resolved purpose of free agents to resist natural opponents of the moral disposition within them.

Kant rejected the notion that morality could be based on nature for a number of reasons. Some had to do with the shortcomings of the sciences of nature and others with the shortcomings of nature as a principle of morality. Like Hobbes and Comte, Kant strove to exploit the resources of modern rationality to secure a foundation for moral judgments that could overcome partisan bickering and the temptations of evil. But Kant could not agree with Hobbes, Comte, and their followers that natural science provided the model for achieving this secure basis. For one thing, Kant believed that a credible ethic had to be absolutely and unconditionally valid, and the only kinds of knowledge relevant to action that natural science can provide are conditional. Natural science can indicate the most effective means to attain a given end, but the utility of that knowledge is conditional on commitment to the end in question. With respect to the determination of ends, natural science can indicate what empirical ends motivate human actions, but these ends vary so much among different peoples and circumstances that knowledge of them cannot provide a secure universal standard.

In the course of searching for an unconditioned and universal moral standard in his *Grundelgung*, Kant ([1785] 1964) fixed on a good will as the only conceivable thing in the world that can be called good without qualification. When he analyzed what constitutes a good will, Kant proposed that acting in accord with a good will entails conforming to duty for its own sake. Through appetitive and egoistic impulses, nature continuously throws up temptations to avoid acting in accord with duty. What is more, even when nature prompts one to perform deeds of a generous sort, that does not make the actions moral, since they have not been executed for the sake of duty. Kant further depreciated nature as a ground for morality by viewing it as the sole arena of deterministic causality, whereas the only secure basis for morality—a good will—requires the agency of human freedom to provide the kind of laws that alone can be formulated by a rational being and followed for their own sake. Natural philosophy, moreover, can never demonstrate the existence of freedom nor document the existence of a good will, the reality of which must be assumed in order to carry out ethical actions.

As a result of these considerations, Kant produced a secular ethic rooted in the proposition that achieving the good requires nature to be transcended and in the assumption that both the need for this transcendence and the means of attaining it derive from the distinctive properties of the human subject. In one guise or another, Kant's theme of the transcending subject became foundational for all subsequent German moral philosophy.

In creating a radical disjunction between the domains of nature and of moral value, Kant introduced a novel mode of conceiving the relationship between the theoretical and the practical. Kant constructed the disciplines of practical philosophy as wholly independent of, and separate from, the disciplines of theoretical philosophy. He did this instead of viewing theoretical understanding as a way to identify a set of human natural potentials whose actualization formed the agenda for a distinctive discipline of practical philosophy, as with Aristotle, and as opposed to regarding practical knowledge as a straightforward application of principles and propositions established by theoretical disciplines, as with the British and French social theorists.

Kant's radical distinction between the worlds of nature and freedom gave expression to thoughtways so deeply embedded in German culture that his ideas were embraced and reworked by hundreds of German philosophers and poets.[2] His articulation of the irreducible reality of a conscious and self-determining subject became the leitmotif of authors in the German tradition. This motif can be discerned in the otherwise dramatically contrasting productions of Kant's onetime student Johann Gottfried von Herder.

Herder's Romantic Revolution

Herder studied with Kant before the latter issued his epochal critiques. It was thus possible for Herder to evince sincere devotion to his professor at Königsberg yet strike off on a different path.[3] It is hard to imagine two more sharply divergent philosophical expressions than those of Kant and Herder. Where Kant enthroned reason, Herder extolled sentiment. Where Kant erected universal standards of morality and justice, Herder espoused cultural relativism. Where Kant made the individual a source of cognitive forms and ethical laws, Herder depicted the collectivity as a matrix of form-giving creativity. And where Kant's argument was precise and logical, Herder's style was evocative and flamboyant.[4]

Even so, Herder celebrated human beings' distinctive capacity for freedom and reason.[5] Herder contrasted humans with other animals, referring to them as "stooping slaves" who possess souls not ripened into reason and are thus condemned to the service of imperious instincts. Humans stand upright; they are free to examine and to choose. Although they are endowed with instincts like other animals, they suppress these instincts as they mature and acquire reason. Their capacity for inner dialogue evinces a marvelous "self-created inner sense of the spirit" (Herder 1969, 141). Even when man abuses his liberty, he remains a king.

However, while Kant found himself logically constrained to represent the voluntarism of human subjects by separating the domain of freedom from that of nature, Herder placed reason and freedom within the domain of nature itself (thus making himself vulnerable to charges of a contradiction between his strong naturalistic determinism and his notion that one can and should resist natural impulses and natural forces). He cast it as a law of nature that "man is a free, thinking, and creative being" (153), and mused "how much it seems Nature hesitated before entrusting ... the great gifts of reason and freedom ... to such a feeble, complicated, earthly creature as the human" (Herder [1784] 1887, 146). During the years when Kant was laying the foundations for an uncompromisingly anti-naturalistic ethics of practical reason, Herder was busy making a revolution of a different stamp.

Kant located the capacity to transcend brutish instinct in the exercise of the faculties of reason. While Herder, too, appreciated human reason, he considered the expression of sentiment to be the prime medium of human transcendence. He described human feeling as one of man's greatest organic advantages, the source of invention and art, and a far greater inspiration for our ideas than we suspect. Among the gifts that nature conferred on humans for the expression of feeling, Herder especially noted the gift of song, available to children and the simplest of peoples. The free and spontaneous forms of self-expression fulfill the true demands of human nature.

For Herder, these forms of self-expression were not the work of individual persons but the creations of an integrated community. They appear, above all, in the language of a people; they embody its historical experience, its whole heart and soul, as Herder was one of the first European thinkers to argue (in a prize-winning essay of 1770). Specifically human creative expressions also appear in a people's music and art, in their myths and religious forms. Herder designated the ensemble of these cultural expressions as the *Volksgeist*, the spirit of a people.

Since every culture or historical period possesses a unique character, Herder believed that efforts to analyze such phenomena as combinations of uniform elements or to subsume them under universal rules tended to obliterate precisely those crucial qualities that constitute them, as the generalizing science of Montesquieu grotesquely demonstrated.[6] From this perspective, the quest for a universal standard of value must seem futile. What appear to be excellent achievements worthy of universal emulation occur only as embedded in a particular configuration. Thus,

> because Athens had exquisite orators, it does not follow that its form of government must likewise have been the best possible, or that because the Chinese moralize so excellently, their state must be a pattern for all others. ... Each [culture] bears in itself the standard of its perfection, totally independent of all comparison with that of others.
>
> *(Herder [1784] 1968, 100, 98)*

By overturning Enlightenment commitments to the ideal of the rational individual beholden to universal standards, Herder evoked a vision of the good based on a set of collective expressions of sentiment that manifest an aesthetic integrity. Humans achieve the good life by living in natural units and do so in societies that transcend the limits of natural circumstance by creating a harmonious shared culture. Central to the ethic he propounded, then, was an injunction to respect the differing cultures manifest by different peoples. This led Herder to a precocious critique of European imperialism for its repression of less civilized peoples. Indeed, it led him to be critical of political repressiveness in all forms. Herder became an ardent foe of absolutism, no matter how enlightened; more generally, he expressed a certain antagonism to the modern state. How ironic that Hegel, the philosopher who did so much to popularize Herder's notion of the *Volksgeist*, was the chief proponent in modern political theory of the state as the historical medium of transcendence.

From Kant to Hegel

Nineteenth-century German social thought began with a series of efforts to ground an ethic on the distinctive creative properties of the human subject. The legacies of Kant and Herder had to be reckoned with. For all their differences, the two men shared a set of assumptions distinctive of the German tradition, which can be represented in terms similar to those I have used for the British and the French traditions. To the question of how the facts of human experience are to be constructed and explained, they respond with the Postulate of Subjective Meaning: *Human phenomena can best be understood by grasping the meanings with which actors imbue their actions.* This entails a method of understanding that in principle diverges from methods used for understanding natural phenomena. For Kant, this was the direct grasp of the self's own legislative activity through *Vernunft*, the faculty of practical reason, which he contrasts with *Verstand*, the faculty used for understanding and explaining natural phenomena. For Herder, it was a method of sympathetic imagination, *Einfühlung*, which he contrasts with the methods of abstraction and objectification used in the natural sciences.

To the question of how secular thought can provide a rational grounding of moral judgments, they respond with the Postulate of Normative Self-determination: *Normative judgments are to be grounded not through some agency external to actors but through codes that free human agents, as individuals or collectivities, promulgate for themselves.* This entails a prescription of unconditional respect for the free expressions of other human agents, which Kant formulates as a categorical imperative and Herder as the only moral absolute.

To the question about the source of human moral dispositions, they respond with the Postulate of Subjective Voluntarism: *Human moral orientations derive from a distinctive human capacity to identify and make choices between good and evil.*

While Kant and Herder thus articulated the German longing for an ethic centered on the nature-transcending qualities of self-determining subjects, their writings contained enough apparent contradictions to busy generations of thinkers in ever-new departures from their philosophies. The first major philosopher to address those contradictions was Johann Fichte. Fichte sought to rescue Kant's philosophy from the error he believed the master had committed in separating a metaphysics of freedom from a metaphysics of nature. His search for an uplifting secular ideal led him to Kant's ethics of duty, which he translated into an injunction to achieve increasing freedom through growing loyalty to one's spiritual ideals. Since the effort to realize one's ideals requires a world of objects on which to act, a primal "moral will" brings into existence the phenomenal world as a field needed for the self-objectification of moral activity. In holding that the ego must posit a non-ego, nature, for its essential field of operation, Fichte sought to complete the Kantian project by locating the noumenal "thing-in-itself" within the transcendental activity of the human mind. Where Herder had overcome the nature-freedom divide by making reason and freedom special "gifts of Nature," Fichte overcame it by making nature an externalization of human spirit: history thus became the story of the continuous struggle of human ideals against the pressures of natural instincts.

Considered the leading philosopher in Germany by the late 1790s, Fichte deeply influenced his young colleague Friedrich von Schelling, who joined him at the University of Jena. Schelling gradually worked himself free from Fichte's subjective idealism, arguing not only that the world of nature is just as real and important as the world of the ego but also that nature gives rise to consciousness, as Herder had held. Even so, Schelling held fast to the Fichtean commitment to voluntarism, maintaining, in words famous among his contemporaries, that "the beginning and end of all philosophy is—freedom."

Schelling's philosophy thus replaced the concept of the ego as supreme principle of philosophy with the concept of natural force. In *Ideas for a Philosophy of Nature*, Schelling ([1797] 2001) argued that mechanical, chemical, electrical, and vital forces were different manifestations of the same underlying cosmic force, a pure activity that continuously seeks to realize itself. He later constructed a theory of stages of knowledge: from sensation and perception to reflection and will. For Schelling, human will becomes the visible, self-conscious part of one world understood as creative energy; before man, spirit slumbers; in man, nature attains consciousness. The real is the rational process of the world developing toward its realization in the final, unified expression of ultimate truth. It is possible to know the world by tracing the logical process through which nature and history move. Self-determination is the primary condition of all consciousness. The process of history consists of the development of human self-determination through the gradual realization of law, which culminates in a sovereign world federation of all sovereign states in which all people are citizens.

Along with Fichte, Schelling gave his friend G. W. F. Hegel ideas that could be used to bridge the gap between Kant and Herder. Following Kant, Hegel perceived a stark opposition between the domains of nature and spirit (*Geist*). "Nature," he wrote, "exhibits no freedom in its existence, but only *necessity* and *contingency*" (Hegel [1830] 2004, 17, §248); spirit, by virtue of its self-consciousness and containing its being within itself, is essentially free. Nature is cyclical and endlessly repetitive, whereas spirit is progressive and continually innovative. Although reason exists in nature, it is not self-conscious but "petrified intelligence," he says, quoting Schelling (Hegel [1830] 1975 37, §24); through the spirit humans differ from animals, not just by thinking but also by the capacity for self-conscious thought. Hegel's lifelong effort was to find a more plausible way to connect the domains of nature and freedom than Kant had done. He did so by looking at the problem as a matter of *historical development*.

Although Kant's quest for a credible ethic was pursued through metaphysics, not historical analysis, he set the stage for Hegel's project with his brief musings on history in the "Idea for a Universal History from a Cosmopolitan Point of View" (Kant [1784] 1963). Kant published this essay in 1784, soon after he had worked out his new philosophical position. Appalled by the record of human history—a tableau of vanity, folly, malice, and destructiveness—Kant wondered if nature might hold some larger plan or purpose for a species whose story otherwise appears to be full of idiocy. He proposed that while the human animal is distinguished by possessing reason, this faculty cannot possibly be developed in the short lifespan nature allots humans; full development of their rational capacities would require an unreckonable series of generations. To achieve this end, nature relies on the mutual antagonism of people—their "unsocial sociability," a disposition to associate with and to oppose one another. Unremitting social conflict first awakens humans from laziness so that they develop their powers; it eventually perfects their self-discipline by creating a universal civic society under the rule of law. Although Kant offered this view of the ultimate destination of humanity in a regime of reason and freedom as a "consoling view of the future," he cautioned that the means nature provides for reaching that destination are unmistakably immoral: "everything good that is not based on a morally good disposition, however, is nothing but pretense and misery" ([1784] 1963, 25, 21).

In searching for a way to save human freedom from naturalistic determinism, Kant made a certain gnawing tension foundational to German moral philosophy. One is required by a categorical imperative to act autonomously—on the basis of moral laws derived from one's own rational activity. However, no amount of searching one's acts or those of others can determine whether that condition has been attained. Worse, the inspirational idea that mankind may attain a more ethical condition in the future rests on a view of history that seems to sanction absolutely proscribed immoral deeds in the present.[7] This is nothing if not a recipe for despair.

Kant's essay arguably served as a template against which Hegel came to stake out his own historicizing philosophy.[8] In his "Idea for a Universal History," Kant ([1784] 1963, 12) had openly invited some philosophical successor to resolve the mystery about history's plan, for which he was merely supplying a clue—to play Newton to his Kepler. Hegel happily accepted the invitation, although he eventually imitated Kant in referring to his own attempt to discern the grand design of history as merely Keplerian (Hegel 1988, 68). In approaching his solution, Hegel incorporated a number of notions from his contemporaries, including Herder's notion of the *Volksgeist* and the ideas of Fichte and Schelling about a historical evolution of *Geist* that culminates in the rule of law.[9]

Like Kant, Hegel admitted that inspection of the ordinary course of human events is demoralizing, that history is a "slaughter-bench, upon which the happiness of nations, the wisdom of states, and the virtues of individuals were sacrificed" (24). And again like Kant, Hegel discerned a latent purpose in history—the progressive realization of humanity's capacities for reason and freedom—and argued that the means of attaining this purpose are not the moral intentions of individuals but selfish interests and social strife. Finally, Hegel also held that the culmination of the drama of history appears at the attainment of universal freedom, which comes about not through unbridled license but through obedience to self-made laws.

In setting forth these views, Hegel sought to eliminate the contradictions that had troubled Kant. He did so, first, by challenging Kant's notion that man's sensuous nature is morally suspect and contains no instructive forces. Hegel followed Herder in acclaiming the passions as the prime creative force in human experience. He called them the woof of the vast tapestry of world history, the driving energy that alone makes the realization of reason possible. He followed Herder, Fichte, and Schelling in finding nonrational expressions, such as myths, images, and religions, to be part of the process of self-expression where human nature realizes itself. He also departed from Kant and followed Herder in considering the agents of human self-realization in history to be not individuals but peoples. He used Herder's metaphor of the organic development of peoples as a way to subordinate considerations of individual morality and happiness (even though his *Philosophy of Right* insists on the individual's right of subjective satisfaction as the distinguishing feature of modernity). Hegel departed from Herder, however, in his attitude toward the nation-state. Where Herder had located human transcendence in culture and waxed critical of the state for its repressive stance toward culture, Hegel—leaning on Fichte and Schelling—held that culture reaches full bloom only when it has advanced to the developmental stage of forming a state.

With these alterations, Hegel attempted to resolve the moral dilemma posed by Kantian philosophy. He overcame the nature-freedom dualism both by subordinating nature, as a fundamentally deficient mode of being that has its substance outside itself, to human freedom and by affirming the natural passions as the efficient cause of reason and freedom in history. He downplayed qualms about individual morality by denying that morality is the highest thing in the world, and he acknowledged circumstances where asserting formally immoral means has served the great end of human progress. He justified this by contesting the assumption that Kant's formal morality and reason constitute an eternally valid standard for morality on grounds that morality cannot exist outside of history. Instead, Hegel historicized reason and morality. That is, he argued that reason and morality take shape through an unfolding process over time, that a person's ethics reflects that of their people (*Volk*) at a certain stage of development, and that morality is fully realized only in the modern state in which freedom achieves full objectivity. In rejecting both Kant's universalistic morality, which stands against reality, and

Herder's relativized morality, which is tied to particular cultural formations, Hegel provided a third way. He viewed all historical moral configurations as stages on the way toward a universally binding ethic that becomes valid only when it becomes real—at the culmination of the historical process.

With his conception of an objective mind, Hegel succeeded in synthesizing two of the major movements of the previous half-century of German thought: the German Enlightenment idea of the state as the encompassing community that realizes the morality of its members, epitomized in Kant's notion of the jural order, and the idea of what came to be known as the German Historical School, with its discovery of the common spirit (*Geist*) of a community. The Hegelian synthesis dominated German philosophy for a full quarter-century after the defeat of Napoleon in 1815. In the decade after Hegel's death in 1831, Hegelians of varied hues staked out diverse positions in defense or emendation of the master (Toews 1980). The breadth and intensity of his hold on the German intellectuals of that time has often been compared to a religious movement.

Notes

1 Luther emphasized that "man has a twofold nature, a spiritual and a bodily" (1957, 7) and characterized the inner person as righteous and free. He held that no external thing has any influence in producing either righteousness or freedom, or unrighteousness or servitude. Consequently, Luther argued that good works do not make a good person, but that a "person himself [must] be good before there can be any good works, and that good works follow and proceed from the good person" (7, 24). Pietism was a form of Christian religiosity that opposed both ecclesiastical establishments and orthodox intellectualism with an emphasis on inner experience, feeling, participation, and introspection. It became organized as a religious movement in Germany in the seventeenth century, although it stems from attitudes that have been attributed to medieval German culture.
2 By the early 1790s, Kant had become a major cultural force in Germany. A decade later, nearly three thousand separate pieces on him had been published. Even Goethe, whose work pointed in a different direction, eventually came to find Kant's critical writings congenial. The poet Hölderlin called Kant the Moses of the German nation (Sheehan 1989, 182; Ermarth 1978, 40).
3 I have had the good fortune to know a philosopher. He was my teacher. ... No cabal, no sect, no prejudice, no desire for fame could ever tempt him in the slightest away from broadening and illuminating the truth. He incited and gently forced others to think for themselves; despotism was foreign to his mind. This man, whom I name with the greatest gratitude and respect, was Immanuel Kant.
(Kant 1963, xxviii)
4 Herder's defection from Kant's philosophical approach was all too apparent to his erstwhile mentor, well before Herder issued a "Metakritik" chiding Kant for trying to separate reason from the other human powers. In a review of the first part of Herder's *Ideen*, Kant observed that Herder failed to present a logical precision in the definition of concepts or careful adherence to principles, but rather a fleeting, sweeping view, an adroitness in unearthing analogies in the wielding of which he shows a bold imagination. This is combined with the cleverness in soliciting sympathy for his subject—kept in increasingly hazy remoteness—by means of sentiment and sensation. (Kant 1963, 27)
5 Isaiah Berlin wrote: Although a great intellectual gulf divides Kant from Herder, they share a common element: a craving for spiritual self-determination as against half conscious drifting along the streams of uncriticized dogma (whether theological or scientific),

for moral independence (whether of individuals or groups), and above all for moral salvation. (1976, 152) Berlin related this shared emphasis on the life of the spirit, which alone liberates humans from the bonds of the flesh and of nature, to the inward-looking tradition of the Pietist movement, which was especially strong in East Prussia where Kant and Herder grew up.

6 "Three wretched generalizations! ... The history of all times and peoples, whose succession forms the great, living work of God, reduced to ruins, divided neatly into three heaps. ... 0, Montesquieu!" (Herder 1969, 217).

7 The predicament resembles that of the Calvinists portrayed by Max Weber: no matter what good deeds they perform, they can never know whether or not they have been chosen to be among the elect who will be saved.

8 In *Kant and the Problem of History*, Galston (1975) persuasively argued that Hegel's view of history resulted from modifying a few of the principles that informed Kant's.

9 Fichte's ideas about alienation and dialectics also figured significantly in Hegel's system.

13

POSITIONS ON CONFLICT IN EURO-AMERICAN AND ASIAN SOCIAL THOUGHT

Philosophical perspectives on social conflict in Western social thought comprise four general positions, formulable by cross-classifying two variables: (1) conflict viewed as inexorable or contingent, and (2) conflict viewed primarily as a negative or a positive phenomenon. A "pessimist" views conflict as negative but inexorable; an "optimist" holds that conflict is inevitable but positive. A "prudential" position views conflict as contingent and entirely negative, and finally, a "provocative" view holds that conflict is a definite positive that needs to be promoted.

These positions can be linked with assumptions about the bodily bases of human aggression. Inexorable views of conflict regard the body as a source of egoistic impulses that well up and initiate aggressive behaviors; contingent views of conflict regard the body as a source of flight or fear. A variant of the prudential position sees the body as a source of malleable plastic energies. In contrast, certain Asian traditions imagine a body that is neither at the mercy of aggressive instincts, nor a scene of conflicting drives, nor utterly lacking in natural structure. In particular, the traditions of yoga, in India, and of aikido, in Japan, depict the body as disposed to a state of calmness and serenity through becoming unified with the mind and spirit. Since the response to attacks can be neutralization in aikido, rather than counterattack or submission, conflict need not be the outcome of aggression. To reduce conflict, the prudential view relies not on external social arrangements, but on internal practices that calm the mind and promote harmony within oneself and with others.

The theory of social conflict includes a number of consensually validated propositions about the causes, forms, levels, dynamics, resolutions, and consequences of interpersonal and intergroup conflict. Regarding philosophical presuppositions about conflict, however, strong differences persist despite agreement on the more empirically ascertainable aspects of conflictual phenomena. I shall articulate some of these differences by constructing four ideal types of perspectives on conflict: pessimistic, optimistic, prudential, and provocative.[1] After discussing the defining features of each perspective and some of their eminent representatives, I shall analyze how these positions relate to assumptions about the natural human body. This analysis will lead to an opening through which certain ideas developed in Asian thought can be included in the discourse about conflict.

Social Conflict as Inexorable

The pessimistic perspective on social conflict has deep roots in Christian theology. Humans are essentially sinful creatures, disposed to attack against their neighbors, causing misery and suffering. Immanuel Kant presented a secular version of this view. Kant found the disposition to engage in conflict ever-present and inherently immoral.[2]

The tenets of Kant's philosophical anthropology have found their way into modern social science through traditions in psychology, ethology, and political science. Freudian psychology, despite vicissitudes of thought regarding the instincts, has tended to assume both an inherent human disposition to aggression that leads to conflict and inexhaustible reservoirs of intrapersonal conflicts that spill over, via externalization and projection, into interpersonal conflicts. Freud held that violent conflict was endemic to human experience—as a means to resolve conflicts of interest and as an expression of an instinctive craving—an "active instinct for hatred and destruction" ([1932] 1939, 90). He bemoaned the destructiveness of modern warfare but held little hope that cultured aversions to war could overcome the aggressive dispositions so deeply rooted in man's biological makeup. He theorized about this by positing a self-destructive "death instinct," producing a constant fund of conflictual energies. Most psychoanalysts considered the destructive instinct as the polar opposite of the sexual instinct. This let them incorporate Freud's pessimistic views on aggression without having to subscribe to what they considered a far-fetched metapsychological construct.

The ethologist N. Tinbergen posited a universal proclivity to intraspecific conflict based on genetically transmitted instincts. Comparing human aggression with aggression in other animals, however, he found that human aggressiveness is distinguished by the fact that it is socially disruptive: "man is the only species that is a mass murderer, the only misfit in his own society" (Tinbergen 1968, 180). This condition comes from a combination of instinctual, cultural, and technological factors. In earlier human periods, and in other species, the impulse to fight gets balanced by the fear response. Now humans have contrived cultural conditions that dampen the impulse to flee from battle, and the technology that permits fighting at a distance eliminates the taming effect personal contact produces in face-to-face encounters. Dismayed about these ineradicable dispositions, which threaten to convulse modern society with destructive warfare, Tinbergen acknowledged the impact of increased population density on the impulse to fight and admitted that the internal urge to engage in combat will be difficult, if not impossible, to eliminate. A similar diagnosis was made a half-century earlier by William James. Despite the acknowledged horrors of modern warfare, modern people have inherited an aggressive nature and a love of glory that inexorably feeds combat; James wrote on the eve of World War I, "our ancestors have bred pugnacity into our bone and marrow, and thousands of years of peace won't breed it out of us" ([1910] 1974, 314).

Political scientists, who espouse a position of "political realism," express a comparably pessimistic position. Long an eminent spokesman for this position, Hans Morgenthau held that the social world results from forces inherent in human nature that make it "a world of opposing interests and of conflict among them" (1960, 4). These conflicts are inexorable and Morgenthau saw no need to glamorize them or consider them benign. Indeed, he cautioned social scientists not to mistake the policy prescriptions that follow from the perspective as *moral*. Morgenthau thought it important to uphold morality as a set of ideals, but urged social scientists and policy-makers to understand that reality consists of conflicts of interest that can neither be understood nor mediated from a moral point of view.

An optimistic position, on the other hand, draws on a philosophic outlook in which conflict figures as an inexorable yet essential source of human well-being. Its proponents hail the Heraclitean dictum that "war is the father of all and king of all." Heraclitus chided those who dreamed of eliminating strife from among gods and men; things exist only insofar as they embody a tension between opposites, and human goods come into being only through strife.

Among ethnologists, Konrad Lorenz has been a prominent advocate of viewing conflict as positive, but inexorable. Conflict has provided adaptive advantages, such as balancing the ecological distribution of members of the same species, selection of the fittest specimens through fights among rivals, mediating the ranking orders need for complex organizations, and instigating ceremonies that promote social bonding. Aggression, he argued, "far from being the diabolical, destructive principle that classical psychoanalysis makes it out to be, is really an essential part of the life-preserving organization of instincts" (Lorenz 1966, 48). If not war, then at least conflict should be called the father of all things. Conflict between independent sources of impulse can produce tensions that lend firmness to systems, much as the stays of a mast give it stability by pulling in opposed directions (95).

The optimistic position was developed in classic sociology through the seminal work of Georg Simmel (1904a, 1904b, 1904c, [1908] 1971). Simmel saw conflict not just as an inexorable feature of human social life, but also as a process with essentially benign consequences. That is, Simmel conceptualized conflict as an essential constitutive feature of social structure. This is because antagonisms maintain distances essential to stable social structures and the expression of conflict preserves association among parties who might otherwise sever relations. Simmel suggested that mutual aversions are indispensable ingredients both of small intimate groups that involve numerous vital relations among their members and of large concentrations of people in modern metropolises. He considered the capacity to accommodate conflict to be a sign of the vitality of intimate relationships.

Simmel's classic analysis was recovered half a century later by Lewis Coser. In *The Functions of Social Conflict*, Coser (1956) refined Simmel's ideas by casting them in the form of discrete, clearly formulated propositions; comparing them with relevant materials from psychoanalysis, psychology, and social psychology; and showing how they could be qualified by the interposition of intervening variables. Although Coser argued that intragroup and intergroup conflicts promote social unification only under specified circumstances, he also identified ways in which the expression of conflictual sentiments enhances the effectiveness and long-term stability of groups.

Social Conflict as Contingent

For all their differences, the pessimistic and optimistic perspectives share the assumption that social conflict is universal and inexorable. A different perspective appears in authors who consider social conflict to be something that can be avoided or minimized. Among such authors, one group regards conflict as essentially negative in its nature and consequences. These authors therefore hold that social conflict can, and should, be kept under check or prevented through appropriate social interventions. The prudential perspective has two main variants: a classic representation such as the one by Thomas Hobbes and another by cultural psychologists like Margaret Mead and Erich Fromm.

The Hobbesian perspective presumes that the pursuit of personal interests disposes all human actors to engage in social conflict sooner or later. This stems both from the promptings of pride and from the need to acquire power to defend one's goods against others. Unrestrained social conflict produces a condition Hobbes famously described as the "war of every man against every man," in which people live in chronic fear and misery. To counter this ever-present possibility, fearful humans institute sovereign authorities. In exchange for the protection against anarchy and civil strife afforded by those authorities, citizens transfer their rights to self-defense. More generally, a Hobbesian perspective sees conflict as always latent but actually contingent. It can and should be forestalled through the establishment of appropriate governing authorities.

An alternative to this perspective comes from authors who hold that the disposition for conflict is not inherent in the human condition but, rather, results from how people are brought up and how their relations are organized. Margaret Mead (1937) was perhaps the first cultural anthropologist to examine this variable across multiple cultures. She found that primitive societies ranged from highly competitive to highly cooperative and that the main determinant of whether people behave in a competitive or a cooperative manner was the cultural conditioning that they experienced. Erich Fromm (1973) pursued the issue more intensively, examining 30 primitive societies from the standpoint of aggressiveness versus peacefulness. Fromm found several—like the Aztecs, the Dobu, and the Ganda—who evince a great deal of interpersonal aggression and violence, both within the tribe and against others. The atmosphere of life within those societies is truly Hobbesian, a condition of constant fear and tension. On the other hand, Fromm found a number of primitive societies where the opposite qualities manifested themselves. Among the Zuni Pueblo Indians, the Mountain Arapesh, and the Mbutu, for example, he found little hostility and violence, little envy and exploitation, virtually no warfare, hardly any crime, and a generally cooperative and friendly attitude. Fromm went on to analyze the specific social conditions that tend to generate aggressive responses, both of the biologically adaptive sort he called defensive aggression and the nonadaptive, purely destructive sorts he called malignant aggression. Psychologists from the behaviorist tradition, like Watson and Skinner, also view conflict as contingent. Since aggression represents a response to frustrating experiences, it can be curbed through the proper reinforcement of nonaggressive dispositions. Whatever the disciplinary orientation, this variant of the prudential perspective views conflict as eradicable through practices which dispose human nature to live in accord with non-conflictual patterns.

Quite the reverse of the prudential perspective is an outlook that advocates social interventions not to eliminate conflict, but to stimulate it—the provocative perspective. Its most extreme versions appear in writers who extol the virtues of war and berate their contemporaries for not being sufficiently martial. Nietzsche's Zarathustra asked: "you say that it is the good cause that hallows even war?" and commented: "I say unto you: it is the good war that hallows any cause"—yet Nietzsche viewed mankind as objectionably timid. This stance appears, among social thinkers, in George Sorel's *Réflexions sur la violence*. Although Sorel proceeded from a radical socialist perspective, his arguments are generalizable and did in fact become utilized by spokesmen for a wide spectrum of ideological positions. Sorel advocated a view of combat that highlights its noble side. The whole of classical history, he argued, was dominated by a heroic conception of war. This idea celebrates the profession of arms as an elite vocation, reflecting the opportunities that great battles afford for submitting to tests of strength and for appealing to the sentiment of glory. Voluntary participation in war and the myths associated with such combat provides the inspiration for the loftiest moral convictions.

Sorelian ideas found their way into twentieth-century apologia both for colonial expansion and for anti-colonial violence. Benito Mussolini cited Sorel's forefather, Proudhon, to claim a "divine origin" for war. Everlasting peace would be depressing and destructive of man's basic virtues, whereas pacifism represents cowardice before sacrifice. Despite having been accepted for opportunistic reasons, fascism rejects all international structures designed to ensure peace. War alone, Mussolini declaimed, "carries to the maximum of tension all human energies and stamps with a seal of nobility the peoples which have the virtue of facing it. All other tests are substitutes which never put man in front of himself" (Borgese 1938, 392).

Writing on the other side of the imperialist divide, psychiatrist Frantz Fanon invoked overtones of Sorelian combat against capitalist oppression to proclaim the ennobling effects of participation in violent struggle with colonial domination. Fanon saw liberation to be possible only after a "murderous and decisive struggle between the two protagonists" (Fanon 1963, 37). He criticized social forms that permit violence to be averted, either by channeling legitimate combative energies into outlets such as dance, spirit possession, or self-destructive symptoms where they are dissipated; or by defusing them through anti-polemical ideational forms like religion, philosophies of human rights, ethics of nonviolence, or a politics of compromise. Nonviolent forms of political opposition—work stoppages in a few industries, mass demonstrations, boycotting of buses or imported commodities—simply represent other forms of action that let people work off their energy and so constitute a kind of "therapy by hibernation" (66). Violent combat alone can liquidate colonialism, regionalism, and tribalism, and thereby introduce into social consciousness the ideas of a common cause, national destiny, and collective history. At the level of individual personality, "violence is a cleansing force. It frees the native from his inferiority complex and from his despair and inaction; it makes him fearless and restores his self-respect" (94).

The provocative perspective on conflict, however, need not be tied to an espousal of physical violence; it can and has been expressed by those who advocate an increase in verbal forms of conflict as a means of promoting social change or as the preferred means of arriving at the truth. Herbert Marcuse helped persuade a generation of intellectuals to follow an ethic of negation on grounds that harmony of opinion was counter-emancipatory. Wayne Booth has described a polemicist position among literary critics that holds that "the more vigorous the conflict, the healthier the body critical" (1979, 4). Such a position appears among those who promote conflict as the best way to approach truth, an epistemological stance that Walter Watson (1985) designated as the agonistic method. Watson cited Machiavelli as one who applies the agonistic method to politics in arguing that the opposition of conflicting parties is needed to preserve liberty.

Bodily Bases of Aggression and Nonaggression

Like much sociological discourse, conflict theory can become highly abstract. Yet its intimate connection with the realities of physical combat makes it easy to relate the discussion of social conflict to the interaction of physical bodies. The tendency to adduce biologically rooted dispositions for the presence or absence of conflict invites us to consider how differing perspectives on conflict might be related to differing assumptions about the human body.

The pessimistic perspective tends to view the human body as a continuously bubbling cauldron of egoistic and aggressive impulses that eventually spill over into combative action. The bodily imagery that underlies this view has been depicted in classical psychoanalysis. Freud saw the human organism as a perpetually renewed source of instinctual energies that well up and produce inner discomfort until they get released. Psychic and somatic symptoms reflect failures in the personality's ability to release those instinctual tensions, which eventually find release through indirect channels. Directly or indirectly, human aggression represents a constantly flowing impulse that emanates from the human body such that humans can never escape the proclivity to destroy either themselves or others.

Although Lorenz took a more positive view of conflict, he too espoused a mechanistic-hydraulic view of aggression, likening aggression to a gas constantly being pumped into a container. In Lorenz's conception, energies accumulate continuously in neural centers for a specific behavior, leading animals and humans to hunt for stimuli in order to trigger the release of those energies. Although Simmel downplayed the salience of instinctive aggressive energies as a source of conflict, he considered the mobilization of such energies useful for the prosecution of conflicts. Even so, Simmel admitted the existence of a pure hostility drive that manifests itself in the institution of combative games.

Insofar as they entertain considerations of the bodily sources of aggression and conflict, those who think of conflict as inexorable tend to see the body as a mechanism that regularly produces aggressive energies. Authors who regard conflict as contingent have a different set of images: either they see the body as producing other impulses that swamp the aggressive instincts or they look at aggressive behavior altogether as not instinctually based.

Hobbes represents the former alternative. The perpetual and restless desire of power after power to which all men are inclined would lead inevitably to constant civil strife were it not for the activation of an even stronger natural inclination: the wish to avoid violent death. Humans are also motivated by a wish to live comfortably by means of conveniences that only a regime of peace can procure. So the impulse to aggress against others gets subordinated to a wish for peaceful coexistence, a condition secured by establishing a sovereign political authority. The logic of Hobbes' argument can be modified to cover a variety of social arrangements designed to prevent conflict. But his logic regarding the bodily bases of action can be left intact: the body is the home of divergent impulses including aggressiveness, but aggression can get inhibited by other propensities that support institutions designed to prevent conflict. This image of the body is not unlike what we find in writers like Nietzsche and Sorel. The latter visualized a natural human disposition to be fierce and combative, a disposition that gets swamped by fear and desires for convenience, thereby deflecting martial impulses into innocuous channels.

A third view of the body appears in authors who reject instinctual determinisms of any sort. The model here presents an organism whose genetic programming is so minimal that it extends only to general response capacities. Without cultural patterns to give some particular shape to human lives, "man's behavior would be virtually ungovernable, a mere chaos of pointless acts … his experience virtually shapeless" (Geertz 1973, 46). Margaret Mead first applied this credo of the cultural anthropologist to the variable of conflict versus cooperation. Bodily dispositions to engage in combat reflect the internalization of symbols and the cultivation of habits promoted by combative cultures, but pacific cultures can just as successfully create nonaggressive dispositions.

Some Asian Views of the Body, Aggression, and Conflict

Although disciplines concerned with bodily healing have recently started to examine what "non-Western" arts might contribute, it is rare that Euro-American social science has an opportunity to draw on the insights and understandings of other traditions. Yet it may be the case that certain Asian traditions afford ways of thinking about conflict that are hard to encompass within available Euro-American paradigms and that the most direct entree into those traditions comes from looking at their distinctive views of the body and aggression. In what follows, I shall discuss the traditions of yoga in India and aikido in Japan, although comparable ideas may also be found in certain aspects of the lore of Taoism in China and of the Korean tradition of *hwarangdo*.

The general thesis I wish to advance is that these traditions imagine a body that is neither at the mercy of aggressive instincts, nor a scene of conflicting drives, nor utterly lacking in natural structure. Rather, the state of being battered about by desires, whether shaped or chaotic, represents human nature in an immature state. Mature humanity exhibits a body that is unified internally and unified with the mind, a being living in inner harmony and with little inclination to aggress against others.

Two thousand years ago, the Sanskrit classic *Bhagavad Gita* represented a state of human joy and fulfillment brought about by a practice that calms the mind and the passions. Unifying the body with the soul and the individual self with the universal spirit, through the practice of yoga, involves a complex of methods that are not only moral and meditative, but physical as well. They include asana, a discipline of holding carefully designed postures, and *pranayama*, exercises in the rhythmic control of the breath. These are not extraordinary practices, the privilege of an exceptional elite or of superhuman creatures, but are available to anyone willing to work hard at them. Exercising every muscle, nerve, and gland in the body, the asanas secure a fine physique, one that is energized, limber, and strong yet not muscle-bound. They are designed to produce a state of superb bodily health, understood as a state of complete equilibrium of body, mind, and spirit.

A millennia after the principles of yoga were codified, aikido, another Asian discipline, was developed with a similar view of the human potential for living with a harmonious body-mind. The art of aikido, developed by the martial artist/religionist Morihei Ueshiba in the 1930s and 1940s, draws on a combination of Asian disciplines, including neo-Confucianism, Shinto, and the martial ways of Budo. Foundational to this art are the notions of unifying the entire bodily system through proper posture and of unifying the body with the mind through focusing one's attention on the bodily center of gravity. The movements that adepts learn for responding to physical attacks require the body-mind system to be centered in this way, and certain exercises have been designed to enhance body-mind harmony. In the words of its founder, aikido "is the way of unifying the mind, body, and spirit" (Saotome 1989, 33).

What does the image of the body, conveyed by yoga and aikido, imply about social conflict? When students of these disciplines stand or sit in the relaxed and centered postures of their practice, they experience a state of calmness. From that, they derive a conviction that there is no inherent or inexorable force driving all human beings to aggress against one another. They also know that, compared to the state of calm they experience, aggression is unpleasant—even when one commits aggressive acts in self-defense. When they sense an impulse to aggress proactively or reactively, they connect it with a primal response that can readily be overcome. The bodily states of yoga or aikido support a belief that conflict is neither inexorable nor desirable, which aligns them with proponents of the prudential perspective. In contrast to the Hobbesian version of that perspective, however, they do not make refraining from aggression dependent on fear. The body in the relaxed and unified state experiences itself as unaggressive, whatever cultural patterns may prescribe.

Yoga and aikido conceive the bodily harmony promoted by their teachings as a model of mature human functioning and thus a model for right living. They also connect it with teachings about interpersonal conflict. They see such conflict as a byproduct of inner discord and neither inexorable nor necessary for the good human life. Yoga complements the state of inner harmony with various *yama*, or ethical disciplines, which cultivate harmony with others. These include the commandment of *ahimsa* or nonviolence. *Ahimsa* is an injunction to show respect to all living creatures. Closely related to this is the principle of *abhaya*, freedom from fear. As a distinguished contemporary yogi put it, "violence arises out of fear, weakness, ignorance or restlessness. To curb it most what is needed is freedom from fear" (Iyengar 1973, 32). Far from basing the understanding of social life on a presumption of ineradicable instincts of aggressiveness and fear, this strand of classic Hindu thought evolved a conception of healthy human functioning in which both fear and combativeness could be avoided.

The preeminent application of yogic principles to contemporary social thought about conflict was the work of Mahatma Gandhi. Gandhi embraced certain well-known notions of the yogic tradition, including *ahimsa* and *satya* (truth).[3] He reworked them into an approach to conflict based on refusal to respond to aggression with counteraggression. Following the yogic philosophy, Gandhi insisted that it is possible—and more effective—to oppose the evil in the wrongdoer without opposing the wrongdoer.

Similar ideas were articulated by the founder of aikido, Morihei Ueshiba. Although Ueshiba created his discipline as a budo, or martial art, he came to insist that in his particular form of budo "there are no enemies." The only enemy consists of the egoistic and aggressive strivings of the immature self, and the only victory worth pursuing is a victory over that immature self. Ueshiba described the goal of his budo as a kind of *ahimsa*, a spirit of loving protection of all living creatures. He dedicated his art to the ideal of promoting peace and harmony throughout the entire world community.

This does not mean that aikido presumes a world wholly free of aggression. Aikido teachings do presume that from time to time some people will, wittingly or not, physically or verbally attack other persons or intrude into their space. But aikido also assumes that the options for response are not restricted to those motivated by the impulses to fight back, to take flight, or to submit obsequiously (and so plant seeds for resentment and later conflict). The aikido position presents a fourth option: by neutralizing the aggression of the attacker, the conflict can be avoided. The person or group attacked can respond in an aiki way, by blending with the energy of the attacker, remaining centered, and redirecting that energy in a way that protects the victim but respects the attacker.

Yoga, satyagraha, and aikido introduce a new position into the inventory of perspectives on conflict developed in social thought. Like the other prudential perspectives, they argue that conflict is not good, because human life does not fulfill itself through discord. Assaulting others bespeaks an expression of the immature self and disrespect for the truth that each person represents—not to mention the horrors brought about by warfare in this century. The virtues of courage, self-respect, and truth espoused by the supporters of conflict can be attained through modes of assertiveness that do not entail aggression against others.

In contrast to the two other variants of the prudential position, the Asian approaches discussed here do not look to external institutions to curb conflict. To be sure, they would not repudiate formal political arrangements as espoused by Hobbes and others, or the effects of benign cultural conditioning as discussed by cultural anthropologists. Their primary emphasis, however, is on internal practices that calm the mind and unify body and spirit. Such practices promote a naturally based harmony that energizes non-conflictual interactions and gets fortified by doctrines supportive of respectful relations with others. Perhaps contemporary discourse about social conflict might benefit from pondering the implications of this piece of Asian social thought.

Notes

1 Calling these constructions ideal types signals my intent to present the perspectives in simplified form so as to clarify the issues. In particular, I note two egregious simplifications: the paper does not make stable distinctions between conflict and such overlapping terms as antagonism, competition, and combat; and in maintaining an opposition between views of conflict as mainly positive or negative, it runs the risk of appearing to support what Boulding rightly described as "the illusion ... that conflict in any amount is either bad or good in itself" ([1962] 1988, 306).
2 From the day of birth, human egoism advances unrestrained. Humans expect opposition on all sides because they know from within that they are inclined to oppose all others. In consequence, the tableau of human history is woven from childish vanity, malice, and destructiveness. To be sure, Kant overlaid this pessimism about the human condition with a secular version of Providence that found in man's "unsocial sociability" the dynamic that leads to civil order and eventually a world state.
3 Gandhi came to call the technique of political action he devised *satyagraha*, the force that is born of truth. He defended its commitment to nonviolence on grounds that truth is absolute, equivalent to God, and "man is not capable of knowing the absolute truth and therefore not competent to punish" (Bondurant 1988, 16).

14

TWO TALES OF ONE CITY

Liben Gebre Etyopiya

On the topic of the, then current, political state of affairs in Ethiopia in 2005, a knowledgeable journalist said to me in Addis: "people here have been attacking one another all year. But they never talk about things they are really mad about." His comment rang a bell. Don't we all know family members who quarrel about things that substitute for what they are really feeling hurt and angry about?

Time and again in October, government and opposition had been on the verge of coming to an agreement that would have prevented the November violence and subsequent imprisonments. For a moment, if possible, let us set aside the question of who is to blame. Let us entertain the hypothesis that whatever the unprovoked harassment of CUD (Coalition for Unity and Democracy) leaders by government security personnel and whatever perceptions the government had about insurrectionary ambitions of the opposition, there was something in the air that enabled the talks—for which the Prime Minister had at one point given assurance that everything was on the table—to break down. They had been talking about parliamentary procedures, access to the press, and the like. But what were the two sides really mad about?

Ever since the Derg was overthrown in 1991, I had heard Ethiopians of different positions hurl insults at one another, accuse one another of the basest motives, and dig ever deeper into the moats that distance them from one another. Since then, I had wondered when the time would come that the underlying issues of their discontent might be addressed and resolved. Perhaps it took the killings and imprisonments of 2005 to force the issue, to get good Ethiopians of different persuasions to thinking in and about a new way.

That takes effort: to get beyond feeling aggrieved and injured although grief and injury are abundant all around; to get beyond pouring blame on one another although there are many things to blame. Perhaps the effort would involve realizing that what has been at stake all along has been two seemingly incompatible narratives about their country's history.

Narrative One

1. Modern Ethiopia is an empire created by a hegemonic Amhara elite under Emperor Menilek II, who conquered and dominated all of the historically separate and independent ethnic groups in the area.
2. It was dominated by a ruling class that had to be overthrown and prevented from regaining power or control of the land of peasants in the conquered territories.
3. The Derg was a ruthless, centrist regime that survived by terrorizing Ethiopian citizens.
4. TPLF (Tigray People's Liberation Front) troops, supported by EPLF (Eritrean People's Liberation Front), were the only viable opposition force to rebel against the Derg. For some 17 years, they had struggled as guerilla fighters and, after enormous sacrifice and suffering, succeeded in defeating the Derg and forcing its much-hated leader to flee.
5. Although they fought during those years under the banner of the Marxist-Leninist League of Tigray, they abandoned communist ideology as the Cold War came to an end and formally embraced liberal democracy.
6. They felt badly treated, after all that sacrifice and suffering, when their victorious entrance into the capital was met with hostility by those who had lived out the Derg years in relative comfort.
7. Once in power, they proceeded to create a novel system of ethnic federalism to ensure dignity for all of Ethiopia's peoples and to prevent a resurgence of private plutocracy through continued state ownership of land and many industries.
8. To ensure the success of their program, they had to spread a network of EPRDF (Ethiopian People's Revolutionary Democratic Front) cadres across the country.

Narrative Two

1. Modern Ethiopia is the outgrowth of a 2,000-year-old polity rooted in Aksum. It became unified and remained independent thanks to the leadership of Emperors Tewodros II, Yohannes IV, and Menilek II.
2. It came to fruition under Emperor Haile Selassie I, who advanced national centralization, instituted ministries and standing armies and, though mostly Shoan Amhara and surrounded by Shoan nobility, included Eritrean, Tigrean, Oromo, and others in the national elite he fostered.
3. The Derg was a ruthless communist regime that survived by terrorizing Ethiopian citizens.

4. Although the EDU (Ethiopian Democratic Union) and the EPRF had been forces to contend with at one time, for about a decade and a half, the TPLF had been the only effective form of competition to the Derg, eventually defeating it and forcing out its despised leader.
5. TPLF troops fought under the Marxist-Leninist League of Tigray. While they had abandoned communist ideology by the end of the Cold War, they never adequately embraced the principles of liberal democracy.
6. Joy at the overthrow of the Derg was muted by apprehension about the revanchist tenor of TPLF anti-Amhara sentiments, their proposal to elevate ethnic groups above the Ethiopian nation, their Leninist political style, and their reluctance to de-collectivize land.
7. Once in power, they excluded other ethnic groups from the center, imposed a system of ethnic federalism without broad national consensus, and continued state ownership of land and many industries. To defend these changes, they consistently harassed opposition parties, clamped down on a free press, and prevented an independent judiciary.
8. To ensure political control, they spread across the country a network of EPRDF cadres, who year after year abused the rights of civilians and did little to promote economic development.

The issues that came to the fore in 1991 and in the making of the Constitution had never been openly addressed and resolved. Beyond whatever strivings for power animated the leaders of the various parties in 2005, it was underlying antagonisms about these contrasting visions of the past and what they implied for Ethiopia's future that fueled an underground current of fire.

This way of framing the matter was suggested to me by a lecture given in Berlin by a seasoned scholar who discussed the essence of the Palestinian-Israeli conflict. He pointed out how chronic hostilities between Israelis and Palestinians flowed from contrasting narratives about their pasts. Jews live with a picture of their past that depicts them as hapless victims, deprived of their sacred land by ruthless Babylonian and Roman conquerors, abused by host societies for millennia thereafter, and subject to an effort at total annihilation so monstrous—*ha-shoah*, the Holocaust—that it gave rise to a new concept in human criminality, genocide. Palestinians live with a picture of their past that depicts them as resident in their land from time immemorial, proud caretakers of the holy places of Christianity and Islam, then confronted by a robust immigrant population that began with intrusive settlements and—through *al nakbah*, the Catastrophe—frightened many from their homes forever and eventually dominated them in their homeland territory. It would seem impossible for peoples with such incompatible stories ever to live together harmoniously—except, the lecturer pointed out, those narratives resembled the incompatible narratives that oriented France and Germany, now friendly neighbors, for a long time and impelled them into three horrible wars within one century.

To be sure, the centuries-old histories of Jews and Palestinians cannot really be said to have a counterpart in opposition between political parties who came into being just decades ago. And so, beyond the contrast of these narratives, we must locate another factor. Perhaps this is what Dr. B. T. Constantinos, in a response to my Getz #2—"Ethiopians in Prison" (www.eineps.org/forum/viewtopic.php?t=7) m)—described suggestively by observing that the Ethiopian political elite has debated the problems of Ethiopia's democratization

> within a particular tradition of political thought, argument and struggle that has origins in the radical student movement; in ideas of "national liberation," "class struggle," "national democratic revolution" spawned by that movement; and in the Marxist-Leninist tradition of political thought, discourse and action that has been a decisive influence over the current political impasse. At a time when the tradition seems a spent force in much of the former second world, including post-Dergue Ethiopia, a toned-down and somewhat reconstructed version of it seems to have gained a new lease on life among Ethiopia's political elite in the country and abroad.

Although Dr. Constantinos and I might disagree on certain details of that diagnosis, we agree on the hallmarks of that tradition: clever talk, arrogance, demonization of the other, presentation of preconditions in tight formulaic terms that are not amenable to alternative formulations and mediation (*shimgilna*), urbanite insurgency, and identification of one's position with the good and the will of the "people."

In this sense, then, the problem is not to move beyond Ethiopian traditions, but to restore the rich traditions of civility, forgiveness, neighborliness, and respect for one another that antedate the uncivility of the Marxist tradition. For this purpose, Ethiopians could scarcely do better than, for example, return to the political culture embodied in that remarkable Ethiopian tradition, the *gumi gayo* of the Boran and Guji peoples, which opens each parliamentary debate with a caution not to look for the worst in what others have said in order to undermine their position and win an argument, but to look for the best they have to offer so as to find a common ground:

> Dubbi qarumman dubbatani miti. Warri qaro qarumman laf keyyaddha.
> (This is not the place for clever talk. Clever people should leave their cleverness behind.)

For today's political elite, that could mean listening to one another's narratives and perhaps even learning something.

15

THE FORMS AND FUNCTIONS OF SOCIAL KNOWLEDGE

The quest to identify a kind of knowledge that enjoys a privileged status over common-sense perceptions and understandings of the world has been pursued since the very beginnings of reflection about how we know. The record of responses to that quest provides a summary of major moments in the history of human speculation. The idea of the Good, the authority of Revelation, the clear and distinct truths of geometry, the controlled outcomes of experimental investigation, the self-understanding by humans of human projects, the demystified grasp of real historic forces, the quantification of metric operations, the analysis of unconscious expressions, the enlightenment that follows disciplined meditation—these are some of the well-known historical candidates for that privileged position.

In the last two centuries in the West, and increasingly throughout the world, the single most popular candidate has been generically known as "science." Far and away the most successful rhetoric for establishing superior warrants for a proposition is to claim that it is scientific and that other contenders should be disqualified because they represent only common sense, pseudoscience, or insufficiently scientific science. Yet the success of this candidate has by no means laid to rest the uneasiness that underlay that historic quest. As the last half-century of debate in the history and philosophy of science has shown, there has been very little consensus concerning what it is that makes a work of science scientific. From Hempel to Popper, from Kuhn to Toulmin, and from Lakatos to Feyerabend, we have witnessed a succession of inconclusive efforts to establish a diacritical marker for scientificity. At this point, it may perhaps be acknowledged that the very notion of "science" belongs to that category of mental constructs that W. B. Gallie referred to as "essentially contested concepts"—concepts that are so closely linked to charged substantive debates, normative issues, and historical contexts that their meaning can never be fixed with a single unambiguous definition (1964, 157–91).

Yet even without the record of those inconclusive efforts—even without the massive evidence that underlies Lakatos' claim that there has been "little agreement concerning a *universal* criterion of the scientific character of theories" (1978, 124)—one might have predicted the futility of any such effort. The notion that there is some single absolute standard of cognitive value belies what has been a major intellectual achievement of the social sciences during the last two centuries—the solid awareness that all human expressions are conditioned by their rootedness in the exigencies of human action. The effort to identify a single diacritical marker for science, like the quest to find some privileged type of knowledge more generally, *must* be inconclusive, because of the irreducible variety of values, norms, and motives that organize all kinds of action, contemplative as well as conative or practical.

To acknowledge that fact, however, is not necessarily to assert that there are no forms of privileged knowledge. Rather, it is to state that sincere adherence to a single criterion of the generically scientific is to commit oneself to a polemical position that invalidates the legitimate claims of other kinds of knowledge. An alternative way to proceed would be to accept the notion of an irreducible plurality of privileged forms of knowledge.

I

Although the perspective I shall finally use to develop this point of view is known to sociologists as the theory of action, let me begin by approaching it from a philosophic perspective. Increased awareness of the plausibility of alternative claims to cognitive privilege has produced a variety of philosophic efforts to deal with the babel of contending intellectual positions in our time. Working on this problem in the area of literary criticism, Wayne Booth has identified five common responses that appear "when we try to decide how to listen to the actual clamor of critics' voices today" (1979, 4)—none of which he finds satisfactory. In incorporating his analysis here, I follow Booth's typology but alter his formulations slightly.

1. The polemicist response—just let everyone get out there and fight, because what the world needs is more assaults on complacency and conformity—is unacceptable because it generates destructive and wasteful exchanges and fosters the vice of misconstruing the ideas of one's intellectual opponents.
2. The semanticist response—just let intellectual antagonists specify the referents of their terms and thus remove ambiguities, and apparent disagreements will disappear—is unacceptable because it assumes that the only real differences among contending intellectual positions are trivial ones, and also because it denies that many concepts remain inexorably ambiguous and consequently depreciates those fruitful inquiries that are stimulated by controversies over such ambiguities.
3. The monist response identifies one of the contending positions as valid and portrays all others as wrong, misleading, or unimportant. A more tolerant

version of this response would encompass those who view alternative approaches as historically valid but currently outmoded positions or as necessary stages in the evolution of current true belief. This response cannot, however, secure universal assent to such invalidation or depreciation of all other positions.
4. The response of skepticism (or relativism, or nihilism) questions the possibility that any position can arrive at statements possessing truth value. The grounds for such a position are enormously varied; its proponents may appeal to the intractable complexity of observed phenomena, to the incorrigible limitations of observers, or to the hopelessness of arriving at mutual comprehension or intersubjective validation among a plurality of knowers. Such a position is ultimately untenable because it rests both on a logical contradiction (the professed certainty about the impossibility of securing statements beyond doubt) and a practical condition (the inhibition of the irrepressible quest for truth).
5. The response of eclecticism acknowledges the valid claims of contending positions or approaches and simply copes with their apparent incompatibility by chopping up the work of others into fragments, salvaging and conjoining whatever of those fragments appear useful. The weakness of this response is its failure to retain the contextual significance of the opposing claims.

In contrast with these responses, Booth espouses a possibility that he terms "methodological pluralism," which holds that "two or more conflicting positions may be entirely acceptable" (1979, 24). Rather than develop de novo the internal texture of such a position, Booth discusses the work of three other critics who, in his judgment, qualify as exemplary proponents of methodological pluralism.

In philosophy proper, many essential elements of a methodological pluralist position were developed during the last half-century by a scholar who has been Booth's mentor as well as my own, Richard McKeon. McKeon has grounded the pluralist position historically by showing ways in which inquiries have been advanced by going through cycles of methodological approaches (1966) and systematically by showing the power of alternative methods to illuminate commonplace notions like freedom and history (1952). Although a position of methodological pluralism appears implicitly or embryonically in the writings of several social scientists, I am unaware of efforts comparable to those of Booth and McKeon in the literature of the social sciences to develop the rationale and implications of that position. Among the few social scientists who have sought to articulate such features are Robert Merton (1976) and Arthur Stinchcombe (1968) in sociology, Henry Briefs (1960) in economics, and Asmarom Legesse (1973) in anthropology.

My own work over the last three decades has been informed by a program that seeks to contribute to a framework for a defensible pluralist position in the social sciences. My dissertation (Levine [1957] 1980) articulated the structure and implications of the divergent principles and methods embodied in the work of Georg Simmel and Talcott Parsons, work that presented two acceptable, yet largely incommensurable, approaches to the study of society. My monographs on Ethiopia sought to illustrate, first, the effect of applying a plurality of observational styles and descriptive modalities to the study of the Amhara tradition and to Ethiopia's modernization and, subsequently, the effect of applying a plurality of explanatory logics to the question of Ethiopia's historical survival as an independent nation (Levine 1974). In pursuing this line of inquiry over the years, I have come to emphasize three considerations that perhaps go beyond the analysis provided by Booth and other advocates of methodological pluralism.

II

I would emphasize that it is no longer productive to limit our advocacy or analysis of pluralism to those rather diffuse entities denoted by such terms as "intellectual approaches" or "methodological orientations." Insofar as an investigator or intellectual school sustains a relatively distinctive and consistent orientation, it necessarily consists of a number of discrete cognitive components. Although these components exhibit mutual affinities in the work of a given person or school, they are not necessarily closely linked and in fact usually exhibit the property of independent variability. Failure to realize this has produced those endless confusions that come from calling someone a positivist, a Marxist, an empiricist, a historicist, a Freudian, a Durkheimian, and the like. To say that someone is a Durkheimian, for example, does that mean he follows the master in using aggregate statistics rather than survey data, in analyzing contextual effects rather than individual properties, in talking about anomie rather than alienation, in positing the relativity rather than the universality of moral norms, or in searching for functional rather than compositional explanations?

To obviate such confusion, I have found it helpful to distinguish between "approaches," the total concrete orientation of a scholar or a research program, and cognitive "features," the constitutive elements of an approach. Each feature represents a discrete aspect or moment of inquiry. What to identify as a discrete cognitive feature is itself a matter of judgment or controversy, but the following have emerged in my work over the last two decades as unavoidable categories:

1. Categorical frameworks—conceptual forms that identify the units of social phenomena and how they are to be understood in combinations
2. Empirical procedures—operation forms that enable one to make observations
3. Descriptive modalities: conceptual forms that specify the types of observations one should make
4. Explanatory logics—conceptual forms that specify how sets of observations are to be construed in relationships of independent and dependent variables
5. Epistemic methods—conceptual forms that organize the strategic pattern of any inquiry or research program
6. Interpretation—conceptual forms that specify how to relate observations of phenomena to notions of what is real
7. Epistemic products—rhetorical forms by which one organizes and makes public the results of inquiry

Some of the variance among divergent approaches reflects differences in the weighting of various features. Thus survey research highlights the feature of empirical procedures; "rational choice" research gives primacy to categorical frameworks; while ethnomethodology stresses the feature of what is called "interpretations." More complex approaches, like Marxian, Freudian, or Weberian social science, pay serious attention to a number of features—one reason why their proponents so often engage in controversy over what is truly the essence of their respective approach.

Every cognitive feature, moreover, can be realized in a variety of ways, which I call "forms." Thus the feature of explanation can take a genetic, a structural, a compositional, or a functional form. Most of the variation and controversy in the social sciences stems from divergences among forms. Just as one finds the "empiricist" and the "theorist" each denouncing what the other does as not "really science" because of their investment in different features or aspects of the cognitive process, so one finds proponents of different forms of the same feature depreciating one another's work in similar ways. It follows from the pluralist position I am advocating, however, that knowledge gained through any form can be valid and indeed can constitute a privileged kind of knowledge when it is pursued on the basis of special training and experience. The name I would give to this type of knowledge is "disciplined."

In addition to transforming a general pluralist appreciation of different approaches into one that appreciates different features and forms, I would stress that the question of the relationship that obtains among divergent forms is genuinely an open question. At this point, at least, I can find no grounds for arguing a priori that the relationship between any two divergent forms is necessarily of a single kind when applied to any problem whatsoever. That relationship can and does take a number of possible forms. It can be the case that divergent forms are *mutually irrelevant*, as when they define and address themselves to wholly different problems. It can be that they *cross-cut* one another, as when they generate different definitions of a similar problem. It can be that they are *competitive*, as when they address a similar problem but lead to different solutions. They can be related in a *collaborative* mode, as when they address different parts of the same problem. Or, when they address different aspects of the same problem, we can view their relationship as *complementary*. Finally, we can see their relationship as lodged in some *architectonic* synthesis when they appear to be performing different tasks that are integrated or integrable in some hierarchical or sequential structure.

III

The third consideration I would stress in articulating a pluralist position is one that brings the array of cognitive forms back into a context of human action. Although the analysis of forms by itself can bring clarity of understanding and enhance the possibilities of mutual comprehension, it remains sterile if not finally tied to some sense of the significance of forms in relation to human purposes. This is so in two senses. To understand the forms as historical products, we must examine the evolutionary context in which they were created and utilized. This not only makes them more fully intelligible but also enables us to ask whether or not the forms we have inherited still serve those matrical purposes, other purposes that have subsequently replaced them, or no good purpose at all. Moreover, the connection to currently defensible purposes provides a central criterion for assessing each cognitive form and indeed for deciding what order of claim to the production of privileged knowledge it may now be said to possess.

The complete pluralist program, then, must include an effort to inventory the array of defensible human purposes no less than an effort to conduct an inventory of cognitive forms. As in the latter case, any schematic inventory must limit itself to a small number of rather broad categories, categories that involve a somewhat arbitrary element of judgment and cannot be specified absolutely. In thinking about the array of purposes that disciplined forms of social knowledge have been thought to serve at some point or other, I have found it convenient to order them by recourse to the well-established categories of the "general theory of action" formulated by Talcott Parsons and many of his colleagues. The central tenets of the Parsonian theory include the following assumptions: (1) that all action is organized toward the attainment of ends; (2) that action is structured in four levels of boundary-maintaining systems, the levels of the behavioral system, the personality system, the social system, and the cultural system; and (3) that each of these systems in turn is organized toward the fulfillment of the four basic systemic functions of marshalling adaptive resources, coordinating energies to attain goals, integrating the elements of the system, and providing support for maintaining the value patterns of the system.

On the basis of the foregoing considerations, then, I have prepared the following paradigm of the forms and functions of social knowledge.[1]

An Action-Theoretic Paradigm for Assessing the Forms and Functions of Social Knowledge

(I) A framework for inquiry into and assessment of alternative types of social scientific work

    (A) Inquiry re: The forms of social science (How does one learn about disciplinary resources?)

        1. What are the properties of each feature? To what kinds of issues is it relevant?

        2. What are the properties of each form? What is it good for? What is it bad for?

        3. How does it relate to other forms? To what extent is it independently variable? What elective affinities/incompatibilities does it have with forms of other features?

(B) Inquiry re: The relationships among different forms
   1. Mutually irrelevant (wholly different problem)
   2. Cross-cutting (different definitions of the problem)
   3. Competitive (similar problem, different solutions)
   4. Collaborative (same problem, different parts)
   5. Complementary (same problem, different aspects)
   6. Architectonic (different tasks, hierarchically or sequentially integrated)

(C) Inquiry re: The functions of social science (How does one produce non-alienated social knowledge?)
   1. What are the defensible objectives of social scientific inquiry? How are they defended?
   2. What are the most appropriate features and forms for each function?

(D) The critical assessment of features and forms (How does one identify excellent, decent, wasteful, alienated, or harmful social science?)
   1. Criteria of validity
      a accuracy
      b logical consistency
      c clarity
      d completeness or scope
   2. Criteria of significance
      a heuristic value
      b appropriateness to content of inquiry
      c appropriateness to purpose of inquiry
      d quality of relevant purposes and values
   3. Criteria of quality of execution
      a extent to which forms are properly or elegantly realized
      b extent to which forms remain linked to defensible purposes

(II) Toward a critical inventory of the forms of disciplined social knowledge

(A) Categorical frameworks (How does one conceptualize the units and organization of social phenomena?)
   1. Choices and markets (Smith, Becker)
   2. Controls and hierarchies (Marx, Dahrendorf)
   3. Affects and connections (Simmel, Bales)
   4. Beliefs and consensus (Durkheim, Benedict)
   5. Needs and mechanisms (Spencer, Parsons)
   6. Themes and patterns (Kroeber, Levi-Strauss)
   7. Intentions and conjoint actions (Toennies, Weber)

(B) Empirical procedures (How does one make observations?)

1. Unobtrusive-noninduced (direct observation, content analysis)
2. Unobtrusive-induced (questionnaires, concealed experiments)
3. Intrusive-noninduced (participant observation)
4. Intrusive-induced (depth interviews, lab experiment)

(C) Descriptive modalities (What does one observe?)

1. Externals (behavior, artifacts)/internals (thoughts, sentiments)
2. Simple properties/rich detail
3. Dominant trends/contradictory tendencies
4. Parts/elements
5. Microscopic/mesoscopic/macroscopic
6. Behavioral system/personality/social system/culture
7. Types of social facts

    a Global
    b Analytic
    c Interactional
    d Institutional

8. First-person/second-person/third-person accounts

(D) Explanatory logics (How does one relate sets of observations construed as independent/dependent variables?)

1. Genetic (explaining y as a consequence of some antecedent process or event)
2. Compositional (explaining y as a result of the properties of its constitutive elements)
3. Structural (explaining y as a consequence of its position in a set of ordered relationships)
4. Functional (explaining y with reference to the needs of x that it fulfills)

(E) Epistemic methods (Where does one start, toward what does one move, and how does one proceed?)

1. Logistic—by construction and decomposition
2. Dialectic—by assimilation and exemplification
3. Problematic—by resolution and question
4. Operational—by discrimination and postulation

(F) Interpretations (How does one relate observations of phenomena to notions of what is real?)

1. Ontological: reality is transcendent, appearances are imperfect manifestations thereof (Plato, Hegel)

2. Entitative: reality is underlying nature, appearances are secondary derivatives thereof (Marx, Freud, LeviStrauss)
3. Essentialist: reality is phenomena, properties, and causes that are natural functions or acquired conditionings (Durkheim, Malinowski)
4. Existentialist: reality is phenomenal, socially constructed (Schutz)

(G) Epistemic products (How does one organize and present findings?)

1. Case studies
2. Narratives
3. Graphs, tables
4. Propositions
5. Ideal types
6. Models
7. Axiomatized systems
8. Discursive syntheses

(III) Toward a critical inventory of the functions of disciplined social knowledge

(A) Cultural functions

1. Grounding a world view (Marx)
2. Grounding normative criteria (Durkheim)
3. Providing aesthetic symbolism (Nisbet)
4. Providing empirical understanding

   a of universals and variants
   b of self-experience and others

(B) Social systemic functions

1. Technical knowledge (Spencer, Coleman)
2. Counsel to rulers/insurgents (Machiavelli, Lenin)
3. Shared beliefs/enhanced communication (Comte, Dewey)
4. Clarifying collective values and enhancing their transmission (Lasswell, Skinner)

(C) Personality functions

1. Increasing consciousness about self and self's situation (Berger)
2. Increasing clarity about one's values (Weber)

(D) Behavioral system functions

1. Enhanced cognitive competence

IV

What, now, is the potential usefulness of a paradigm of this sort? First, it enables us to analyze more efficiently the structure of a given approach by constraining us to identify and locate the forms of its central defining features. Second, it may facilitate constructive communication among proponents of different approaches and provide a less polemical way for them to talk about their differences. Above all, it provides a more coherent way for critics to assess the value of different kinds of social knowledge—to indicate what kinds of social knowledge may legitimately claim privileged states and why.

Section I.D. of the paradigm schematizes three sets of appropriate criteria. There is no mechanical way to indicate the relative weighting of these criteria. That is a matter of value judgment that will vary with the background and purposes of each critic. What this part of the paradigm can do is constrain critics to be aware of a broader range of legitimate criteria than they would be likely to acknowledge otherwise and prod them to be more articulate in defending the criteria they choose to stress.

One set of criteria concerns the validity of cognitive efforts. These are the criteria familiar to scientists, who, however, are not always aware that the criteria are seriously competitive among themselves. Disciplined work that ranks high according to all of these criteria has a very special claim to privilege with respect to its truth value. Yet validity has never been the exclusive general criterion for assigning special merit to scientific work. Not only may one criterion of validity be sacrificed for another—as when accuracy is sacrificed for logical consistency, or scope is sacrificed for accuracy—but other kinds of criteria may or should be invoked as well. What may be called the criteria of significance also became prominent. These include: (1) the extent to which a given finding, idea, or research program opens up new areas of discovery or new ways of looking at some part of the world; (2) the consideration of how appropriate a given cognitive form is to the type of phenomena being studied; (3) the consideration of how appropriate a given cognitive form is to the purpose of the inquiry; and (4) the quality of the purpose served and the values embodied in or promoted by the research program.

Finally, there are criteria that have to do with what may be called the quality of execution of a program. Two chief criteria of this sort stand in chronic tension with one another. On the one hand, there is the consideration of how well a given form is realized in practice. To what extent is its integrity respected? What is the level of technical ability with which it is employed? How elegantly is its script performed? On the other hand, there is the consideration of how closely the execution of form remains linked to defensible purposes. It is often the case that the integrity of a form is sacrificed on behalf of a given purpose; it is perhaps even more often that the integrity of purpose is sacrificed to the intrinsic requirements of the form. Yet no final claim to privileged knowledge can be made without addressing these two concerns.

These remarks have been abstract and schematic. I hope they have been sufficiency clear and suggestive to elicit some support for their central thrust: that the time is ripe for articulating a self-conscious pluralist program in the social sciences in which the point will be not to scrap the demarcationist project, but to sophisticate it.

Note

1 The typology presented under II.C.7. is based on Lazarsfeld and Menzel (1961). Typology II.D. may be viewed as a transmutation of Aristotle's four causes. Typologies II.E. and II.F. are adapted from McKeon ([1966] 1998).

BIBLIOGRAPHY

Adler, Mortimer J. 1948. "War and Peace in Western Thought." *Common Cause, I*, pp. 407–411.
Adler, Mortimer J. 1977. *Philosopher at Large: An Intellectual Autobiography*. New York: Macmillan.
Al-Ghazali. 1995. *Al-Ghazali, On Disciplining the Soul [KitabRiyadat al-nafs] and On Breaking of the Two Desires [KitabKasr al-Shahwatayn]: Books XXII and XXIII of the Revival of the Religious Sciences [IhyaUlum al-Din]*. Trans. T. J. Winter. Cambridge: Islamic Texts Society.
Albert Einstein Institution. 2014. "About Us." www.aeinstein.org/about/.
Alexander, Jeffrey C. 1983. *The Modern Reconstruction of Classical Thought: Talcott Parsons*. Berkeley, CA: University of California Press.
Alexander, Jeffery C. 1993. "'Formal Sociology' is not Multidimensional: Breaking the 'Code' in Parsons' Fragment on Simmel." *Teoria Sociologica* 1(3): 101–114.
Anno, Motomichi. 1999. "Interview with Motomichi Anno Sensei." Conducted by Susan Perry, translated by Mary Heiny and Linda Holiday. *Aikido Today Magazine*July 11.
Arendt, Hannah. 1978. *The Life of the Mind/Thinking*. New York: Harcourt, Brace, Jovanovich.
Aristotle. 1984. *The Politics*. Trans. Carnes Lord. Chicago: University of Chicago Press.
Aron, Raymond. [1970] 1978. "On the Historical Condition of the Sociologist." In *Politics and History: Selected Essays*, trans. and ed. M. B. Conant. New York: Free Press, pp. 62–82.
Aubrey, John. 1949. *Brief Lives and Other Selected Writings*. Ed. Anthony Powell. London: The Cresset Press.
Baker, Keith M. 1975. *Condorcet: From National Philosophy to Social Mathematics*. Chicago: University of Chicago Press.
Barker, E. 1934. "Stoicism." *Encyclopedia of the Social Sciences*, XII. New York: Macmillan, pp. 407–410.
Beaulieu, Søren. 2005. *After O'Sensei: On the Dynamics of Succession to a Charismatic Innovator*. Unpublished Master's thesis. University of Chicago, Master of Arts Program in Social Science.

Becker, Carl. 1932. *The Heavenly City of the Eighteenth Century Philosophers*. New Haven, CT: Yale University Press.
Bellah, Robert. 1957. *Tokugawa Religion*. Glencoe, IL: Free Press.
Bellah, Robert. 1964. "Religious Evolution." *American Sociological Review* 29(3): 358–374.
Bellah, Robert. 2011. *Religion in Human Evolution*. Cambridge, MA: Harvard University Press.
Benedict, Ruth. 1934. *Patterns of Culture*. New York: Houghton Mifflin.
Berdyaev, Nicolas. 1948. *The Russian Idea*. New York: Macmillan.
Berdyaev, Nicolas. [1937] 1960. *The Origin of Russian Communism*. Ann Arbor, MI: The University of Michigan Press.
Berlin, Isaiah. 1976. *Vico and Herder: Two Studies in the History of Ideas*. New York: Vintage.
Berlin, Isaiah. 1990. "Joseph de Maistre and the Origins of Fascism: III." *The New York Review of Books*, October 25: 61–65.
Blanc, Louis. 1847. *Histoire de la révolution française*. Brussels: Société typographique Belge.
Bloom, Allan. 1987. *The Closing of the American Mind: How Higher Education Has Failed Democracy and Impoverished the Souls of Today's Students*. New York: Simon and Shuster.
Boehm, Max. 1931. "Cosmopolitanism." *Encyclopedia of the Social Sciences*, IV. New York: Macmillan, pp. 457–461.
Bondurant, Joan V. 1988. *Conquest of Violence: The Gandhian Philosophy of Conflict*. Rev. ed. Princeton, NJ: Princeton University Press.
Bonhoeffer, Dietrich. 1963. *The Communion of Saints: A Dogmatic Inquiry into the Sociology of the Church*. Trans. R. Gregor Smith. New York: Harper & Row.
Booth, Wayne C. 1979. *Critical Understanding: The Powers and Limits of Pluralism*. Chicago: University of Chicago Press.
Borgese, G. A. 1938. *The March of Fascism*. London: Victor Gollancz.
Boulding, Kenneth. [1962] 1988. *Conflict and Defense: A General Theory*. Lanham, MD: University Press of America.
Bowen, Murray. 1978. *Family Therapy in Clinical Practice*. New York: Aronson.
Brailsford, H. N. 1932. "Internationalism." *Encyclopedia of the Social Sciences*, VIII. New York: Macmillan, pp. 214–218.
Briefs, H. W. 1960. *Three Views of Method in Economics*. Georgetown Economic Studies. Washington, DC: Georgetown University Press.
Brown, Kevin L. 1994. *Fleshing out Economic Man: The "Utilitarian Dilemma" in Historical Perspective*. Ph.D. dissertation, University of Chicago.
Buber, Martin. 1957a. "Genuine Dialogue and the Possibilities of Peace." In *Pointing the Way: Collected Essays*, ed. and trans. M. Friedman. New York: Harper & Brothers, pp. 232–239.
Buber, Martin. 1957b. "The Demand of the Spirit and Historical Reality." In *Pointing the Way: Collected Essays*, ed. and trans. M. Friedman. New York: Harper & Brothers, pp. 177–191.
Buber, Martin. 1957c. "What Is To Be Done?" In M. Friedman, ed. and trans., *Pointing the Way: Collected Essays*. New York: Harper & Brothers, pp. 109–111.
Buber, Martin. [1938] 1965. *Between Man and Man*. Trans. Ronald Smith. New York: Macmillan.
Buber, Martin. 1992. *On Intersubjectivity and Cultural Creativity*. Ed. S. N. Eisenstadt. Chicago: University of Chicago Press.
Buber, Martin. [1923] 2004. *I and Thou*. New York: Scribner.
Burke, Kenneth. 1945. *A Grammar of Motives*. New York: Prentice Hall.
Burke, Kenneth. 1965. *Permanence and Change: An Anatomy of Purpose*. New York: Bobbs-Merrill.

Burke, Kenneth. 1984. *Attitudes Toward History*. Berkeley, CA: University of California Press.
Camic, Charles. 1989. "Structure after 50 Years: The Anatomy of a Charter." *American Journal of Sociology* 95(1): 38–107.
Camic, Charles, ed. 1997. *Reclaiming the Sociological Classics: The State of the Scholarship*. Malden, MA: Blackwell Publishers.
Caplow, Theodore. 1968. *Two Against One: Coalitions in Triads*. Englewood Cliffs, NJ: Prentice-Hall.
Carroll, James. 2001. *Constantine's Sword: The Church and the Jews—A History*. New York: Houghton Mifflin.
Chaadaev, Peter. 1913. "Lettres sur le philosophie d'histoire, I and II," and "Apologie d'un fou," in *Sochinenia i pis'ma*, ed. M. Gershenzon. Moscow.
Ciepley, David. 2006. *Liberalism in the Shadow of Totalitarianism*. Cambridge, MA: Harvard University Press.
Coleman, James S. 1957. *Community Conflict*. Glencoe, IL: The Free Press.
Comte, Auguste. 1875. *System of Positive Polity*. 4 vols. London: Longmans, Green, and Co.
Comte, Auguste. [1822] 1974. "Plan of the Scientific Operations Necessary for Reorganizing Society." In *The Crisis of Industrial Civilization: The Early Essays of Auguste Comte*, ed. Ronald Fletcher. London: Heinemann, pp. 111–181.
Comte, Auguste. [1825] 1974. "Philosophical Considerations on the Sciences and Savants." In *The Crisis of Industrial Civilization: The Early Essays of Auguste Comte*, ed. Ronald Fletcher. London: Heinemann, pp. 182–213.
Comte, Auguste. 1974. *The Crisis of Industrial Civilization: The Early Essays of Auguste Comte*. Ed. Ronald Fletcher. London: Heinemann.
Comte, Auguste. [1853] 2009. *The Positive Philosophy of Auguste Comte*. 2 vols. Trans. Harriet Martineau. New York: Cosimo Classics.
Condorcet, M. J. A. N. de Caritat, Marquis. 1802. *Outlines of an Historical View of the Progress of the Human Mind*. Baltimore, MD: Fryer.
Coser, Lewis. 1956. *The Functions of Social Conflict*. Glencoe, IL: The Free Press.
Coser, Lewis. 1967. *Continuities in the Study of Social Conflict*. New York: The Free Press.
Dahrendorf, Ralf. 1959. *Class and Class Conflict in Industrial Society*. Stanford, CA: Stanford University Press.
Deploige, Simon. [1911] 1938. *The Conflict between Ethics and Sociology*. Trans. C. Miltner. London and St. Louis: Herder.
Dewey, John. 1916. *Democracy and Education*. New York: Macmillan.
Dewey, John. 1925. *Experience and Nature*. Chicago: Open Court.
Dewey, John. 1937a. "President Hutchins' Proposal to Remake Higher Education." *The Social Frontier* 3(22): 103–104.
Dewey, John. 1937b. "Higher Learning in America." *The Social Frontier* 3(24): 167–169.
Dewey, John. 1939. "No Matter What Happens—Stay Out." *Common Sense* 8(3): 11.
Dewey, John. 1969. *The Learning Society*. New York: New American Library.
Dewey, John. [1922] 1988. *Human Nature and Conduct*. New York: Holt.
Dewey, John. [1915] 1990. *The School and Society*. Rev. ed. Chicago: University of Chicago Press.
Dostoevski, Fyodor. [n.d.] *The Brothers Karamazov*. New York: Modern Library.
Dostoevski, Fyodor. [1872] 1936. *The Possessed*. New York: Modern Library.
Dostoevski, Fyodor. 1949. *The Diary of a Writer*, Vol. II. New York: Charles Scribner's Sons.
Dollard, J., Doob, L. W., Miller, N. E., Mowrer, O. H., and Sears, R. R. 1939. *Frustration and Aggression*. New Haven, CT: Yale University Press.
Durkheim, Emile. [1892] 1960. *Montesquieu and Rousseau*. Trans. Ralph Manheim. Ann Arbor, MI: University of Michigan Press.

Durkheim, Emile. [1898] 1973. "Individualism and the Intellectuals." In *Emile Durkheim On Morality and Society*, ed. Robert N. Bellah. Chicago: University of Chicago Press, pp. 43–57.
Durkheim, Emile. [1899] 1973. *Two Laws of Penal Evolution*. Chicago: University of Chicago Press.
Durkheim, Emile. [1900] 1973. "Sociology in France in the Nineteenth Century." In *On Morality and Society*, ed. Robert N. Bellah. Chicago: University of Chicago Press, pp. 3–22.
Durkheim, Emile. [1893] 1984. *The Division of Labor in Society*. New York: The Free Press.
Easwaran, Eknath. 1999. *Nonviolent Soldier of Islam: Badshah Khan, a Man to Match His Mountains*. Tomales, CA: Nilgiri Press.
Eidelson, Roy J. and Eidelson, Judy I. 2008. "Dangerous Ideas: Five Beliefs that Propel Groups Toward Conflict." *American Psychologist* 58(3): 182–192.
Einstein, Albert and Freud, Sigmund. [1932] 2010. *Why War?* Los Angeles: Sequoia Free Press.
Eisenstadt, S. N. 1992. *Jewish Civilization: The Jewish Historical Experience in a Comparative Perspective*. Albany, NY: State University of New York Press.
Eisenstadt, S. N. 1996. *Japanese Civilization: A Comparative View*. Chicago: University of Chicago Press.
Eisenstadt, S. N. 2003. *Comparative Civilizations and Multiple Modernities*. Leiden: Brill.
Eisler, Riane. 1987. *The Chalice and The Blade: Our History, Our Future*. New York: Harper & Row.
Elias, Norbert. [1939] 2000. *The Civilizing Process: Sociogenetic and Psychogenetic Investigations*. Rev. ed. Oxford: Blackwell Publishing.
Ermarth, Michael. 1978. *Wilhelm Dilthey: The Critique of Historical Reason*. Chicago: University of Chicago Press.
Evans-Pritchard, E. E. 1970. *The Sociology of Comte: An Appreciation*. Manchester: Manchester University Press.
Fanon, Franz. 1963. *The Wretched of the Earth*. New York: Grove Press.
Feuerbach, Ludwig. [1843] 1903. "Grundsätze der Philosophie der Zukunft." In *Sämmtliche Werke*, Vol. II, ed. Wilhelm Bolin and Friedrich Jodl. Stuttgart: Fr. Fromanns Verlag.
Fisher, Robert, Ury, William, and Paton, William. 1991. *Getting to Yes*. 2nd ed. Boston, MA: Houghton Mifflin.
Folberg, Jay and Golann, Dwight. 2011. *Mediation: The Roles of Advocate and Neutral*. New York: Aspen Publishers.
Folberg, Jay and Taylor, Alison. 1984. *Mediation: A Comprehensive Guide to Resolving Conflicts Without Litigation*. San Francisco, CA: Jossey Bass.
Foucault, Michel. 1980. *Power, Knowledge: Selected Interviews and Other Writings 1972–1977*. Ed. Colin Gordon. New York: Pantheon.
Freud, Sigmund. [1932] 1939. "Letter to Albert Einstein." In *Civilization, War and Death: Psycho-Analytical Epitomes*, No. 4, ed. John Rickman. London: Hogarth Press.
Frisby, David, ed. 1994. *Georg Simmel: Critical Assessments*. 3 vols. New York: Routledge.
Fromm, Erich. 1973. *The Anatomy of Human Destructiveness*. New York: Holt, Rinehart and Winston.
Fujimura, J. H., Blick, D. A., Rajagopalan, R., Kaufman, J. S., Lewontin, R. C., Duster, T., Ossorio, P., and Marks, J. 2014. "Clines without Classes: How to Make Sense of Human Variation." *Sociological Theory* 32(3): 208–228.
Gallie, W. B. 1964. *Philosophy and the Historical Understanding*. London: Chatto and Windus.
Galston, William A. 1975. *Kant and the Problem of History*. Chicago: University of Chicago Press.
Geertz, Clifford. 1973. *The Interpretation of Cultures*. New York: Basic Books.
Gelles, Richard J. and Straus, Murray. 1979. "Determinants of Family Violence: Toward a Theoretical Integration." In *Contemporary Theories About the Family*, ed. Wesley R. Burr, Reuben Hill, F. Ivan Nye, and Ira L. Regiss. New York: The Free Press, pp. 549–581.

Gleason, William. 1995. *The Spiritual Foundations of Aikido*. Rochester, VT: Destiny Books.
Goldberg, Steven. 2005. "The Secrets of Successful Mediators." *Negotiation Journal*, 21(3) 365–376.
Gorski, Philip. 2003. *The Disciplinary Revolution*. Chicago: University of Chicago Press.
Habermas, Jürgen. 1984. *The Theory of Communicative Action*. Vol. I. Trans. T. McCarthy. Boston: Beacon Press.
Halévy, Elie. [1901–4] 1966. *The Growth of Philosophic Radicalism*. Trans. Mary Morris. Boston: Beacon Press.
Haumant, Émile. 1913. *La Culture Française en Russie, 1700–1900*. Paris: Hachette & Cie.
Hecht, David. 1947. *Russian Radicals Look to America*. Cambridge, MA: Harvard University Press.
Hegel, G. W. F. [1830] 1975. *Hegel's Logic: Being Part One of the Encyclopaedia of the Philosophical Sciences*. Trans. W. Wallace. Oxford: Clarendon Press.
Hegel, G. W. F. 1988. *Introduction to the Philosophy of History*. Trans. Leo Rauch. Indianapolis, IN: Hackett.
Hegel, G. W. F. [1830] 2004. *Philosophy of Nature: Being Part Two of the Encyclopaedia of the Philosophical Sciences*. Trans. A. V. Miller. Oxford: Oxford University Press.
Hensler, Deborah R. 2003. "Our Courts, Ourselves: How the Alternative Dispute Resolution Movement Is Re-Shaping Our Legal System." *Pennsylvania State Law Review* 108(1): 165–179.
Herder, Johannes G. [1784–91] 1887. *Sammtliche Werke*. Vol. XIII. Berlin: Weicimannsche.
Herder, Johannes G. [1784] 1968. *Reflections on the Philosophy of the History of Mankind*. Chicago: University of Chicago Press.
Herder, Johannes G. 1969. *Herder on Social and Political Culture*. Ed. and trans. F. M. Barnard. Cambridge: Cambridge University Press.
Hirschman, A. O. 1977. *The Passions and the Interests*. Princeton, NJ: Princeton University Press.
Hobbes, Thomas. [1861] 1909. *Leviathan*. Oxford: Clarendon Press.
Hobbes, Thomas. [1843] 1966. *The English Works of Thomas Hobbes of Melmesbury*. Ed. Sir William Molesworth. 11 vols. Darmstadt: Scientia Verlag Aalen.
Hobbes, Thomas. [1642] 1972. "The Citizen" [De Cive]. In *Man and Citizen*, ed. Bernard Gert. Garden City, NY: Doubleday.
Hobbes, Thomas. [1658] 1972. "On Man" [De Homine]. In *Man and Citizen*, ed. Bernard Gert. Garden City, NY: Doubleday.
Horne, Thomas A. 1978. *The Social Thought of Bernard Mandeville: Virtue and Commerce in Early Eighteenth-Century England*. New York: Columbia University Press.
Howard, Michael. 1991. *The Lessons of History*. New Haven, CT: Yale University Press.
Hume, David. [1751] 1975. *An Inquiry Concerning the Principles of Morals*. In *Hume: Moral and Political Philosophy*, ed. Henry D. Aiken. New York: Hefner Press.
Huntington, Samuel. 1993. "The Clash of Civilizations." *Foreign Affairs* 72(3): 22–49.
Hutcheson, Francis. 1755. *A System of Moral Philosophy*. Vol. I. London: A. Millar; Glasgow: Robert & Andrew Foulis.
Hutcheson, Francis. [1725] 1971. *An Inquiry into the Original of our Ideas of Beauty and Virtue*. New York: Garland Publishing.
Hutcheson, Francis. [1728] 1971. *Illustrations on the Moral Sense*. Ed. Bernard Peach. Cambridge, MA: Harvard University Press.
Hutchins, Robert M. 1930. "Inaugural Address: 19 November 1929." *University Record* 16: 8–14.
Hutchins, Robert M. 1931. "The Chicago Plan." *Educational Record* 12: 24–29.
Hutchins, Robert M. 1935. *The University of Utopia*. Chicago: University of Chicago Press.

Hutchins, Robert M. [1934] 1936. "The Higher Learning II." In *No Friendly Voice*. Chicago: University of Chicago Press.
Hutchins, Robert M. 1936. *No Friendly Voice*. Chicago: University of Chicago Press.
Hutchins, Robert M. 1937. "Grammar, Rhetoric, and Mr. Dewey." *Social Frontier* 3(23): 137–139.
Hutchins, Robert M. 1943. *Education for Freedom*. Baton Rouge, LA: Louisiana State University Press.
Hutchins, Robert M. 1969. *The Learning Society*. New York: New American Library.
Ikegami, Eiko. 1995. *The Taming of the Samurai*. Cambridge, MA: Harvard University Press.
Iswolsky, Helene. 1943. *Soul of Russia*. New York: Sheed & Ward.
Iyengar, B. K. 1973. *Light on Yoga*. New York: Schocken Books.
James, William. [1910] 1974. "The Moral Equivalent of War." In *Essays on Faith and Morals*, ed. R. B. Perry. New York: New American Library, pp. 311–328.
Janowitz, Morris. [1968] 1991. "Theory and Policy Engineering versus Enlightenment Models." In *Morris Janowitz on Social Organization and Social Control*, ed. James Burk. Chicago: University of Chicago Press, pp. 86–96. Originally "Sociological Models and Social Policy," Archives for Philosophy of Law and Social Philosophy LV (1969): 307–19.
Joas, Hans. 2013. *The Sacredness of the Person: A New Genealogy of Human Rights*. Washington, DC: Georgetown University Press.
Kagan, Robert A. 2001. *Adversarial Legalism: The American Way of Law*. Cambridge, MA: Harvard University Press.
Kano, Jigoro. 1932. "The Contribution of Judo to Education." *Journal of Health and Physical Education* 3, 37–40, 58.
Kano, Jigoro. 1990. "The Life of Jigoro Kano." *AikiNews*, 85.
Kant, Immanuel. [1784] 1963. Idea for a Universal History from a Cosmopolitan Point of View. In *On History*, ed. Lewis White Beck. Indianapolis, IN: Bobbs-Merrill, pp. 11–26.
Kant, Immanuel. [1785] 1964. *The Moral Law: Groundwork of the Metaphysics of Morals* (Grundelgung zur Metaphysik der Sitten). Trans. H. J. Paton. New York: Harper & Row.
Keeley, Lawrence. 1996. *War Before Civilization*. New York: Oxford University Press.
Kerr, Michale. 1988. "Chronic Anxiety and Defining a Self." *The Atlantic Monthly*, September: 35–58.
Kotev, Stephen. 2001. *Aikido and Conflict Resolution*. Unpublished.
Koyré, Alexandre. 1927. "Russia's Place in the World: Peter Chaadaev and the Slavophils." *Slavonic and East European Review* 5(15): 594–608.
Koyré, Alexandre. 1929. *La Philosophie et le problème national en Russie au début du XIXe siècle*. Paris: Champion.
Kriesberg, Louis. 2007. *Constructive Conflicts: From Escalation to Resolution*. Lanham, MD: Rowman and Littlefield.
Kriesberg, Louis. [1998] 2014. *Constructive Conflicts: From Escalation to Resolution*. Lanham, MD: Rowman and Littlefield.
Lakatos, I. 1978. *The Methodology of Scientific Research Programs*. Cambridge: Cambridge University Press.
Lampert, E. 1947. "Some Trends in Russian Social Thought of the Nineteenth Century." In *Russian Review III*. London: Penguin.
Laslett, Peter, ed. 1960. "Introduction." In *Two Treatises of Government* by John Locke. New York: New American Library.
Lazarsfeld, P. F. and Menzel, H. 1961. "On the Relation between Individual and Collective Properties." In *A Comparative Analysis of Complex Organizations*, ed. A. Etzioni. New York: Holt, Reinhart and Winston, pp. 422–440.

Lear, Jonathan. 2000. *Happiness, Death, and the Remainder of Life*. Cambridge, MA: Harvard University Press.
Legesse, A. 1973. *Gada: Three Approaches to the Study of African Society*. New York: Free Press.
Lepenies, Wolf. 1988. *Between Literature and Science: The Rise of Sociology*. Cambridge: Cambridge University Press.
Levenson, Edgar. 1983. *The Ambiguity of Change*. New York: Basic Books.
Levine, Donald N. 1974. *Greater Ethiopia: The Evolution of a Multiethnic Society*. Chicago: University of Chicago Press.
Levine, Donald N. 1978. "Book Review of Robert K. Merton, *Sociological Ambivalence and other Essays*." *American Journal of Sociology* 83(5): 1277–1280.
Levine, Donald N. [1957] 1980. *Simmel and Parsons: Two Approaches to the Study of Society*. With a new introduction. New York: Arno Press.
Levine, Donald N. 1985. *The Flight from Ambiguity*. Chicago: University of Chicago Press.
Levine, Donald N. 1991a. "Martial Arts as a Resource for Liberal Education: The Case of Aikido." In *The Body: Social Process and Cultural Theory*, ed. M. Featherstone, M. Hepworth, and B. S. Turner. London: Sage, pp. 209–224.
Levine, Donald N. 1991b. "Simmel and Parsons Reconsidered." *American Journal of Sociology* 96(5): 1097–1116.
Levine, Donald N. 1994a. "Simmel e Parsons riconsiderate/Simmel und Parsons neu betrachtet." *Annali di Sociologia/Soziologisches Jahrbuch* 10. Translation of "Simmel and Parsons Reconsidered," 1991.
Levine, Donald N. 1994b. "Further Comments Regarding Parson's Chapter on Simmel and Tönnies: A Response to Teoria Sociologica 1(93), 13–156." *Teoria Sociologica* 2(94): 360–374.
Levine, Donald N. 1995. *Visions of the Sociological Tradition*. Chicago: University of Chicago Press.
Levine, Donald N. 2005a. *Powers of the Mind: The Reinvention of Liberal Learning in America*. Chicago: University of Chicago Press.
Levine, Donald N. 2005b. "Putting Voluntarism back into a Voluntaristic Theory of Action." In *Die Ordnun der Gesellschaft: Festschrift Geburtstag von Richard Münch*, ed. H.-J. Aretz and C. Lahusen. Frankfurt am Main: Peter Lang, pp. 161–178.
Levine, Donald N. 2006a. "The Masculinity Ethic and the Spirit of Warriorhood in Ethiopian and Japanese Cultures." *International Journal of Ethiopian Studies* 2(1/2): 161–177.
Levine, Donald N. 2006b. "Somatic Elements in Social Conflict." In *Embodying Sociology: Retrospect, Progress, and Prospects*, ed. Chris Shilling. London: Wiley, 37–49.
Levine, Donald N. 2006c. "Merton's Ambivalence Towards Autonomous Theory—and Ours." *Canadian Journal of Sociology* 31(2): 235–243.
Levine, Donald N., Carter, Ellwood B., and Gorman, Eleanor Miller. 1976a. "Simmel's Influence on American Sociology, I." *American Journal of Sociology* 81(4), 813–845.
Levine, Donald N., Carter, Ellwood B., and Gorman, Eleanor Miller. 1976b. "Simmel's Influence on American Sociology, II." *American Journal of Sociology* 81(5), 1112–1132.
LeVine, Robert A. and Campbell, Donald T. 1972. *Ethnocentrism: Theories of Conflict, Ethnic Attitudes, and Group Behavior*. New York: John Wiley and Sons.
Lichtenstein, Aaron. 1981. *The Seven Laws of Noah*. New York: The Rabbi Jacob Joseph School Press.
Lidz, V. 1993. "Parsons and Simmel: Convergence, Difference, and Missed Opportunity." *Teoria Sociologica* 1(3): 130–142.
Lively, Jack. 1971. "Introduction." In *The Works of Joseph de Maistre*. Trans. Jack Lively. New York: Schocken.
Lorenz, Konrad. 1966. *On Aggression*. New York: Harcourt, Brace, and World.

Lukes, Steven. 1972. *Emile Durkheim: His Life and Work*. New York: Harper & Row.
Luther, Martin. 1957. *Christian Liberty*. Trans. W. A. Lambert. Philadelphia: Fortress Press.
McKeon, Richard. 1952. *Freedom and History: The Semantics of Philosophical Controversies and Ideological Conflicts*. New York: Noonday Press.
McKeon, Richard. [1952] 1954. "Love and Philosophical Analysis." In *Thought, Action and Passion*. Chicago: University of Chicago Press, pp. 30–53.
McKeon, Richard. 1966. "Philosophy and the Development of Scientific Methods." *Journal of the History of Ideas* 27(1): 3–22.
McKeon, R. [1952] 1987. "A philosopher mediates on discovery." In *Rhetoric: Essays in Invention and Discovery*, ed. M. Backman. Woodbridge, CT: Ox Bow Press, pp. 194–220.
McKeon, Richard. [1956] 1990. "Dialogue and Controversy in Philosophy." In *Freedom and History*. Chicago: University of Chicago Press, pp. 103–125.
McKeon, Richard. 1990. *Freedom and History and Other Essays*. Chicago: University of Chicago Press.
McKeon, Richard. [1966] 1998. Philosophic Semantics and Philosophic Inquiry. In *Selected Writings of Richard McKeon*, Vol. I, ed. Zhava K. McKeon and William G. Swenson. Chicago: The University of Chicago Press, pp. 209–221.
McKeon, Richard. [1969] 1998. "Fact and Value in the Philosophy of Culture." In *Selected Writings of Richard McKeon*, Vol. I, ed. Zhava K. McKeon and William G. Swenson. Chicago: The University of Chicago Press, pp. 429–435.
Maistre, Joseph de. 1971. *The Works of Joseph de Maistre*. Trans. Jack Lively. New York: Schocken.
Mandeville, Bernard. [1714] 1924. *The Fable of the Bees: or, Private Vices, Publick Benefits*. Ed. F. B. Kaye. 2 vols. Oxford: Oxford University Press.
Manuel, Frank E. 1962. *The Prophets of Paris*. New York: Harper & Row.
Marriott, McKim. 2004. "Varna and Jāti." In *The Hindu World*, ed. Sushil Mittal and Gene R. Thursby. London: Routledge, pp. 357–382.
Martin, Jay. 2002. *The Education of John Dewey*. New York: Columbia University Press.
Maynard, John, Sir. 1946. *Russia in Flux*. London: Gollancz, Ltd.
Mazour, Anatole. 1937. *The First Russian Revolution, 1825*. Berkeley, CA: University of California Press.
Mead, Margaret. 1937. *Cooperation and Conflict among Primitive Peoples*. New York: McGraw-Hill.
Mearsheimer, John J. 2011. "Imperial by Design." *The National Interest*, 111 (January/February): 16–34.
Melnick, Jed. 2013. "Lost Opportunities in Mediation." *Westlaw Journal, Securities Litigation and Regulation* 19(4): 1–4.
Melzer, Arthur M. 1990. *The Natural Goodness of Man*. Chicago: University of Chicago Press.
Menand, Louis. 2001. *The Metaphysical Club*. New York: Farrar, Strauss, and Giroux.
Mendes-Flohr, Paul. 1989. *From Mysticism to Dialogue: Martin Buber's Transformation of German Social Thought*. Detroit, MI: Wayne State University Press.
Mendes-Flohr, Paul. 2004. "Die Gesellschaft: An Early Transdisciplinary Project." In *The Dialogical Turn: New Roles for Sociology in the Postdisciplinary Age*, ed. Charles Camic and Hans Joas. Lanham, MD: Rowman and Littlefield, pp. 105–114.
Merton, R. K. [1938] 1968. "Social Structure and Anomie." In *Social Theory and Social Structure*. New York: Free Press, pp. 185–214.
Merton, R. K. [1942] 1973. "The Normative Structure of Science." In *The Sociology of Science*, ed. N. Storer. Chicago: University of Chicago Press, pp. 267–280.
Merton, R. K. [1957] 1973. "Priorities in Scientific Discovery." In *The Sociology of Science*, ed. N. Storer. Chicago: University of Chicago Press, pp. 286–324.
Merton, R. K. 1973. *The Sociology of Science*, ed. N. Storer. Chicago: University of Chicago Press.

Merton, R. K. 1976. *Sociological Ambivalence*. New York: Free Press.
Milioukov, Paul, Seignobos, Charles, and Eisenmann, Louis. 1932. *Histoire de Russie*. Vol. II. Paris: Presses universitaires de France.
Mills, C. Wright. [1940] 1963. "Situated Actions and Vocabularies of Motive." In *Power, Politics and People*, ed. Irving Louis Horowitz. New York: Oxford University Press, pp. 439–452.
Morgenthau, Hans. 1960. *Politics Among Nations*. 3rd ed. New York: Knopf.
Morning, Ann. 2014. "Does Genomics Challenge the Social Construction of Race?" *Sociological Theory* 32(3): 189–207.
Morris, Ivan. 1975. *The Nobility of Failure: Tragic Heroes in the History of Japan*. New York: Holt, Rinehart, and Winston.
Mueller, John. 2004. *The Remnants of War*. Ithaca, NY: Cornell University Press.
Murata, Naoki. 2005. "From 'Jutsu to Dō: The Birth of Kōdōkan Judo." In *Budo Perspectives*, ed. Alexander Bennett. Auckland: Kendo World, pp. 147–148.
Nomad, Max. [1939] 1961. *Apostles of Revolution*. New York: Collier.
Parsons, Talcott. 1935. "The Place of Ultimate Values in Sociological Theory." *International Journal of Ethics* 45(3): 282–316.
Parsons, Talcott. 1951. *The Social System*. New York: Free Press.
Parsons, Talcott. [1939] 1954. "The Professions and Social Structure." In *Essays in Sociological Theory*. New York: Free Press, pp. 34–49.
Parsons, Talcott. [1947] 1954. "Certain Primary Sources and Patterns of Aggression in the Social Structure of the Western World." In *Essays in Sociological Theory*. New York: Free Press, pp. 298–322.
Parsons, Talcott. 1966. *Societies: Evolutionary and Comparative Perspectives*. Englewood Cliffs, NJ: Prentice-Hall.
Parsons, Talcott. [1937] 1968. *The Structure of Social Action*. 2 vols. New York: Free Press.
Parsons, Talcott. 1971. *The System of Modern Societies*. Englewood Cliffs, NJ: Prentice-Hall.
Parsons, Talcott. 1978. *Action Theory and the Human Condition*. New York: Free Press.
Parsons, Talcott. 1986. "Social Science: A Basic National Resource." In *The Nationalization of the Social Sciences*, ed. Samuel Z. Klausner and Victor M. Lidz. Philadelphia, PA: University of Pennsylvania Press, pp. 41–112.
Parsons, Talcott. 1989. "A Tentative Outline of American Values." *Theory, Culture, and Society* 6(4): 557–612.
Parsons, Talcott with Platt, G. M., and Smelser, N. J. 1973. *The American University*. Cambridge, MA: Harvard University Press.
Parsons, Talcott and Smelser, Neil. 1956. *Economy and Society*. Glencoe, IL: Free Press.
Patterson, O. 1991. *Freedom in the Making of Western Culture*. New York: Basic Books.
Peyre, Henri. 1960. "Foreword." In *Montesquieu and Rousseau* by Emile Durkheim. Trans. Ralph Manheim. Ann Arbor, MI: University of Michigan Press, pp. v–xvi.
Piazza, Antonio. 2004. *The Physics of Aikido and the Art of Mediation*. Unpublished.
Pinker, S. 2011. *The Better Angels of our Nature*. New York: Viking.
Plamenatz, John. 1963. "Introduction." In *Leviathan* by Thomas Hobbes. New York: Meridian Books.
Plochmann, George Kimball. 1990. *Richard McKeon: A Study*. Chicago: The University of Chicago Press.
Pogson Smith, W. G. 1909. "Introduction." In *Leviathan* by Thomas Hobbes. Oxford: Clarendon Press.
Proust, Jacques. 1962. *Diderot et L'Encyclopedie*. Paris: Armand Colin.
Qutb, Sayyid. 1980. *Milestones*. Beirut: The Holy Koran Publishing House.
Rhee, C. H., van, ed. 2005. *European Traditions in Civil Procedure*. Antwerpen: Intersentia.

Robertson, Roland and Turner, Bryan S., eds. 1991. *Talcott Parsons: Theorist of Modernity*. London: Sage Publications.
Rosenberg, Marshall B. 2005a. *Nonviolent Communication: A Language of Life*. Encinitas, CA: Puddle Dancer Press.
Rosenberg, Marshall B. 2005b. *Speak Peace in a World of Conflict*. Encinitas, CA: Puddle Dancer Press.
Rosenberg, Marshall B. 2012. *Living Nonviolent Communication: Practical Tools to Connect and Communicate Skillfully in Every Situation*. Louisville, CO: Sounds True.
Rousseau, J.-J. [1782] 1861. *The Confessions of Jean-Jacques Rousseau*. London: Reeves and Turner.
Rousseau, Jean Jacques. 1917. *A Lasting Peace through the Federation of Europe*. London: Constable and Co., Ltd.
Rousseau, Jean Jacques. [1772] 1947. *Considerations on the Government of Poland*. Minneapolis, MN: Minnesota Book Store.
Rousseau, Jean Jacques. [1762] 1987. *On the Social Contract*. Trans. Donald A. Cress. Indianapolis, IN: Hackett.
Rousseau, Jean Jacques. [1752] 2005. *On the Origins of Inequality*. Trans. G. D. H. Cole. New York: Cosimo Classics.
Said, Edward W. 2001. "The Clash of Ignorance." *The Nation* 273(12): 11–13.
Saint-Simon, Henri de. 1859. *Oeuvres Choisies de C.-H. de Saint-Simon*. Vol. I. Bruxelles: Van Meenen.
Saint-Simon, Henri de. [1825] 1964. "New Christianity." In *Social Organization, The Science of Man and Other Writings*, trans. and ed. Felix Markham. New York: Harper & Row, pp. 81–116.
Saint-Simon, Henri de. [1952] 1964. *Social Organization, The Science of Man and Other Writings*. Trans. and ed. Felix Markham. New York: Harper & Row.
Sandomirsky, Vera. 1949. "We Who Loved Thee, O Russia." In *Common Cause, III*.
Saotome, Mitsugi. 1989. *The Principles of Aikido*. Boston & Shaftesbury: Shambhala.
Saotome, Mitsugi. [1986] 1993. *Aikido and the Harmony of Nature*. Boston and London: Shambhala.
Saposnek, Donald. 1998. *Mediating Child Custody Disputes: A Strategic Approach*. San Francisco, CA: Jossey-Bass Inc.
Scheff, Thomas J. [1994] 2000. *Bloody Revenge: Emotions, Nationalism, and War*. Boulder, CO: Westview Press.
Schelling, F. W. J., von. [1797] 2001. *Ideas for a Philosophy of Nature as Introduction to the Study of this Science*. Cambridge: Cambridge University Press.
Schmitt, Carl. [1927] 2006. *The Concept of the Political*. Chicago: University of Chicago Press.
Schneiderman, Howard G. 2013. "Protestantism and Progress, Redux." In *Protestantism and Progress*, ed. Ernst Troeltsch. New Brunswick, NJ: Transaction, pp. vii–xix.
Schneiderman, Howard G. 2015. "Folkways and the Rise of Modern Sociology." In *On Folkways and Mores: William Graham Sumner, Then and Now*, ed. Phillip D. Manning. New Brunswick, NJ: Transaction, pp. 59–76.
Shackelton, Robert. 1961. *Montesquieu: A Critical Biography*. Oxford: Oxford University Press.
Shaftsbury, Anthony Ashley Cooper, Earl of. [1711] 1900. *Characteristicks of Men, Manners, Opinions, Times, Etc.*, ed. John M. Robertson. 2 vols. London: Grant Richards.
Sharp, Gene. 1990. *Civilian-Based Defense*. Princeton, NJ: Princeton University Press.
Sheehan, James. 1989. *German History 1770–1866*. Oxford: Oxford University Press.
Shiao, Jiannbin Lee. 2014. "Response to Hosang; Fujiura, Bolnick, Rajagopalan, Kaufman, Lewontin, Duster, Ossorio, and Marks; and Morning." *Sociological Theory* 32(3): 244–258.
Shibata, Beth. 2004. "Throw versus Release: The Effect of Language and Intention on Aikido Practice." www.aiki-extensions.org.

Sidgwick, H. [1886] 1954. *Outlines of the History of Ethics*. London: Macmillan.
Sidgwick, H. [1892] 1994. "Review of Simmel, Einleitung in die Moralwissenschaft." Mind 1: 434. Reprinted in *George Simmel: Critical Assessments*, Vol. I, ed. David Frisby. London: Routledge.
Simmel, Georg. 1904a. "The Sociology of Conflict, I." *American Journal of Sociology* 9(4): 490–525. Trans. Albion W. Small.
Simmel, Georg. 1904b. "The Sociology of Conflict, II." *American Journal of Sociology* 9(5): 672–689. Trans. Albion W. Small.
Simmel, Georg. 1904c. "The Sociology of Conflict, III." *American Journal of Sociology* 9(6): 798–811. Trans. Albion W. Small.
Simmel, Georg. 1906. *Die Religion*. Frankfurt am Main: Rütten & Loening.
Simmel, Georg. 1918. *Lebensanschauung: Vier metaphysische Kapitel*. München: Dunker & Humblot.
Simmel, Georg. [1907] 1971. "Exchange." In *Georg Simmel on Individuality and Social Forms*, ed. D. N. Levine. Chicago: University of Chicago Press, pp. 43–69.
Simmel, Georg. [1908] 1971. "Conflict." In *Georg Simmel: On Individuality and Social Forms*, ed. D. N. Levine. Chicago: University of Chicago Press, pp. 70–95. Translation of "Soziologie der Geselligkeit."
Simmel, Georg. [1910] 1971. "Sociability." In *Georg Simmel: On Individuality and Social Forms*, ed. D. N. Levine. Chicago: University of Chicago Press, pp. 127–140. Translation of "Soziologie der Geselligkeit," GSG 12.
Simmel, Georg. [n.d.] 1971. "Freedom and the Individual." In *Georg Simmel on Individuality and Social Forms*, ed. Donald N. Levine. Chicago: University of Chicago Press, pp. 217–226.
Simmel, Georg. [1890] 1989. "Über sociale Differenzierung." In *Georg Simmel Gesamtausgabe*. GSG 2. Frankfurt am Main: Suhrkamp.
Simmel, Georg. [1892–93] 1991. *Einleitung in die Moralwissenschaft*. 2 vols. GSG 3. Frankfurt am Main: Suhrkamp.
Simmel, Georg. [1898] 1992. *Die Selbserhaltung der Socialen Gruppe*. GSG 5. Frankfurt am Main: Suhrkamp.
Simmel, Georg. [1908] 1992. *Soziologie: Untersuchungen über die Formen der Vergellschaftung*. Ed. Otthein Rammstedt. Frankfurt am Main: Suhrkamp.
Simmons, E. J. 1940. *Doestoevksy: The Making of a Novelist*. New York: Oxford University Press.
Simmons, E. J. 1946. *Leo Tolstoy*. Boston, MA: Little, Brown, & Co.
Smith, Adam. [1776] 1976. *An Inquiry into the Nature and Causes of the Wealth of Nations*, ed. Edwin Carman. 2 vols. in 1. Chicago: University of Chicago Press.
Smith, Adam. [1759] 1982. *The Theory of Moral Sentiments*. Indianapolis, IN: Liberty Classics.
Smith, Thomas and Stevens, G. 2002. "Hyperstructures and the Biology of Interpersonal Dependence." *Sociological Theory* 20(1): 106–130.
Soloviev, Vladimir. 1918. *The Justification of the Good*. New York: Macmillan Co.
Soloviev, Vladimir. [1889] 1948. *Russia and the Universal Church*. Introduction and Part III. London: MacLelose and Co., Ltd.
Sorokin, Pitirim A. 1928. *Contemporary Sociological Theories*. New York: Harper & Brothers.
Spencer, Herbert. 1972. *On Social Evolution*. Ed. J. D. Y. Peel. Chicago: University of Chicago Press.
Starobinski, Jean. 1990. "Rousseau in the Revolution." *The New York Review of Books*, April 12, 47–50.
Steiner, Mark E. 1995. "The Lawyer as Peacemaker: Law and Community in Abraham Lincoln's Slander Cases." *Journal of the Abraham Lincoln Association* 16(2): 1–22.
Stinchcombe, A. L. 1968. *Constructing Social Theories*. New York: Harcourt, Brace and World.

Stipanowich, Thomas J. 2010. "Arbitration: The New Litigation." *University of Illinois Law Review* 1: 1–60.
Strauss, Leo. 1936. *The Political Philosophy of Hobbes: Its Basis and Its Genesis*. Trans. Elsa M. Sinclair. Oxford: Clarendon Press.
Sumner, William Graham. [1907] 2002. *Folkways: A Study of the Sociological Importance of Usages, Manners, Customs, Mores, and Morals*. Mineola, NY: Dover Publications, Inc.
Thilly, F. [1893] 1994. Review of Simmel, Einleitung in die Moralwissenschaft. Philosophical Review 3: 637–40. Reprinted in *Georg Simmel: Critical Assessments*, Vol. I, ed. David Frisby. London: Routledge.
Timmerman, David M. and Schiappa, Edward. 2010. *Classical Greek Rhetorical Theory and the Disciplining of Discourse*. New York: Cambridge University Press.
Tinbergen, N. 1968. "On War and Peace in Animals and Man: An Ethologist's Approach to the Biology of Aggression." *Science* 160(3835): 1411–1418.
Tocqueville, Alexis de. [1835] 2000. *Democracy in America*. New York: Perennial Classics.
Toews, John Edward. 1980. *Hegelianism: The Path Toward Dialectical Humanism*. Cambridge: Cambridge University Press.
Tolstoy, Leo. 1894. *Kingdom of God Is within You*. London: Scott.
Tolstoy, Leo. [1900] 1911. "Patriotism and Government." In *Essays and Letters*. Trans. Aylmer Maude. London: Oxford University Press, pp. 238–261.
Tolstoy, Leo. [1887] 1934. "On Life." In *On Life and Essays on Religion*. Trans. Aylmer Maude. London: Oxford University Press, pp. 1–167.
Tolstoy, Leo. [1904] 1934. "Church and State." In *On Life and Essays on Religion*. Trans. Aylmer Maude. London: Oxford University Press, pp. 331–346.
Tucker, Robert C., ed. 1972. *The Marx-Engels Reader*. New York: Norton.
Tuttle, Russell H. 2014. *Apes and Human Evolution*. Cambridge, MA: Harvard University Press.
Ueshiba, Kisshomahu. 1984. *The Spirit of Aikido*. Trans. TaietsuUnno. New York: Kodansha International.
Voltaire, F. M. A. de. 1935. *Dictionnaire philosophique*. With an Introduction by Julien Benda. 2 vols. Paris: Garnier.
Ward, F. Champion, ed. [1950] 1992. *The Idea and Practice of General Education: An Account of the College of the University of Chicago*. Chicago: University of Chicago Press.
Warner, Stephen R. 1978. "Toward a Redefinition of Action Theory: Paying the Cognitive Element its Due." *American Journal of Sociology* 83(6): 1317–1349.
Watson, Walter. 1985. *The Architectonics of Meaning: Foundations of the New Pluralism*. Albany, NY: State University of New York.
Watson, Walter. 1991. "McKeon: The Unity of His Thought." Paper presented at the Conference on Pluralism and Objectivity in Contemporary Culture: Departures from the Philosophy of Richard McKeon, University of Chicago, March 13–14.
Weber, M. 1968. *Economy and Society*, ed. G. Roth and C. Wittich. 3 vols. New York: Bedminster Press.
Weil, Shalva. 2010. "On Multiple Modernities, Civilizations, and Ancient Judaism: An Interview with Professor S. N. Eisenstadt." *European Societies* 12(4): 451–465.
Weinstein, Daniel. 2004. Talk to J. D. students at Northwestern School of Law. Unpublished.
Westbrook, Robert B. 1991. *John Dewey and American Democracy*. Ithaca, NY: Cornell University Press.
Wilson, William S. 1982. *Ideals of the Samurai: Writings of Japanese Warriors*. Burbank, CA: Ohara.
Wrangham, R. and Peterson, D. 1996. *Demonic Males*. Boston, MA: Houghton Mifflin.
Young, Nigel. 1984. "Why Peace Movements Fail: An Historical and Social Overview." *Social Alternatives* 4(1): 9–17.

INDEX

Acrimony 2
Addams, Jane 12
Aiki approach 34
Aikido 21, 29, 32–41, 49, 52, 113–114, 117–118, 120–123, 181, 188–190
Anti-Semitism 5, 48
Arendt, Hannah 1, 2
Aristotle 1, 2, 46, 103–105, 107, 109–112, 125–126, 139–145, 151, 205
Aron, Raymond 5
Assimilation of ideas 3

Baehr, Peter 3
Bakunin, Michael 70, 71, 82
Becker, Carl 61, 201, 207
Bellah, Robert 27, 48, 95, 207, 208
Benedict, Ruth 16, 201, 207
Bentham, Jeremy 146, 153
Berdyaev, Nicholas 65, 67, 69–70, 80–81, 207
Bloom, Allan 124, 178, 207
Bonald, Joseph de 82, 156, 158–160, 163, 168
Booth, Wayne 186, 196–198, 207
Boulding, Kenneth 33, 190, 207
Bridging devices 3
Buber, Martin 11–12, 18, 20, 45, 53, 113, 115–117, 121, 123, 207
Burke, Kenneth 3–4, 7, 160, 207
Bushido 27–28

Camic, Charles 86, 213
Caplow, Theodore 95

Caricature 2–3, 5–6
Civilizations 44–45, 48, 50, 52, 74, 209–210
Clash of civilizations 14, 42–43, 210
Coleman, James S. 34–203
Combat, combativeness 2–3, 15–16, 18–22, 24–27, 38–41, 44, 48, 73, 118, 122, 148, 182–183, 185–187, 190
Competitive individualism 38
Comte, Auguste 23–24, 84–85, 95, 102, 114, 152, 154, 158–169, 172, 203, 209
Condorcet, M.J.A.N de Caritat, Marquis 61, 68, 70, 82, 153, 157–161, 163
Conflict, legal 30, 35–36
Controversy 1–5, 7, 18, 30, 35, 124, 199, 213
Cooley, Charles Horton 12, 127
Cooperation 3, 4, 6, 66, 115, 187
Coser, Lewis 95, 183–184
Cultural relativism 6

Dahrendorf, Ralf 201
Debate 1–3, 18, 88, 107, 111, 114, 132, 135–136, 145, 195
Debunk, debunking 3–5
Demonization 2, 3, 194
Dewey, John 12, 14, 84, 101, 103, 105–106, 108, 110–111, 114, 124–136, 159, 203, 213
Diagnostic rationality 102, 106, 108, 111
Dialogue 1–7, 11–12, 14–15, 18–20, 25, 42, 44–45, 48, 115, 117, 123, 134, 136, 145, 148, 161, 165, 167–168
Diderot 63, 153, 165, 214

Disengagement 2, 169
Dogmatism 2, 4
Dollard, John 18
Dostoevski, Fyodor 59, 70–77, 81–82
Durkheim 5, 22–23, 58, 84–89, 92–93, 96–97, 103, 108, 110–111, 114, 153, 155–156, 160, 164–170, 198, 201, 203, 209, 213

Eisenstadt, Shmuel 42–43, 45, 47, 50, 53, 207, 209
Eisler, Riane 19, 209
Elias, Norbert 24, 209
Engagement 3, 19, 28, 32, 38, 121, 133, 136, 169
Ethiopia, Ethiopian 14, 39, 49–51, 191–194, 197–198, 212
Ethnocentrism 6, 7, 43, 212
Euro-American litigation 32
Evolution, evolutionary 16, 24, 26, 29–30, 32, 78, 85, 87–88, 90–92, 95, 98, 166, 169, 178, 197, 200, 207, 209–10

Fanon, Frantz 185, 209
Feurbach, Ludwig 116, 209
Fichte, Johann 176, 178, 180
Freud, Sigmund 14–15, 85, 87, 92, 103, 110, 117–120, 182, 186, 203
Freudian 110, 112, 182, 198–199
Friendship 1, 146, 149
Fromm, Erich 16, 34, 184–185

Gandhi, Mohandas 20, 47–48, 50, 52–53, 189–190
Geertz. Clifford 187, 209
Genuine dialogue 11, 117, 207
Grammar of motives 4, 207

Habermas, Jurgen 45, 108, 115, 210
Harper, William Rainey 127
Hegel, G. W. F. 23, 69, 81, 127, 175–180, 202, 210
Herder, Johannes G. 153, 175–180, 207, 210
Hirschman, A.O. 85, 210
Hobbes, Thomas 15–16, 85, 114, 139, 140–149, 151–154, 160, 172, 184, 187, 189–190, 210, 214
Holmes, Oliver Wendell 12
Hume, David 85, 136, 149–150, 153, 171, 210
Huntington, Samuel 42
Huntington thesis 42–44
Hutchins, Robert Maynard 14, 98, 124–126, 130–136, 210

Ideological 3–6, 42, 47, 106, 123, 165, 185
Intercommunication 11
Interhuman 11, 44, 113, 115, 117, 123

James, William 12, 13, 20, 182–183
Janowitz, Morris 101
Japanese civilization 47
Jewish 49–53, 77
Jihad 49–53
Joas, Hans 22, 213
Judaism 52, 53, 59

Kagan, Robert 30
Kant, Immanuel 63, 66, 90, 93, 102–105, 107, 110–111, 153, 171–172, 175–180, 182, 190, 209
King, Martin Luther, Jr. 20, 47
Knowledge 65 and passsim
Kriesberg, Louis 47

Labeling 2, 3, 6
Lavrov, Peter 70–71
Litigation 15, 21, 25–26, 30–32, 34, 37
Locke, John 145
Lorenz, Konrad 16, 45, 183

Maistre, Joseph de 82, 156–161, 168, 207, 212–213
Mandeville, Bernard 145–149, 151, 154, 210
Mannheim, Karl 3
Manuel, Frank E. 168, 213
Martial arts 25–26, 28–30, 32, 48, 113, 118
Marx, Karl 103, 105, 110–111, 123, 201, 203
Marxist, Marxian 6, 69, 71, 108, 192–194, 198–199
McKeon, Richard 1–5, 7, 14, 96–101, 103, 106–112, 125, 197, 205, 213
Mead, George Herbert 12, 125, 135–136, 159
Mead, Margaret 184, 187, 213
Mediation 21, 29, 31–32, 36–41, 194, 209
Mendes-Flohr, Paul 115–116, 213
Merton, Robert 14, 85, 93–95, 212–214
Mill, John Stuart 84
Mills, C. Wright 4, 214
Montesquieu 61, 63, 85, 114, 153–160, 167–168, 180
Morality 14, 28, 46, 79, 81, 84–85, 87–89, 91, 93, 95, 133, 141, 143–144, 147, 149–151, 154–155, 158, 164–166, 171–172, 178–179, 183
Mores 6, 90, 215
Morgenthau, Hans 16, 183

Motives 4, 16, 33, 84–85, 87, 92, 108, 152, 191, 196
Mueller, John 20, 22
Muslim 47, 49, 50–52

Nietzsche, Friedrich, 11, 115–117, 123, 185, 187
Nomad, Max 71, 21

Park, Robert 84, 108, 127
Parsons, Talcott 85–88, 91–102, 106, 109–113, 119, 139, 197, 200–201, 212, 214–215
Pattern variables 87, 94
Peirce, C.S. 11–12
Pejorative labeling 3, 6
Philosophes 14, 59, 61–66, 80–82, 158–159
Pluralism 99, 109, 111, 197–198, 207
Polemics, polemical 45, 135, 185–186, 196, 204
Politics 2–3, 46, 69, 103, 107, 110, 124, 140, 168, 186
Pragmatism, pragmatist 3, 12, 101, 125, 127, 135
Psychoanalysis 118, 183–184, 186

Rationality 84, 95, 100, 102, 104–106, 108, 110–111, 115, 124, 172
Relativism 6–8, 197
Rieff, Phillip 3
Rousseau, Jean Jacques 153–160, 166–168, 215

Saint-Simon, Henri de 67, 70, 158–162, 167–169, 215
Samurai 26–28, 32, 36, 41, 48
Scheff, Thomas 18, 215
Schelling, F.W.I., von 69, 176–178, 215
Shaftesbury, Earl of 145–149, 151, 153, 171

Simmel, Georg 5, 11, 14, 30, 34–36, 45, 85, 88–93, 95, 114–117, 119, 123, 183, 187, 197, 201, 216
Skepticism 81, 94, 197
Smith, Adam 84, 150
Social conflict 14, 32, 95, 177, 181–182, 184, 186, 188, 190
Social knowledge 200–201, 203–204
Sorel, George 185, 187
Sorokin Pitirim 97, 139, 216
Spencer, Herbert 23–24, 146, 160, 201, 203, 216
Sumner, William Graham 5–8, 23–24, 43, 84, 87, 90, 215

Theory-practice nexus 103, 106
Therapeutic relationships 113
Therapist(s) 18, 40, 117, 119, 121–122
Thomas, W.I. 84, 127
Tocqueville, Alexis de 160
Tolstoy, Leo 59, 72, 75–77, 80–82
Troeltsch, Ernst 5, 6, 216

Ueshiba, Morihei 10, 14, 19, 48, 50–51, 53, 117–119, 123, 188–189
Universalism 57–59, 61, 64–67, 69–81, 94
University of Chicago 1, 96–97, 124, 126, 130, 135
Unmasking 3
Utilitarianism 86, 95, 114

Veblen, Thorstein 5, 108
Voltaire, F.M.A. 61, 63–64, 66, 159, 163

Watson, Walter 99, 107–108, 111, 185–186
Weber, Max 2, 4, 6, 24, 84–86, 92, 95–97, 99, 100, 102, 109–110, 180, 199, 201, 203

Taylor & Francis eBooks

Helping you to choose the right eBooks for your Library

Add Routledge titles to your library's digital collection today. Taylor and Francis ebooks contains over 50,000 titles in the Humanities, Social Sciences, Behavioural Sciences, Built Environment and Law.

Choose from a range of subject packages or create your own!

Benefits for you
- Free MARC records
- COUNTER-compliant usage statistics
- Flexible purchase and pricing options
- All titles DRM-free.

Benefits for your user
- Off-site, anytime access via Athens or referring URL
- Print or copy pages or chapters
- Full content search
- Bookmark, highlight and annotate text
- Access to thousands of pages of quality research at the click of a button.

REQUEST YOUR FREE INSTITUTIONAL TRIAL TODAY

Free Trials Available
We offer free trials to qualifying academic, corporate and government customers.

eCollections – Choose from over 30 subject eCollections, including:

Archaeology	Language Learning
Architecture	Law
Asian Studies	Literature
Business & Management	Media & Communication
Classical Studies	Middle East Studies
Construction	Music
Creative & Media Arts	Philosophy
Criminology & Criminal Justice	Planning
Economics	Politics
Education	Psychology & Mental Health
Energy	Religion
Engineering	Security
English Language & Linguistics	Social Work
Environment & Sustainability	Sociology
Geography	Sport
Health Studies	Theatre & Performance
History	Tourism, Hospitality & Events

For more information, pricing enquiries or to order a free trial, please contact your local sales team:
www.tandfebooks.com/page/sales

The home of Routledge books

www.tandfebooks.com